Alternative Learning Styles in Business Education

NATIONAL BUSINESS EDUCATION YEARBOOK, NO. 17

Editors: **B. BERTHA WAKIN**
State University of New York at Albany
Albany, New York

CHARLES F. PETITJEAN
State University of New York at Albany
Albany, New York

Published by:

National Business Education Association
1906 Association Drive
Reston, Virginia 22091

ALTERNATIVE LEARNING STYLES IN BUSINESS EDUCATION

Copyright 1979 by

NATIONAL BUSINESS EDUCATION ASSOCIATION
1906 ASSOCIATION DRIVE
RESTON, VIRGINIA 22091

$10.00

LIBRARY OF CONGRESS CARD NO. 79-87550
ISBN 0-933964-00-5

Contents

PART I

Foreword

Life, in general, is made up of alternatives, and we, as human beings, are responsible for making the decisions related to these alternatives. How we make use of the *where* and *how* of such alternatives in our profession of business education is the theme of this Yearbook.

Business teachers have always been well informed concerning the presentation of material to those who want to learn about business. However, alternatives imply "other" or "something different" from which a choice can be made. Thus, the pattern under which any one business teacher functions will be an alternative to that of any other business teacher. No one teacher can be expected to know about all the alternatives; the possibilities are endless. Neither can a yearbook be all-inclusive. Although readers may take exception to some patterns described as alternatives in this book, it is the hope of the editors that each reader will at least consider the alternatives presented.

The Yearbook was developed in two parts. Part I presents the *where*— where a learner can go to learn about business, starting with our school systems in a traditional sense and continuing through life. Business is learned in many settings other than in the formal classroom; unquestionably, much learning takes place on the job, through individual reading, and through everyday experiences.

Part II is the *how*—the methodology of teaching and learning. Much has been written about methods, and teachers involved with a particular level of education and in a particular subject matter field try to keep up with the appropriate literature. The attempt here has been to develop a cross section of ideas that ultimately become alternatives for each reader.

This publication would not be possible without the contributions and cooperation of many people. The editors are indebted to the members of NBEA who support the publications program of the Association, to the administrative and editorial staff in the headquarters office for their patience and advice, and certainly to the individual authors whose outstanding efforts made this Yearbook possible. We hope the readers will find this book provocative, challenging, and useful.

B. Bertha Wakin
Charles F. Petitjean
Editors

Part I

CHAPTER 1

Business Education in Public and Private Schools

It seems appropriate that an "alternatives" Yearbook starts with a look at the traditions in business education that have brought us to where we are today. While we as business educators assume that we know our discipline and its heritage, this chapter develops that knowledge into a clearly defined pattern. It establishes a base upon which we can understand that which follows regarding the "alternatives" of today and tomorrow.

Section A: At the Secondary School Level

EUGENE JONES

Northeast Louisiana University, Monroe

Education has experienced a number of movements during the last quarter century. The movements reflect political, social, economic, and technological changes and have generated new patterns in the teaching/learning process.

At least four of the major movements in education have had a significant impact on business education. These include the academic education, special-needs education, vocational education, and career education movements. These movements have created numerous alternatives in business education. They have expanded the choices business educators have in regard to (1) *who* is provided business education, (2) *what* business education is provided, (3) *when* business education is provided, (4) *where* business education is provided, and (5) *how* business education is provided.

While business educators cannot assume that all available alternatives are good ones, they likewise cannot assume that the traditional patterns in business education are good ones either. Rather, they must choose those alternatives which, when combined, constitute a sound teaching/learning process. To do this, the identification and understanding of available alternatives are necessary. An analysis of the movements in education that have influenced business education will help.

MOVEMENTS IN EDUCATION AFFECTING ALTERNATIVES IN BUSINESS EDUCATION

The academic education movement. In the 1950's, such critics of education as Hyman Rickover and James Conant, spurred on by the threat of

Communism, the beginning of the space race, and the continuation of war, feared that American schools had strayed too far from the basics. They called for a renewed emphasis on disciplines such as math, science, and language. Jerome Bruner in his book, *The Process of Education*, brought to the attention of educators, as well as the public, the importance of structure in the organization of school subjects. The interest in organizing and sequencing subject matter into discipline-centered curriculums permeated the entire field of education. Curriculums in the high school became, for the most part, college preparatory.

A real contribution of the academic movement was that it caused business educators to examine and evaluate the subject matter in business education courses. The value of some business content was questioned. Gaps and voids in other business subject matter were discovered, and new content was added. The sequence of content within and among courses was studied, and revised business education curriculums emerged.

The special-needs education movement. As the academic education movement continued, some educators became concerned that it was going too far. A counter movement focused concern on those who were neither college bound nor academically talented. Concern grew for those with learning disabilities due to mental, physical, social, or economic handicaps. Funds from both public and private sources were made available to improve the education of those with learning disabilities.

Business education participated and benefited from the special-needs education movement. Whole populations of students who had been neglected previously were offered instruction in business education. Business educators experimented with new instructional strategies, and both materials and media were developed. A major contribution of this movement was the experimentation that led to the development and use of materials, media, and methods with more varied populations of learners, some of whom had previously been thought to have neither interest, aptitude, nor ability to profit from instruction in business education.

The vocational education movement. The vocational education movement rose from a concern that individuals should not only have a general education which is needed to become academically literate, but they should have sufficient specialized education to develop marketable skills needed to secure, hold, and advance on a job. Legislation provided funding for developing improved programs in occupational education. It was during this period that office education received funding for the first time.

It is interesting to note that during the vocational education movement, the secondary school vocational programs moved from subject-matter-oriented programs to employer-needs-oriented programs to employee-needs-oriented programs. It is this change of emphasis that provided the most significant contribution to business education. Business education changed from teaching a highly subject-oriented program in which shorthand was taught for the sake of shorthand, bookkeeping for the sake of book-keeping, etc., to a job-oriented program. Jobs in the business occupations were analyzed, and business education moved toward offering task-oriented training that would satisfy employer needs. Recognizing that task training was too narrow, business education expanded its programs to equip students with a broader education that would prepare them for a whole cluster of jobs.

The career education movement. The overkill represented by the divergent views in the earlier movements led to the realization that ultimately and finally all education can and should contribute to the preparation of the individual for participation in a chosen career. All possible occupations were classified into 15 occupational clusters. The entire educational process from kindergarten through postdoctoral study is viewed as being phases in career education. The early school years are viewed as contributing to career awareness followed by education contributing to career orientation. Secondary and postsecondary education contribute to career preparation. Easy exit from and reentry into a variety of educational programs to secure needed education for job placement or advancement is a basic feature of career education.

The career education movement contributed to the alternatives in business education by helping to break down the sharp dichotomy that had existed between general education and vocational education. The skills and knowledges found in basic business subjects are equally as important to career preparation as are those in office, distributive, and entrepreneurial subjects. Business education has likewise become more respectable to both students and teachers in other fields of study. They recognize that business education can, in varied degrees, contribute to the preparation for careers in each of the 15 clusters.

Numerous alternatives in business education in the secondary schools have emerged from the movements in education during the last 25 years. These alternatives are not the product of any one of the movements, but rather the end result of the movements collectively. These alternatives can be classified into three broad categories: (1) alternatives in the statement of objectives for business education, (2) alternatives in the organization *for* instruction in business education, and (3) alternatives in the organization *of* instruction in business education. A review of these alternatives reveals numerous opportunities for improving business education patterns of instruction.

ALTERNATIVES IN THE STATEMENT OF OBJECTIVES FOR BUSINESS EDUCATION

Stating objectives has been and will always be a critical task in the teaching/learning process. Since the early part of the century, the philosophy of business education has encompassed a twofold function. It is widely accepted that business education in the secondary schools should contribute to the general education of all individuals by providing basic business education and to the vocational education of individuals preparing for business careers by providing practical job preparatory education for office, distributive, and entrepreneurial occupations.

While there tends to be general agreement concerning the overall objectives of business education in the secondary schools, the ways in which the objectives have been or should be implemented remain controversial. The controversy stems from the alternatives available for stating the objectives so that application of the philosophy of business education can be made to the classroom program. Three approaches to stating objectives are available: the general objectives approach, the taxonomy of objectives approach, and the behavioral objectives approach.

Use of broad, general objectives. Traditionally, objectives have been stated in terms which specify learning experiences and outcomes. Objectives stated in this form are often very broad and general. Examples of such statements are:

- To develop an understanding
- To increase skills
- To help acquire a knowledge
- To aid in learning a concept
- To instill an appreciation.

General objective statements are concerned with the acquisition of information, knowledges, understandings, concepts, attitudes, and appreciations needed to develop or modify behavior. Educators skilled in the use of general objectives can state them in hierarchical order by specifying the information needed to develop knowledges, the knowledges needed to develop understandings, the understandings needed to develop concepts, the concepts needed to develop attitudes, the attitudes needed to develop appreciations, and the appreciations needed to develop or modify behavior in desired directions. General objective statements indicate whether learning is to be at an acquaintanceship level or at a mastery level. Such statements, however, fail to specify the degree of mastery.

While statements of general objectives can be meaningful if the desired instructional outcomes are specified, such objectives often state the process rather than the product. When this happens, the instruction focuses on learning activities and experiences rather than on learning outcomes.

Use of a taxonomy of educational objectives. In the late 1950's and early 1960's, Benjamin Bloom, D. R. Krathwohl, and others developed an interesting taxonomy of educational objectives in which all possible learning outcomes were classified into three categories: the cognitive domain, the affective domain, and the psychomotor domain. Each domain is further divided into levels of outcomes. The levels within the cognitive domain include knowledge, comprehension, application, analysis, synthesis, and evaluation, with knowledge being the lowest level and evaluation the highest. The affective domain includes the receiving, responding, valuing, organization, and characterization by a value or value complex levels of outcomes. Such levels as perception, set, guided response, mechanism, and complex overt response have been suggested for the psychomotor domain. The taxonomy offers a tool for systematically checking sets of objectives in business education to see that all desired types and levels of outcomes have been accounted for.

4

Use of behavioral objectives. In the late 1960's and early 1970's, a great deal of enthusiasm and support for behavioral or competency-based objectives appeared in the professional literature. Robert F. Mager helped to popularize behavioral objectives by identifying a three-step approach to stating objectives in behavioral terms. These steps include defining the terminal behavior, identifying the conditions under which behavior is to occur, and specifying the criteria of acceptable performance. Such an approach allows greater specificity in the statement of teaching/learning objectives.

All three approaches have appropriate applications to business education. The three types of objectives are complementary rather than conflicting. Preparing a set of objectives for a business education program, a course, or a unit of study may begin with statements of general objectives which are then analyzed by using the taxonomy of objectives. Later, the set of objectives may be further refined by stating them in behavioral terms.

One may also work in the reverse direction by first preparing a set of behavioral objectives. These may then be checked for completeness by using the taxonomy of objectives. Later, the objectives may be generalized into broader statements for ease in working with them.

One may also start with the taxonomy to identify and select a set of objectives and then work in either the direction of general objectives or of behavioral objectives. Because the alternatives in stating the objectives for business education are so compatible, the identification, selection, and evaluation will probably involve all three approaches in the preparation of a set of objectives.

ALTERNATIVES IN THE ORGANIZATION FOR INSTRUCTION

During the last quarter century, educators have become more and more concerned about where certain types of learning should occur. Much work has been done to modify the organization for instruction. The work has involved changes in both the external and the internal organization of schools.

External organization. In the educational ladder represented by kindergarten-elementary-secondary-postsecondary education, radical changes have occurred at the secondary level. Traditionally, the secondary schools referred to the junior high school with grades 7 and 8 or 7, 8, and 9; and high school with grades 9, 10, 11, and 12 or 10, 11, and 12. Today, middle schools have become a part of many secondary schools. The middle schools generally include grades 6, 7, and 8 or grades 5, 6, 7, and 8. Sometimes grade 9 is a part of the middle school. The purpose of the middle school is to provide programs designed to meet the specific needs of preadolescents and early adolescents rather than to provide programs which merely imitate the senior high school programs.

Much work needs to be done in both middle schools and junior high schools to improve business education offerings. In many schools, business education is not available before the ninth grade. When it is, the offerings are frequently watered-down versions of general business and typewriting. Having a good business education program in the middle and junior high schools remains a promising alternative. But what would constitute a good program remains a nagging question.

Another alternative in the organization for instruction is found in nongraded schools. In such schools, grade levels, labels, and expectations are removed. Students progress at their own rates. Individualization is the key factor. While the ungraded program is still not widely accepted as a pattern for middle schools and high schools, it is likely to become a more viable alternative as teachers acquire greater expertise in handling individual differences.

Alternative schools provide still another choice in the organization for instruction. Students who either cannot function at all or function poorly in the traditional secondary school may be given the opportunity to acquire instruction from a school other than the traditional campus-based one.

The forms of alternative schools include (1) the community-based schools, (2) the home-based schools, (3) the employer-based schools, and (4) the residential-based schools. Business education is commonly offered in all types.

The community-based schools include such schools as storefront schools or schools without walls. Rather than attending campus schools, students meet off campus in some other type of building. In some cases, the classes are held in several different places.

With the advent of educational television and correspondence courses, more business education courses and programs are offered in home-based schools. Instruction is received in the home, and students come to schools or teachers go to the homes for testing and/or counseling only.

Employer-based schools may also be an alternative for some students. Students receive instruction while on the job. Classrooms may be provided by the employer at the job location with teachers sent to the employer-based stations to instruct the students enrolled in such programs.

The residential schools provide some students with the alternative of living at the school. The school is the student's home. Students frequently elect to go to residential schools to receive specialized education not offered in the local school.

A final alternative related to the external organization of schools concerns their sponsoring agents. While most business education is still provided by public secondary schools, business education programs continue to increase in private and parochial schools.

Internal organization. Departmentalization by discipline or field of study has been the traditional form of organization in secondary schools, and business education has commonly been a separate department in most schools. Increasingly, secondary schools are using an interdisciplinary or interdepartmentalized approach in providing certain types of instruction. Consumer education and economics, for example, are areas of instruction in which many secondary schools use an interdisciplinary approach. Business education teachers may team-teach with teachers from social studies, home economics, or other departments. In other schools, the same course may be offered by a number of departments.

Time is another element which is being reallocated in secondary schools to provide an alternative in the organization for instruction. Flexible scheduling is replacing the traditional periods in which students meet 45-50 minutes at the same time each day for five days a week during one year to earn one unit of credit. Flexible scheduling permits the use of time modules of different lengths at varied times during the week. A student may earn more or less than one unit of credit for a certain subject during a year. Flexible scheduling complements sound teaching and learning principles in business education and should probably receive more consideration when future instructional programs in business education are being planned.

Closely related to flexible scheduling is the block programming used in many schools. COE and other business education programs frequently utilize a block of time extending beyond the 45-50 minute time frame.

Another alternative related to time is the minicourse offerings which are popular in some schools. Rather than offering the traditional one-semester or one-year course, the course is broken into shorter units of instruction. Students may elect the number of minicourses desired.

Class size provides the basis for still another alternative in the internal organization for instruction. The magic number of 30 students to a class is being challenged. In some secondary schools, business teachers will have classes as large as 100 or more for certain subjects and as small as 10 or less for others. The nature of the content and the instructional methods determine the size of the group.

Individualized instruction is becoming more widely accepted and implemented by business teachers. As more and better instructional materials and media become available, teaching on a one-to-one basis will likely become more acceptable.

Another alternative facing business education teachers is related to student characteristics. While homogeneous groupings were touted for almost all classes a few decades ago, the need for a social setting which integrates students with varied backgrounds, abilities, and other characteristics has been recognized. Currently, a push is on to "mainstream" students. Students with mental or physical handicaps who were previously placed in special classes are being returned to the regular classroom.

ALTERNATIVES IN THE ORGANIZATION OF BUSINESS EDUCATION INSTRUCTION

Another large group of alternatives in business education is related to how instruction is provided. In other words, the organization of instruction lends itself to many choices. The three factors which influence instructional strategies and systems are materials, media, and methods.

Both the kinds and volume of instructional materials have greatly increased during the last quarter century. With the funding made available to education by federal legislation, the opportunity to experiment with varied forms of materials has been made possible. While the textbook and workbook remain popular, audiovisual materials are regular supplements in many classrooms. Software to be used with instructional media, such as films, transparencies, filmstrips, film loops, videotapes, and programs for computer-assisted instruction, are budgeted in a fashion similar to textbooks and workbooks in many school systems. Programmed instructional materials and learning activity packets are also appearing in greater numbers. Both of these permit schools to offer better individualized instruction.

Technology is providing improved hardware at lower costs. Teachers are able to use instructional media more frequently. Overhead projectors, movie and filmstrip projectors, opaque projectors, and tape recorders and players are readily accessible to teachers in many schools. The use of videotapes, closed circuit TV, and educational television is also increasing. Inroads are being made into the use of computer-assisted instruction.

Business education teachers are becoming more proficient in methodology and appear to have a better command of pupil-oriented methods of instruction. They continue to accept their roles as facilitators of learning rather than merely transmitters of information. Thus, the traditional lecture, question-and-answer, and discussion methods are being either supplemented or replaced by problem solving, committee work, simulations, games, role playing, and other less formal methods. Teachers are electing a variety of alternative methods.

Instructional strategies that utilize a singular form of material, medium, and methodology have generally failed. For example, a course taught by using only programmed materials has not been successful. No one kind of material, media, or method is likely to be an appropriate alternative. Rather, it is the proper mix of materials, media, and methods that will produce satisfactory results. The possible combinations are innumerable; therefore, the alternatives for the organization of instruction are endless.

SUMMARY OF ALTERNATIVES IN BUSINESS EDUCATION IN SECONDARY SCHOOLS

Many alternatives are available to business educators as they plan patterns of instruction. The alternatives are, for the most part, the products of changes reflected in the major educational movements in the last quarter century. These movements have provided business educators with choices concerning who will be taught, what will be taught, how it will be taught, where it will be taught, and when it will be taught.

The major opportunities for improving instructional patterns in business education in the secondary schools are related to the alternatives available in stating objectives, in organizing for instruction, and in the organization of instruction. The combination of objectives, school organization, and instructional organization will determine the effectiveness and efficiency of business education instructional strategies in the secondary school.

Section B: At the Postsecondary Level

DONALD E. ENGLISH and JACK E. JOHNSON

East Texas State University, Commerce

This section will review the status of business education programs at post-secondary levels. An introductory section on the development of business education since the Colonial Period will preface three distinct periods of program changes in business education: (1) the 1950's, (2) the 1960's, and (3) the 1970's. To conclude the chapter, a clairvoyant approach will be taken to identify a few of the important technological discoveries that will inevitably create a new dimension for business education in the 1980's.

COLONIAL PERIOD

Business education is often thought of as a recent development in education; however, the history of business education can be traced as far back as to the Colonial Period in the late 1700's. The business courses most frequently taught during this time were arithmetic, bookkeeping, and penmanship; and the schools where these subjects most frequently appeared were the writing and reckoning schools, private schools, academies, and evening schools. Although many of these schools were teaching business subjects, the courses were not in any organized curriculum. Many of the classes were temporary in nature, sometimes only meeting for one session.

As the academies began to teach the business subjects during the latter part of this period, a more organized business curriculum developed. However, even in the academies there is evidence that the teachers of business subjects were not as well qualified as those in the academic subjects.

PRIVATE BUSINESS SCHOOL ERA

Records of private business schools date back as far as the 1820's, but it wasn't until sometime between 1850 and 1900 that private business schools became the dominant force in teaching business subjects. In fact, the private business schools were really the first schools devoted exclusively to teach these courses. Among the most influential schools during this period were the Bryant and Stratton Schools, which by 1865 had expanded into a chain of 44 institutions in 44 different cities.

There are many reasons why private business schools flourished during this period. With the growth of business and industry in the United States, it was essential that there be more training in business subjects, which the high schools were not then teaching. The private business schools were able to fill a void that existed in the educational system.

Veterans returning from the Civil War needed vocational training, and the private business schools were prepared to provide it. By this time, the use of shorthand in business was increasing, and in addition, the first prac-

9

tical typewriter had been invented. Training in these two skills areas became part of the private business school curriculum.

During the early 1900's, the number of private business schools declined. Then, with the onset of World War I, women were needed in business to take the place of men who had vacated their positions to assist in the War effort, and a large number of them enrolled in private schools for business training. After the War, the returning veteran needed some type of vocational training, and he also logically turned to the private business schools.

From Colonial history through World War II, the private business schools contributed significantly to business education. So pronounced were these contributions that Daughtrey credited the following innovations to the private business schools:

1. Organizing business teachers into a professional society
2. Using a typewriting textbook
3. Holding meetings for improving instruction in business subjects
4. Offering basic business subjects (though then considered vocational)
5. Developing a methodology in teaching business subjects
6. Originating collegiate-level business instruction
7. Individualizing instruction.[1]

COLLEGIATE SCHOOLS OF BUSINESS

The collegiate schools of business began to develop after the Civil War amidst an expansion in business and industry. The Wharton School of Finance and Commerce at the University of Pennsylvania, organized in 1881, was the first successful collegiate school of business. After 1917 the collegiate schools of business began to develop rapidly. The reasons for this rapid expansion were the need for higher education in an industrial society, more students graduating from high schools, and a raise in the minimum age for employment. Also, in 1916 the American Association of Collegiate Schools of Business (AACSB) was organized (the name was changed in 1972 to the American Assembly of Collegiate Schools of Business). This organization helped to give the business curriculum status. The requirements for membership in the Association were quite stringent; they insisted that collegiate programs in business require courses in finance, accounting, management, statistics, and business law.

The courses most frequently taught during the 1920's were accounting, finance, economics, and money and banking. Very few courses in the secretarial science or business education area were offered in collegiate schools of business, and even as late as 1940, many of them were not in favor of giving credit for skills subjects such as typewriting and shorthand. College credit for skills courses did not receive attention until the late 1940's.

JUNIOR COLLEGES

The idea of the junior college is not new. It was first suggested by

---

[1]Daughtrey, Anne Scott. *Methods of Basic Business and Economic Education.* Cincinnati: South-Western Publishing Co., 1974, p. 10.

Edmund J. James as early as 1885. However, it was not until 1901 that the first public junior college was established at Joliet, Illinois. The main objective of the early junior colleges was to fulfill the requirements of the first two years of a baccalaureate degree. Since their establishment there has been a tremendous increase in the number of such schools and in their enrollments. Today there are more than 1,200 junior colleges educating over 4 million students.

Eells conducted a study in 1930 of 279 junior colleges in the United States and found that only 134 (48 percent) of the junior colleges were offering commercial subjects at that time.[2] Since then, business subjects in junior colleges have grown in numbers and in enrollments.

The goals of the junior college expanded quickly as enrollments mushroomed. Not only were junior colleges concerned with preparing students for eventual transfer to a four-year school, they were also interested in developing terminal vocational programs for students.

TEACHER EDUCATION

During the Colonial Period there was no formal training for business teachers. What was provided was either through the apprenticeship method or by private instruction. It was thought that anyone could teach the business subjects if students could be persuaded to attend the classes. Very little thought was given to the formal preparation of business teachers until about 1900. Throughout the early 1900's most of the business teachers were trained in private business schools, and they often did not receive training in the liberal arts or in professional education. Much of their preparation consisted of highly specialized training in a particular concentration. Progress was slow in the development of business teacher training programs. By 1922, there were approximately 37 colleges and universities offering some training for business teachers. During the 1930's there was a trend toward colleges and universities providing more academic and professional education for business teachers. Most business teachers by the late 1940's were being trained in colleges and universities that offered teacher education degrees, and by the 1950's, it was common for most business teachers to be certified after completing a four-year business teacher education program.

THE NEED FOR POSTSECONDARY BUSINESS EDUCATION

The progression of business education courses from the high school level to the postsecondary level began most aggressively in the decade from 1930 to 1940. This "upgrading" was due to a variety of reasons. One was the fact that vocational subjects were promoted from the ninth and tenth grade levels to the eleventh and twelfth grade levels. Secondly, many authorities and professionals in business education at that time (as well as community leaders and business proprietors) believed that high school students were not receiving sufficient training at the ninth and tenth grade

---

[2]Eells, Walter Crosby. *The Junior College.* Boston: Houghton Mifflin Co., 1931, p. 489.

levels to allow them to succeed in the business world. Thirdly, the depression of the thirties created a time of low employment; and an additional year of business training for these people would keep the students out of the job market, thus ensuring a lower rate of unemployment. And finally, the thirteenth year of education was supported for the simple reason that many of the academically prepared youth did not possess a skill that would allow them to enter the job market.

Thus, by 1950, business education was prospering in the aftermath of an extremely successful beginning in the 1930's and 1940's. Business curriculums were firmly established in a variety of postsecondary institutions. Most popular among these institutions were the junior colleges, private business schools, collegiate schools of business, and four-year colleges.

BUSINESS EDUCATION PROGRAMS
IN THE 1950'S

Junior colleges. The junior colleges of the 1950's provided postsecondary education to those students who could not otherwise obtain it because of restrictive entrance requirements at a few of the four-year colleges and universities, because of financial problems of attending a postsecondary school that was not locally supported, because of the distance to a suitable four-year postsecondary school, and a variety of other reasons. Many junior colleges required the entering student to be a high school graduate. In a limited sense, junior colleges operated as stepping-stones to four-year collegiate institutions, because universities would often accept credit for courses taken at a junior or community college. Instructors and administrative personnel from the junior college system strongly supported the belief that credit for junior college courses should transfer to four-year institutions, if for no other reason than that the same textbooks were used in the junior college classroom to teach identical courses. With few exceptions, two-year graduates were allowed to transfer the two-year course credits to four-year colleges and universities. However, many students looked upon their education in the junior college as a terminal venture. Therefore, they used the skills and knowledges they gained in this educational environment to seek employment upon graduation.

Enrollments in junior colleges rose rapidly in the 1950's, primarily due to three positive influences: (1) the increasing number of students in secondary schools during the 1950's necessitated a parallel increase in the number of postsecondary schools to provide further training for graduating high school seniors; (2) many universities were raising their entrance requirements, thus forcing some students into junior colleges for the first two years of their collegiate education; (3) junior colleges were frequently less expensive for students to attend, because they were located closer to the students' homes.

The junior college business education programs in the 1950's were predominantly terminal in nature, and they provided a variety of vocational skills for those graduating from different programs. Joplin Junior College in Missouri provided both a one-year and two-year program in the secretarial

12

curriculum. The Joplin secretarial curriculum was terminal in nature (see Table 1), as evidenced by the number of vocational courses in the program listed in the school's 1952 catalog:

TABLE 1. Joplin Junior College Secretarial Curriculum

Subject	Semester Hours for Beginning Students	Semester Hours for Advanced Students
Shorthand	14	6
Introduction to Business	2	2
Typewriting	9	3
Business Arithmetic	3	3
Secretarial Typewriting	2	4
Office Practice	—	3
Business Law	—	3
Accounting	6	—

The curriculum at Lasell Junior College at Auburndale, Massachusetts, placed more emphasis on the liberal arts courses in their merchandising curriculum, which appears in Table 2. The increased emphasis in general education courses, as listed in the 1952 catalog, may have been associated with a goal to provide students with the maximum number of credits so they could transfer to a four-year institution as a first-semester junior.

TABLE 2. Lasell Junior College Merchandising Curriculum

First Year	Second Year
English	Retail Training
Public Speaking	Economics
Clothing	Psychology
General Survey	Physical Education
Appreciation of Color, Line, and Design	Electives
Applied Chemistry	
Social Problems	
Foods (or an elective)	
Physical Education	

Thus, in the Joplin program and in the Lasell program, the two primary goals of junior college education in the 1950's—four-year college preparatory and terminal (vocational) education—were realized.

Private business schools. The 1950's also revealed a tremendous growth in private business schools. Enrollments ranged from just a few dozen to literally hundreds of students. The private schools usually offered students the choice of one of four options: six-month programs, one- or two-year programs, or up to four-year programs. Entrance was permitted year around, and there was no definite length of time established for course completion.

As was true with many of the earlier private business schools, the most popular business courses were found in the accounting curriculums and the secretarial curriculums. As the success of these business-oriented programs became evident with growing enrollments, a few of the private schools instituted business administration programs for those students who wanted to prepare for the managerial and supervisory aspects of business operations.

Table 3 identifies a typical program that was popular in the private business schools during the 1950's.

TABLE 3. Typical Private Business School Program

Program	Weeks of Study
General Business	36
Stenographic	36
Accounting	42
Stenographic-Secretarial	42
Secretarial	60
Accounting-Finance	84
Executive-Secretarial	84

The curriculum of the private business schools was obviously much more comprehensive than Table 3 reveals. The private schools also offered courses in business administration, journalism, and other specialty areas.

Private business schools often sold their services by the month or by the course. The usual tuition rate for attending a private school averaged about $25 a month. Teachers' salaries were widely dispersed, ranging from $150 per month and up to $350 per month in some of the wealthier schools. The average school enrollment was less than 200 students. Private business schools built their reputation on the success of the students they trained. Thus, it was in their best interests to maintain a close liaison with the local business establishments. Most of the curriculums were therefore based on what the community needed and what the students desired.

The National Council of Business Schools provided guidance on minimum requirements for private business school curriculums. Table 4 reveals the minimum time requirements for the standard courses of study.

TABLE 4. Minimum Time Requirements for Standard Courses of Study

Program	Weeks of Study
Stenographic	36
Junior Accountancy	36
Secretarial	48
Executive Secretarial	72
Business Administration	72

Collegiate schools of business. Although the role of the collegiate schools of business was varied, their general purposes were (1) to provide the student with a general understanding of business, (2) to provide the student with a specialty in business, (3) to provide the student with leadership training, and (4) to provide the student with a foundation in business ethics. These goals were considered to be essential to any person desiring to enter the profession of business management.

The subject matter taught in collegiate schools of business covered many aspects of business administration. Table 5 shows some of the most frequently taught courses.

The inclusion of business teacher training and secretarial studies as an integral part of the collegiate schools of business curriculum during the 1950's (as revealed in Table 5) would be a remote possibility today. Collegiate schools of business have always been opposed to training in the secretarial areas of shorthand and typewriting because they were not considered "professional" in nature. However, they did recognize that such training

TABLE 5. Typical Courses Taught in Collegiate Schools of Business

Accounting	Insurance
Banking and Finance	Labor
Business Ethics	Management (including organiza-
Business Law	tion, production, personnel,
Business Teacher Training	office management)
Distribution (including adver-	Public Finance and Taxation
tising, marketing, selling,	Real Estate
and retailing)	Secretarial Studies
Economics	Statistics and Business Cycles
Foreign Trade	Transportation and Public Utilities

provided students with a usable skill with which they could gain employment and hopefully progress to a position that more appropriately challenged their professional business background in business administration. The practice of enrolling in secretarial skills courses to gain a marketable skill, however, did not always prove to be a guarantee that an office position could be secured. The one problem associated with this practice was that these courses were usually offered in the freshman and sophomore years, and by the time the students graduated, they had all but lost the marketable skills they needed for job-entry proficiency. Thus, it was not long before the secretarial and business teacher training courses disappeared from the professional schools of business.

The majority of instruction in the collegiate schools of business related to large-scale business organizations with an almost purposeful neglect for the small-scale business operations. It appears rather ironic that such would be the emphasis when one considers the fact that small-scale business operations (in today's standards) were predominant on the American business scene in the 1950's.

The faculty of the collegiate schools of business usually came from the economics departments, from business establishments in the nearby communities, or (when a sufficient number of persons had graduated from the collegiate programs) from within their own ranks. The methods of instruction were few, with most of the learning coming from a strict lecture method

15

with limited discussion. A formal test was given once or twice during the course to see if the students had grasped the intent of the instructor's lectures. Only a few of the business instructors encouraged alternative methods of teaching such as student participation, research, or interpretation. Term papers were often assigned, but since the list of topics was restricted, students soon realized that changing a word or two in a previous assignment would fulfill the term paper requirements.

One of the most popular collegiate schools of business in the 1950's was the Wharton School of Commerce at the University of Pennsylvania. Its accounting curriculum appears in Table 6, taken from a school catalog of the early 1950's. The freshman and sophomore year courses were taken by all students, and specialization did not begin until the beginning of the junior year. At that time a student could enroll in one of many programs such as general business, accounting, corporation finance, investments, economics, industrial management, insurance, marketing, real estate, and other concentrations. Notice in this curriculum that no mention is made of the secretarial or business education courses that infiltrated the earlier curriculums of the collegiate schools of business. Approximately 40 courses were required for a student to graduate from this program, half of which related to a business administration base. An interesting feature of this accounting curriculum is that about 10 of a student's courses could be taken as electives, something not often found in today's accounting curriculums.

TABLE 6. Wharton School of Commerce Accounting Curriculum

Freshman Year	Credits
Physical Education	2
English Composition	4
English Language and Literature	4
Elementary Accounting	5
Economic Geography	5
American Government	5
Legal Bases of Business Transactions	5
Principles of Economics	5
Industries of the U.S.	5

Sophomore Year	
Physical Education	2
Advanced English Composition (first term)	2
Nineteenth Century Novelists (second term)	2
3 courses from the following:	
Business Finance	
Insurance	
Elements of Marketing	18
Business Statistics	
Transportation and Communications	
Introduction to Sociology	4
Other University Subjects	6
Electives	10

Junior Year	*Credits*
Physical Education	2
Advanced Accounting	6
Cost Accounting (one term)	3
Industrial Accounting (one term)	
or	3
Financial Accounting Systems (one term)	
Two courses from the following:	
Business Finance	
Insurance	
Elements of Marketing	12
Business Statistics	
Transportation and Communications	
Advanced Economics, Political Science,	
or Sociology	4
Other University Subjects	8
Electives	6
Senior Year	
Physical Education	2
Senior Seminar in Accounting	4
Income Tax Accounting (one term)	3
Auditing (one term)	3
Other University Subjects	8
Electives	24

Four-year colleges and universities. The liberal arts colleges were popular four-year institutions in the 1950's, although they were hardly what could be called "liberal arts" because they offered courses that were technical and professional in nature. Business administration courses such as finance, law, industrial management, and accounting were the first business courses to be offered in liberal arts colleges, and the number of students majoring in business administration increased significantly in the 1950's.

Teacher's colleges of the 1950's specialized in the preparation of public school teachers. There was a variety of different types of teachers colleges, including state teachers colleges, city teachers colleges, private teachers colleges, and university teachers colleges. The state teachers colleges were among the earliest to develop business teacher curriculums. They specified that teachers wishing to obtain a teaching certificate had to take a core of courses and also a specialized curriculum within their area of concentration. The core courses were the same for all students, whether they were pursuing a major or minor in English, science, mathematics, art, etc. Specialized curriculums were offered in shorthand, typewriting, accounting, and general business. The catalog of East Texas State University at Commerce offered a typical business teacher education program in the 1950's (Table 7).

TABLE 7. East Texas State University Teacher Education Program

Freshman	Sophomore
English (2 courses)	English (2 courses)
History (2 courses)	Physical Science (2 courses)
Physical Science (2 courses)	Teaching as a Profession
Mathematics	Educational Psychology
General Education	Elementary Shorthand
Elementary Accounting	Advanced Shorthand
Physical Education (2 courses)	Elementary Accounting
	Physical Education (2 courses)
	Minor (1 course)

Junior	Senior
The Secondary School Pupil	Student Teaching in the
Principles of Secondary	Secondary School
Education	General Education
Methods of Teaching	Business Administration
Business Subjects	(3 advanced courses)
Principles and Practices of	Minor (4 courses, including
Teaching in Secondary	2 advanced)
Schools	
Government	
Social Science	
Principles of Accounting	
(2 courses)	
Business Administration	
(advanced course)	
Minor (1 course)	

The teacher education program was not housed in a department of business education at East Texas State, but rather as a special program in the Department of Business Administration. It was designed especially for students preparing to teach secondary school business education. In addition to the methods course in business education and the student teaching experience, students were required to complete five additional courses in education: (1) Teaching as a Profession, which basically studied the career opportunities of a teacher; (2) Educational Psychology, a course similar to the educational psychology course of today that studies the aspects of psychology that influence the effectiveness of learning and teaching; (3) The Secondary School Pupil, designed to study the progressive development of the older student toward adulthood; (4) Principles of Secondary Education, offered to inform a student about the instructional materials that were available in secondary school teaching; and (5) Principles and Practices of Teaching in Secondary Schools, a study of educational practices which were effective in secondary school teaching.

BUSINESS EDUCATION PROGRAMS IN THE 1960'S

Junior colleges. In 1960, there were close to 700 junior colleges with a total enrollment of over 900,000 students. These junior colleges had 18,000

18

full-time and over 12,000 part-time faculty. Junior colleges were most numerous in California in 1960, with the total enrollment reaching more than 200,000 students in both public and private institutions. A popular offering at the Metropolitan Junior College at Los Angeles was the stenographic sequence. Its 1960 catalog offered a more liberal choice of courses for potential stenographers, as shown in Table 8. Although the purposes of junior

TABLE 8. Metropolitan Junior College Stenographic Curriculum

First Year, 1st Semester	Credits
Communications (English 1 or 21)	3
Psychology 9	1
Secretarial Science 1	2
Secretarial Science 7	1½
Secretarial Science 10	5
General Education Electives	2
Physical Education	½
First Year, 2nd Semester	
Communications (English 45)	3
Political Science 10	2
Secretarial Science 2	2
Secretarial Science 11	5
General Education Elective	3
Physical Education	½
Second Year, 1st Semester	
History 11	3
Office Machines 22, 23	1
Secretarial Science 3	2
Secretarial Science 12	5
Secretarial Science 33	1
General Education Electives	2
Physical Education	½
Second Year, 2nd Semester	
Accounting 1-1 or 23	1
Mathematics 30-1	1½
Health Education 10	2
Secretarial Science 8	1
Secretarial Science 13	5
Secretarial Science 30	1
General Education Electives	3
Physical Education	½

colleges in the 1960's were varied, the two most popular goals were terminal training and preparation for a continuing program at a four-year collegiate school. The Metropolitan stenographic sequence appeared more terminal in nature, as evidenced by the fact that over half the courses in the two-year program were secretarial. However, the secretarial curriculum of Corning Community College in New York shown in its 1960 catalog emphasized a

19

preparatory program for continued work on a bachelor's degree at a collegiate school, as Table 9 reveals. Only one-third of the courses in this program were secretarial.

TABLE 9. Corning Community College Secretarial Curriculum

First Year	Fall Semester	Spring Semester
English, Freshman	3	3
Principles of Economics	3	3
College Accounting	3	3
Fundamentals of Business	2	2
Typewriting	2	2
Shorthand	3	3
Physical Education	1	1
Second Year		
Business Mathematics	3	
Business Elective		3
Office Management	3	
Secretarial Workshop	7	10
Science or Elective	3	3
Speech	2	2
Physical Education	1	1

Private business schools. The executive secretarial curriculum at Goldey-Beacom School of Business in Delaware specified an Associate in Arts Degree for two-year graduates in its 1960 catalog. The total number of credits required for this program was 79, and the example appearing in Table 10 illustrates that the private business schools offered a curriculum similar to that of the junior college secretarial curriculum. However, at Goldey-Beacom more emphasis was placed on basic business core courses such as principles, contracts, sales, psychology, and business behavior. Also, most of the electives were business content courses.

TABLE 10. Goldey-Beacom School of Business Secretarial Curriculum

First Semester	Credits
Principles of Accounting 1	4
Business Mathematics	6
Principles of Business	6
Penmanship	1
Law of Contracts and Negotiable Instruments	3
Principles of Typewriting	2
Second Semester	
Principles of Accounting 2	4
Shorthand Theory 1	4
Law of Sales, Bailments, Agency, Real Property	3
Business Correspondence	3
Word Study and Vocabulary Building	3
Business Psychology	3
Typewriting	2

Third Semester	Credits
Shorthand Theory 2	4
Shorthand Dictation and Transcription	4
Typewriting	2
Business Machines	2
Elective	3
Secondary English Techniques	3

Fourth Semester	
Advanced Dictation and Transcription	4
Filing Systems	2
Typewriting	1
Secretarial Office Procedures	4
Elective	3
Business Behavior	3

Four-year colleges and universities. In the 1960's, business teacher education was often housed physically in a College of Education. A teaching certificate could be obtained in one of several areas: secretarial, bookkeeping/accounting, distributive education, or comprehensive (a special program for students who wished to be certified in all areas of business education). The University of North Dakota followed this pattern in the 1960's, and Table 11 shows the curriculum for a major in business education with a comprehensive emphasis, as outlined in the 1962-64 undergraduate catalog. The courses listed are departmental; university general education courses and professional education courses required for graduation are not identified.

TABLE 11. University of North Dakota Comprehensive Business Education Program

Course	Credits
Elements of Accounting	6
Intermediate Typewriting	2
Advanced Typewriting	2
Shorthand	6
Advanced Shorthand	3
Advanced Dictation and Transcription	3
Records Administration	2
Orientation to Business Education	3
Methods for Teachers of Bookkeeping in High School	2
Methods of Teaching Shorthand and Office Practice	2
Principles of Adding, Calculating, and Posting Machines	2
Principles of Secretarial Office Machines	2
Cooperative Business Education	3
Business Law	3
Secretarial Practice	3
Improvement of Instruction in Typewriting	2
*Principles of Economics I	3

*Not a departmental requirement.

21

The University of North Dakota also offered a four-year program for secretarial training through the College of Business and Public Administration, as many four-year colleges and universities did in the 1960's. The justification for such a program was provided in the 1962-1964 catalog:

The business man of today is demanding much more of his secretary than a mere knowledge of shorthand and typewriting. He wants one who is familiar with office methods, including the most efficient methods of filing; one who can relieve him of a large amount of routine work pertaining to an office. The broader the foundation one has in the understanding of business principles, business organization and management, and business law, along with the most effective methods in office work, the more sure one will be of promotion.

As the promotional literature reveals, the four-year secretarial curriculum provided the secretary with a broad background not only in the skills but also in the related aspects of business administration. The four-year secretarial program is illustrated in Table 12.

TABLE 12. University of North Dakota Four-Year Secretarial Program

(Junior and Senior Years Only)

Junior Year	First Semester	Second Semester
Business Law	3	3
Principles of Marketing	3	
Money and Banking	3	
Office Management		3
Business Reports and Letter Writing		3
Shorthand	3	3
Electives: With the approval of the Dean and the Chairman of the Department.		

Senior Year		
Corporation Finance	3	
Business Policies and Management		3
Advanced Shorthand	3	
Secretarial Practice		3
Personnel Management		3
Electives: With the approval of the Dean and the Chairman of the Department.		

BUSINESS EDUCATION PROGRAMS IN THE 1970'S

Junior colleges. Business education programs in postsecondary institutions have expanded tremendously in the 1970's. The junior colleges have continued to grow throughout the country in the past decade, and their purposes have amplified as well. In its 1977 catalog, Cabrillo College at Aptos, California, defines its purposes as follows:

1. Two-year curricula which are equivalent to freshman and sophomore years at a university or college. These programs permit the student to transfer to a four-year institution with full junior standing.

2. One- and two-year curriculum in preparation for employment in a number of semi-professional, industrial, business, and technical fields. These programs are designed to meet the employment needs of employers for both pre-service and in-service aspects of students' careers.
3. A general education program for personal enrichment and cultural development. Courses in this area help the students to increase their individual ability as citizens and improve community, home and family living.
4. Courses designed to make up high school deficiencies, permitting further education and training at the college level.
5. A program of guidance and orientation making individuals aware of their special ability and aptitudes so that they may make a wise choice of a vocational goal and secure the maximum benefits from their college experiences.

The purposes which Cabrillo College has listed are similar to those given by many junior colleges. Their curriculum continues to support the two basic purposes of the junior colleges that were prevalent in the 1950's and 1960's—to provide vocational training and to provide the first two years of a student's collegiate education so that the student may be admitted as a junior to a four-year college or university. In addition, other important services of Cabrillo College are to provide a general education program for all students, to permit many youth to eliminate high school deficiencies, and to establish a career orientation for all students so that they may consider the programs that will best meet their needs, abilities, and aspirations. This final goal incorporates the need of providing career education for all students, a goal noticeably absent in junior college catalogs of earlier years.

In the Cabrillo two-year program, 56 hours minimum may transfer to a four-year collegiate program—26 general education hours and 30 specialized hours. The program offering a specialization in office occupations at Cabrillo College appears in the 1977 catalog and is illustrated in Table 13.

TABLE 13. Cabrillo College Office Occupations Specialization*

Course	Credit Hours
Accounting Practice	4
Business Math	3
Business Communications	3
Personnel Relations	3
Introduction to Business	3
Machine Calculation	1-3
Typing	3-8
Office Practice	3
Office Work Experience	5-7
Electronic Data Processing	3
Machine Transcription	2
Filing and Records Management	3
Machine Transcription	2
Personal Development	2
Business Grammar	3

*30 Total Hours Needed

Boca Raton College in Florida is an independent coeducational institution where students graduating from the two-year program may earn an associate of arts degree in liberal arts and general business. To obtain the A.A. degree, students must complete a business core curriculum, which consists of 21 semester hours in communication skills, social and behavioral sciences, and arts and humanities. The business core from the Boca Raton 1977 catalog is shown in Table 14. After the business core has been com-

TABLE 14. Boca Raton College Business Core

Courses	Semester Hours
Communication Skills	
English Composition I	3
English Composition II	3
English Speech Communication	3
Social and Behavioral Sciences	
History or Behavioral Science Elective	3
Arts and Humanities	
Visual or Performing Arts Elective	3
Liberal Arts Electives	6
Total Hours in Business Core	21

pleted, the student may study in one of several specializations, one of which may be secretarial administration. Table 15 reveals the secretarial administration specialization.

TABLE 15. Boca Raton College Secretarial Administration Specialization

Courses	Semester Hours
Accounting I	3
Business Law 1	3
Business Elective	3
Introduction to Business	3
Elementary Typewriting	3
Intermediate Typewriting	3
Advanced Typewriting	3
Elementary Shorthand	3
Intermediate Shorthand	3
Dictation and Transcription I	3
Dictation and Transcription II	3
Office Practice I	3
Office Practice II	3
Total Hours in Concentration	39

Data processing has become quite popular in junior college programs in the 1970's, and the need for preparing qualified personnel in this area has caught the attention of many junior college administrators. Paris Junior College in Texas, for example, offers an associate of arts degree program in data processing. In addition to the general education requirements for the degree, the 1977 catalog shows that a student is expected to complete the sequence of courses listed in Table 16 to obtain a data processing background.

TABLE 16. Paris Junior College Data Processing Program

First Semester

Business Communications
Neat/3
Introduction to Computer Data Processing
Introduction to Unit Record Equipment
Orientation
Physical Education

Second Semester

Introduction to Business
Business Math
Human Relations in Business
Basic COBOL Language
Physical Education
Basic RPG II

Third Semester

Principles of Management
Office Machines
Advanced COBOL Language
Principles of Accounting
Elective

Fourth Semester

Business Law
Computer Operations
Advanced COBOL Applications
Principles of Accounting
Government

Private business schools. Private business schools in the 1970's have developed a comprehensive program in literally every aspect of business education. In metropolitan centers around the country, programs have been developed for students wishing to obtain vocational skills in typewriting, shorthand, data processing, word processing, and office skills in the legal and medical professions. One such program exists in Dallas, Texas, at the Executive Secretarial School. This private school, like many in the country, is accredited by the Accrediting Commission of the Association of Independent Colleges and Schools. The commission is recognized by the U.S. Office of Education as the official accrediting agency for business schools. The objectives of Executive are stated as follows in its 1978 catalog:

1. To achieve a superior level of skill in shorthand, typewriting, and transcription
2. To instill in each student the means for developing self-confidence in communication skills
3. To develop a practical knowledge of all phases of secretarial procedures and techniques

25

4. To provide a background in business administration subjects broad enough to enable graduates to progress to executive levels
5. To offer general education courses that will enrich a young woman's personal life and prepare her for better citizenship as well as increase her employment competency.

A minimum of 920 clock hours is required for graduation from the executive secretarial program, and 1,238 clock hours are required for graduation from the legal secretarial program. Courses in the school begin in June, September, and February, thus making it possible for a student to enroll for classes during any one of the three sessions. The subjects offered in the executive secretarial course appear in Table 17. Executive offers a placement service to assist students in their program and after graduation. All graduates have lifetime access to the services of the placement office.

TABLE 17. Executive Secretarial School
(Executive Secretarial Course)

Subjects	Clock Hours
Executive Seminars	40
Secretarial Procedures	50
Records Management	10
College Typewriting	260
Business Communications	50
Power Reading	35
Gregg Shorthand Theory	90
Dictation/Transcription	255
Secretarial Accounting	70
Business Office Machines	35
Executive Woman	24
Total Clock Hours	920

Four-year colleges and universities. Through the 1950's, skills subjects were prevalent in business education programs in many postsecondary schools. Then in the 1960's, additional emphasis was placed on basic business and management courses. In the 1970's business education included a multi-faceted curriculum in skills courses, basic business, consumer education, word processing, business communications, data processing, records and office management, and accounting. The consumerism movement prompted immediate action in curriculum revision, and various schools throughout the country have initiated programs in this area. Word processing programs have been included at such schools as Utah State University and the University of Wisconsin—Eau Claire as well as other four-year colleges. The purposes of the word processing courses at Utah State University are summarized in the 1977 catalog: "Development of proficiency at transcribing from magnetic medium machines, acquaintance with automatic typewriter operations."

The University of Wisconsin—Eau Claire provides a word processing course for students majoring in office administration. This course provides

" . . . an in-depth study in which participants compare paperwork costs, design word processing systems and reprographics programs for existing businesses, and experiment with selected electronic typewriting systems, dictation/playback systems and copier systems," according to the 1975 catalog.

Office administration/management and administrative services have received increased emphasis during the 1970's. Utah State's program for students wishing to pursue a bachelor of science degree in office administration appears in Table 18. The purpose of this program is summed up as follows: "Duties and responsibilities of the office manager, types of organization, methods of control, office arrangement and equipment, job analysis, selection, employment and training of employees."

TABLE 18. Utah State University Office Administration Program

Intermediate Typewriting	Law and the Consumer
Advanced Typewriting	Law of Contractual and Organi-
Dictation & Transcription	zational Relations
Business Machines	Business Statistics
Key Punch	Management Concepts
Word Processing	Corporation Finance
Office Practice	Fundamentals of Marketing
Supervised Work Experience	Behavioral Dimensions of
Office Data Systems	Management
Business Communications	Accounting (two courses)
Office Management	Introduction to Computer Science
Managing Personal Finances	Economics (two courses)
	Mathematics
	General Psychology

Other general education and business core courses are
taken to complete a bachelor's degree
in office administration.

The University of North Dakota has long been a leader in business education, both at the undergraduate and graduate levels. The undergraduate student enrolled in business education may enroll in one of four options: comprehensive, secretarial, accounting, and vocational office education. For the nonbusiness education major, programs in executive secretarial and administrative office services are available. The administrative office services major is, according to the 1962-64 undergraduate catalog:

> . . . designed to prepare office administration students for positions in administrative support services (office) area of modern organizations—office administration, records administration, reprographics and word processing, office services, and data processing. The option is recommended for students seeking primarily nonsecretarial supervisory positions in offices or in a nonteaching major.

This major requires the student to complete 33 general education credits and 35 business core credits. In addition, courses in one of the two options shown in Table 19 are required.

27

TABLE 19. University of North Dakota Administrative Office Services Major

Executive Secretarial Administration	Credits
Shorthand	4-10
Typewriting	4
Records Administration	2
Office Machines	2
Office Management	3
Business Reports and Letter Writing	3
Secretarial Office Machines	2
Organizational Behavior	3
Personnel Management	3
Executive Secretarial Procedures	3
Records Administration II	
or	3
Office Management II	

Administrative Office Services	
Intermediate Typewriting	2
Records Administration I	2
Records Administration II	3
Office Management I	3
Office Management II	3
Office Support Services Seminar	3
Business Reports and Letter Writing	3
Office Machines	2
Personnel Management	3
Organizational Behavior	3

The purposes of the basic records management and office management programs at the University of North Dakota reflect the current content for many office management programs throughout the country. The following course descriptions outline the essence of the office management and records administration course content:

Records Administration I: Study of modern filing systems and equipment, extensive practice in applying indexing rules and in filing correspondence, designing records systems for large and small offices.

Records Administration II: The application of basic principles to the creation, maintenance and disposition of both hard-copy and automated records and information; cost analyses, systems analyses, and work measurement methods applied to records administration; administration of basic microfilm systems and administration of active and inactive records centers.

Office Management I (offered through the Management Department): Principles and approaches to organization of administrative office services which includes: design and layout of productive office interiors; equipment selection and utilization; office systems and procedures analyses methods, tools and techniques, personnel recruitment, selection, training, and administration.

Office Management II: Management concepts applied to administrative support systems; planning, developing, analyzing, and controlling costs of office support systems; noncomputer and reprographic systems analyses and cost control;

legislative and legal restraints applied to information processing; and field experiences.

Arizona State University in its 1977 catalog offers several course options for business majors through the administrative services sequences which provide students with "the preparation for careers in one of the following: office management, secretarial administration, and business education." All business education majors must take a core of 15 courses which include the following: office management, records management, theory of administration communications, business report writing, and electronic data processing. In addition, students may select courses from the following:

Elements of Business Enterprise
Business Communications
Business Law
Business and Legal Environment
Small Business Administration
Legal Environment of Business
Business Research Methods
Seminar: Professional Report Writing
Research Methods

The Arizona State curriculum places heavy emphasis on communications, permitting the student several courses in which he/she may enroll.

Northern Illinois University has recognized the need for several specializations in business education. In the four-year program, the general education courses are identical for all specialties; however, the departmental requirements vary substantially from a high of 60 hours in the stenographic specialization to a low of 40 in the general clerical specialization. The program, taken from the 1977 catalog, offers students an option in five areas, as Table 20 reveals.

TABLE 20. Northern Illinois University Business Education Specializations

Specialization	Stenographic	General Clerical	Distributive Education	Office Education	Secretarial Administration
General Education	37	37	37	37	37
Departmental	60	40	41	50	46
Extradepartmental	15	15	24	16	18
Prerequisites	9	6	3	9	6
Electives	13	16	19	13	17

The administrative services option is also popular at the University of Wisconsin—Eau Claire. The program at Eau Claire offers three courses in administrative management for both undergraduate and graduate students. The purpose of each of these courses appears as follows in the 1977-1978 catalog:

Administrative Management: Office administration and supervision, and the contribution of such services to business. Emphasis on supervision and evaluation of office personnel, salary administration, incentive plans, in-service programs, and development of effective office communications systems.

Advanced Administrative Management: An in-depth study of the laws affecting the first-line supervisor, methods for productivity increases through work measurement techniques and motivation, and an examination of budgetary controls in the office.

Seminar in Administrative Services Management and Consulting: Designed to integrate and apply the background knowledge developed in administrative services to comprehensive office problems. Includes the development of consultative techniques and procedures in administrative services.

As stated in the earlier pages of this chapter, the American Assembly of Collegiate Schools of Business (AACSB) formulated a specific core of business administration courses to be completed by students obtaining majors in business. This "core" also applies (in many instances) to students who are pursuing a teaching degree in business. Certain universities do not require the business core courses because business teacher education students receive their degree from a School of Education rather than a School of Business.

The University of Rhode Island offers a typical business degree program accredited by AACSB and illustrated in its 1976 catalog. The curriculum appearing in Table 21 reveals the courses a student would complete for a social business/secretarial concentration.

TABLE 21. The University of Rhode Island
Social Business Secretarial Concentration

Freshman Year

Elementary Typewriting
Advanced Typewriting
Introduction to Quantitative
    Analysis for Business
    and Economics
Introduction to Computing
    in Management
Electives

Sophomore Year

Elementary Accounting
Managerial Statistics
Economic Principles
Introduction to American
    Education
Psychology of Learning
General Psychology
Business Communications

Junior Year

Accounting for Business
    Teachers
Elementary Shorthand
Business Machines
Law in a Business Environment
Advanced Shorthand
Financial Management
Fundamentals of Management
Methods and Materials in
    Secondary Schools
Marketing Principles

Senior Year

Dictation and Transcription
Methods and Materials of
    Teaching Business Subjects
Operations Management
Business Policy
Seminar in Teaching
Supervised Student Teaching

BUSINESS EDUCATION PROGRAMS IN THE 1980'S

The decade of the 1980's will soon be upon us, and with it will come new methodologies, refined concepts, and challenging opportunities in business education. Today's programs will require continued evaluation and analysis to ensure that stagnation does not occur in any of the rapidly expanding specialties within the profession. In the latter years of the 1970's, we began to realize that business education was assuming a larger and more demanding role in the training of teachers, office workers, and managers. The business world has demanded that we expand our horizons, and we must react to that challenge if we hope to continue supplying competently trained individuals.

Programs in business education are today making progress to fulfill these demands. In data processing, we have initiated new programs to educate keyboard operators, systems analysts, and programmers. But we cannot stop now, for as rapidly as we develop new programs to train these people, computer technology will demand even greater emphasis in these areas. When the third generation concept materialized so that we could generate suitable training programs, we were immediately challenged by the impact of a fourth generation of computers requiring new software programs.

The rapidly expanding information explosion forced us into the world of word processing, CRT terminals, keyboarding, and electronic playback systems. The curriculums revealed in this chapter have suggested an awareness of these advancing technologies through the increasing integration of data processing and word processing courses in the curriculums of post-secondary schools.

The information explosion has also created a need for expanding our records management emphasis at the postsecondary levels. Whereas in the last decade students enrolled in a records management course to learn how to file with alphabetic, subject, geographic, and alphanumeric systems, we now find that students must also be aware of the rapidly expanding technologies of micrographics and reprographics in the storage of important documents. The records manager has emerged as an influential factor in the everyday operation of a business, equally as important as the office manager and personnel manager. Thus, we will see an increased emphasis in this specialization within business education.

Typewriting is one of the oldest and most popular courses in business education. Although we see an increasing use of electronic playback systems in business offices today, the courses in typewriting at the postsecondary schools are not necessarily in a recession. Quite contrary to this position, typewriting is on a threshold of expansion in these schools for two reasons: (1) an increasing number of adults who return to school recognize the necessity of obtaining a personal skill in typewriting so that they may use it in their personal business and in many other facets of their personal lives; (2) with the advent of data processing in the decade of the 1980's, there will be an increasing need for "keyboarders," the people who operate the keyboards of various computer input systems. With these influential factors affecting typewriting, the inclusion of typewriting into the curriculums of the 1980's will be as realistic and essential as it was in previous years.

Communications skills are going to become more important in future curriculums, partially because of our society's continuous demand for information through advanced word processing systems and management information systems. Educators are also recognizing the need for an expanding communications program because of their belief that adults hoping to realize any degree of success in life must possess a working knowledge of the art of communications.

It would be safe to surmise that business educators are innovative and that many workable suggestions have come from the ranks of those who are convinced that various alternatives must be employed to accomplish our objectives and to sustain our goals. The traditional environment of today will yield to newer and better methods of teaching our youth for tomorrow. We must recognize the continuous need for these innovations just as surely as we have recognized and implemented a variety of practicable alternatives to teaching business education subjects in the 1970's: office simulation, competency-based education, individualized instruction, nontraditional classrooms, and many other alternatives that have permitted us not one but several instructional choices.

CHAPTER 2

One need not stop learning at the conclusion of formal public education. When a group of business people recognize that they have common needs and interests, there have developed plans for self-improvement. This has led to the formation of professional groups whose objectives then tend to meet the needs of their constituents. In this chapter Dr. Sanders identifies a number of such organizations which have developed and made available to their members "alternative" learning in business education. Annually, thousands of business employees at varying levels of background knowledge take advantage of the opportunity to improve their skills and to grow within the management structure. In some instances they are rewarded with credit toward a degree and/or professional certification.

Business Education Through Professional/Organizational Groups

MARGARET MCKENNA SANDERS

Western Michigan University, Kalamazoo

Educators have long recognized the necessity of lifelong education and have pursued it through various means including taking courses, reading, and attending conferences, seminars, or workshops. Business, too, recognizes this necessity, and this chapter will discuss one way in which lifelong business education may be pursued—through professional/organizational groups.

It is a cliché to say that the rate of change and the increase in knowledge is at a point where it is difficult to keep abreast of those elements and activities needed for personal professional growth and advancement. Nor can employees be expected to have obtained all necessary skills prior to employment. Specialized job skills must be added to the foundation of intellectual abilities an employee may have. Development of the individual on the job neither can nor should be limited to the classroom. In the final analysis, the individual must accomplish his or her own development. The extent of a person's ambition and interest in the preparation for effective performance and advancement influences the person's rate of growth and development.

Professional associations provide a variety of training experiences. Some of these are limited to technical fields, such as engineering or accounting; others are concerned with general problems of management or administration. Participation in the activities of such groups exposes an individual to current thinking in the area and also provides contact with personnel from other organizations with similar problems.

Many of the organizations offer certification programs for their members and others employed in the profession. These programs take different forms bu usually have experience requirements and include one or more examinations. They result in the person being designated as "certified" in the area. Examples include the Certified Professional Secretary, Certified Administrative Manager, and Certified Public Accountant.

To list and discuss all of the groups which offer business learning to their members would be impossible. They include the Administrative Management Society, the American Institute of Banking, the Association for Systems Management, the American Management Associations, the American Marketing Association, the National Association of Purchasing Management, the American Institute of Banking, the Data Processing Management Association, the National Association of Secretaries (International), the National Association of Educational Secretaries, the National Association of Legal Secretaries, the International Word Processing Association, the National Association of Accountants, the American Society for Personnel Administration, the International Association of Printing Craftsmen, the National Association of Realtors, Certified Life Underwriters, and many others. Most of these groups are organized on a chapter basis; they hold periodic meetings on local, regional, national, and even international levels. They publish journals and technical reports and have lending libraries to help their members keep abreast of significant advances in their fields.

In addition, organizations like the Institute for Professional Education, the Dartnell Institute of Management, Dale Carnegie Associates, and private management consultants provide seminars on a wide variety of topics which may be presented publicly or may be custom-designed for a particular company.

This chapter will discuss in detail the educational activities of eight professional organizations. Their activities are representative of most such organizations. Further information about particular organizations is readily available from the director or executive secretary or local chapters of the organization.

ADMINISTRATIVE MANAGEMENT SOCIETY

The Administrative Management Society was founded in 1919 as the National Office Management Association (NOMA). It now has over 150 chapters in the United States, Canada, and Jamaica and helps to keep today's professional administrative managers abreast of current trends and practices in the areas of management development, administrative services, personnel, systems and information management, and finance.

Its publications include *Management World, Guide to Management Compensation, Office Salary Survey,* and numerous courses and manuals made available to its members. Conducted on an annual basis, the AMS salary survey provides up-to-date weekly salary data for 20 clerical and data processing jobs in major cities and regions in the United States and Canada, as well as statistics on office unionization; paid vacations and holidays; company policies on pension plans, health and life insurance, hospitalization, and long-term disability. The annual survey on middle management personnel reports annual base compensation, insurance benefits, company payment of benefits, holidays and vacations, pension plans, and sick leave. Every two years a survey of turnover rates for office personnel is conducted covering over 2,600 companies in 80 major cities in the United States and Canada. AMS has a management information center which provides information on professional subjects for members at no charge and a library which makes available to the members books, magazines, and reports on virtually every phase of administrative management.

Meetings are held at local, regional, and international levels. Chapter meetings feature speakers and panel discussions and a variety of seminars and conferences. Business expositions held under the auspices of many local chapters are showcases for management tools. They provide an opportunity for managers to see, test, and compare the latest equipment and services available. Chapters within particular geographical areas are linked together to provide annual area conferences which offer stimulating management programs of mutual interest.

Held annually in a different major city, international conferences project the latest thinking on administrative management problems and managerial techniques through seminars, workshops, panel discussions, and films. Special one- and two-day educational programs on topics of timely importance to the forward-looking administrative manager are held throughout the year.

Recognizing the importance of the profession of administrative management, AMS launched a professional accreditation program in 1970 which gives qualified managers the opportunity of attaining the professional designation "Certified Administrative Manager." Candidates are required to pass a series of examinations and to meet other qualifications of experience, character, and leadership ability. The C.A.M. examination, which is offered in the spring and fall of each year at local testing centers, is a thorough five-part exam aimed at measuring the candidate's knowledge of the skills, concepts, and fundamentals of administrative management. A certificate and membership in the Academy of Certified Administrative Managers are issued to those persons who qualify.

AMERICAN INSTITUTE OF BANKING

The American Institute of Banking is the educational division of the American Bankers Association. Its purpose is to inform, educate, and train the men and women who work in banks. Its educational offerings are available only to its members. It has developed over 50 courses and seminars and the textbooks and instructional materials to accompany them.

The AIB program is offered through five study methods—chapters, study groups, study teams, correspondence study, and accelerated in-bank study. The Institute offers four certificates, each of which represents a different level of academic achievement. They are Basic, Standard, Advanced, and General. Students earn certificates based on the number of credits taken within a designated content area for each certificate. The areas of study include foundations of banking, banking functions, management and supervision, and language and communications. The AIB offers two types of courses—academic offerings which teach theories and principles at a conceptual level, and skill offerings which promote the acquisition of new or improved skills or techniques. An AIB course may employ several different formats—formal classroom instruction, seminar, or workshop.

AMERICAN MANAGEMENT ASSOCIATIONS

American Management Associations is the world's largest organization devoted to the development of professional management. Its 52,000 individual and organization members come from every state in the Union, every Canadian province, and more than 100 nations. The privileges of membership include AMA periodicals on important phases of management, AMA Executive Books, AMA Survey Reports, and free use of AMA's Management Information Service.

AMA's Center for Management Development puts on some 2,200 courses every year. These courses cover every area of job training and career development, for each level of employee from secretary to president.

AMA offers live programs, in-company programs, books, periodicals, and home study in subjects such as accounting, advertising, affirmative action, auditing, budgeting, career planning, cash management, collective bargaining, communication, compensation, creativity, credit management, customer service, data communications, direct mail, electronic data processing, employee fringe benefits, financial management, forecasting, human resource management, insurance, inventory management, job evaluation, legal aspects of management, management by objectives, marketing, materials management, office management, personnel management, printing and reprographics, public relations, real estate management, records management, sales management, secretarial development, supervision, telecommunications, time management, wage and salary administration, and many others.

AMERICAN MARKETING ASSOCIATION

The American Marketing Association is an organization of professional people engaged in marketing activities. The purpose of the Association is the advancement of the discipline of marketing. Through its predecessor units, the Association traces its inception from 1915; the present organization resulted from a 1937 consolidation of the American Marketing Society and the National Association of Marketing Teachers. With a membership of approximately 18,000, the Association is a vehicle for interchange between marketing practitioners, marketing educators, and marketing students.

Conferences at the local, national, and international levels offer a wide variety of educational opportunity. Recent conferences included such topics as Women and Marketing: Role Changes and Opportunities; Ag-Chem

Marketing: An Expanded Role in a Changing Environment; Attitude Research; and The New Role of the Marketing Professional.

Numerous publications are available through the Association. They include books, monographs, bibliographies, proceedings, and films. The *Journal of Marketing* is a national, quarterly publication for marketing executives and teachers of marketing which makes available information on new marketing discoveries, new techniques, new ideas, new trends, and new views on old problems The *Journal of Marketing Research* is a scientific journal which publishes the best available articles dealing with fundamental research in marketing and with marketing research practice. Focusing on the latest ideas and developments in marketing research, JMR articles deal with philosophical, conceptual, or technical aspects of marketing research and its applications. *Marketing News* is a biweekly tabloid newspaper which reports activities of the Association, its divisions, chapters, and committees as well as of the marketing field in general.

The *Annual Review of Marketing* provides the professional marketer with an integrated review and yearly updating of the various subfields within marketing. Articles specify practical implications of current marketing thought. Each is an original review and synthesis of the published literature in the major fields of marketing including buyer behavior; legal, economic, and political environment; retailing; wholesaling; marketing management, planning, and strategy; research and forecasting; distributing; pricing; product promotion; sales management; industrial marketing; and international marketing.

ASSOCIATION FOR SYSTEMS MANAGEMENT

The Association for Systems Management is an organization of systems specialists which was formed in 1947 to accelerate the personal development of its members and the systems profession. It does this through chapter and national activities; committee functions in research, education, and public relations; extended programs in local and regional areas in education and research; and the promotion of high standards of work performance.

Among the benefits it offers to the members of its more than 125 chapters are: monthly chapter meetings which regularly feature a variety of solid educational programs and provide an opportunity for members to meet and benefit from continuing contact with knowledgeable systems professionals; local and regional seminars, workshops, or conferences which provide specialized educational opportunities in the areas of management information systems, data processing, data communications, organization planning, and written communications; an annual conference which offers two and a-half days of intensive educational programming; publication of the *Journal of Systems Management* which reports on significant advances and techniques in the field of systems management; publication of bimonthly technical reports in the specialized areas of data processing, data communications, management information systems, organization planning, and written communications; and a technical reference library and technical inquiry service.

In addition, a structured approach to developing essential management skills is provided by the ASM Management Development Program. This trilevel program, for which certificates are awarded at each level of accomplishment, is designed to acquaint systems analysts and managers with the latest management philosophies and practices and to provide a broader understanding of the relationships of systems to corporate aims and objectives.

NATIONAL ASSOCIATION OF EDUCATIONAL SECRETARIES

The National Association of Educational Secretaries is a professional association for educational office personnel in the United States. It is dedicated to the professional growth and recognition of educational office personnel as members of the educational team. It has an active in-service program, an active Professional Standards Program, and provides numerous publications for its membership.

The Professional Standards Program was established by members to measure their services and skills as educational office personnel. It includes seven kinds of certificates, each with specific requirements in education, experience, and professional activity. Subject areas include accounting, government, English, psychology, records management, supervision, history of education, school law, and human relations.

NAEA annually sponsors three national conferences and an institute held each summer on a university campus. Numerous publications including a quarterly magazine, *The National Educational Secretary*, are sent to members. State and local organizations sponsor meetings, seminars, and conferences.

NATIONAL ASSOCIATION OF PURCHASING MANAGEMENT

The National Association of Purchasing Management has a membership of nearly 23,000 members and has a strong certification program. The Association offers seminars on a wide range of topics in conjunction with local purchasing management associations, as well as programs on college or university campuses. A list of recent seminars included the following topics: Energy Supply Laws and Regulations, Legal Aspects of Purchasing, Improving Management Skills and Communications, Product Life Cycle, How To Audit Purchasing Departments Effectively, Warehousing and Material Handling, Word Processing, Office Systems, and Communication. In addition, review courses for the N.A.P.M. Certification Examination are conducted. For certification, tests are offered twice a year in Purchasing, Materials Management, and Business Management.

NATIONAL SECRETARIES ASSOCIATION (INTERNATIONAL)

The National Secretaries Association (International) has over 30,000 members in more than 700 chapters in the United States, Canada, Mexico, and other countries. Its education-minded members attend regular meetings, sponsor workshops and seminars, and conduct study courses in a wide range of secretarial topics. They also receive *The Secretary*, a monthly magazine of interest to secretaries.

The Institute for Certifying Secretaries, a department of NSA, administers its CPS program through which a person who has successfully completed an examination and who has met the secretarial experience requirements may be designated a Certified Professional Secretary. As stated by the Institute, the purposes of the CPS program are to improve secretarial personnel by giving specific direction to an educational program and by providing a means of measuring the extent of professional development, to provide secretaries with the assurance that comes from having attained a professional educational standard, to promote the professional identity of the exceptional secretary, to assist management in selecting qualified secretaries, and to plan and sponsor additional programs of continuing development for the Certified Professional Secretary.

The CPS examination is given each May in approved colleges and universities. It is based upon an analysis of secretarial work with emphasis on judgment, understanding, and administrative ability gained through education and work experience. The areas tested are Environmental Relationships in Business, Business and Public Policy, Economics of Management, Financial Analysis and the Mathematics of Business, Communications and Decision Making, Office Procedures.

CONCLUSION

It is evident from the above descriptions that education for business is available through professional/organizational groups for those who will take advantage of it. An added plus for those who take an active part in such organizations—serving on committees, as committee chairpersons, and as officers at local, regional, and national levels—is that such service offers an opportunity to develop managerial skills and provides experience in management in a setting other than on the job.

CHAPTER 3

The traditional K-12 lockstep, followed by formalized college attendance, is no longer the sole mode of education. This chapter identifies much, if not all, of what is being done in business education in nontraditional settings and provides an excellent introduction to Part II of the Yearbook which presents the "how" of nontraditional business education.

Business Education in Nontraditional Settings

ANNE E. SCHATZ
Northern Michigan University, Marquette

DONALD BUSCHE
Saddleback College, Mission Viejo, California

NAOMI H. MORTON PHARR
Norfolk State College, Norfolk, Virginia

Since the early sixties, a wave of innovation has engulfed education and educational practices throughout the world. Concepts in the organization and structure of knowledge are changing. School programs are often no longer a continuous discourse divided into chapters of equal importance. They are becoming modular systems allowing for the creation of packages which can themselves be divided into interchangeable blocks. Paths imposed on students are no longer linear. Learning resources are diversified, particularly by multimedia approaches to learning.[1]

School time is no longer cut into uniform slices. Its pace varies, and diversified work replaces lockstep, uniform advancement for all.

Innovation has not only affected teaching methodologies and learning activities, it has also influenced reorganization of the school, adding to a growing list of nontraditional learning environments. The typical school building has lost much of its importance in countries with limited resources. Experience has shown that shortcomings in school installations, equipment, and buildings can be largely compensated for by new relationships between teachers and learners, by setting up a new kind of educational atmosphere. In fact, on the whole, progress within schools themselves goes hand in hand with improved practical links between schools and society.

Gould defines nontraditional study as an attitude.

Nontraditional study is more an attitude than a system and thus can never be defined except tangentially. This attitude puts the student first and the institution second; concentrates more on the former's needs than the latter's conve-

---

[1]Faure, Edgar. *Learning To Be.* Paris: UNESCO, 1972. pp. 137-54.

nience; encourages diversity of individual opportunity rather than uniform prescription; and de-emphasizes time, space, and even course requirements in favor of competence and, where applicable, performance. It has concern for the learner of any age and circumstances, for the degree aspirant as well as the person who finds sufficient reward in enriching life through constant, periodic, or occasional study.[2]

How familiar is the teacher of today with nontraditional settings? What do these terms mean as they apply to nontraditional settings: open school . . . free school . . . school without walls . . . school without schools . . . satellite colleges . . . adult education . . . continuing education . . . learning centers . . . alternative high schools . . . external degrees . . . family college . . . weekend college . . . ?

It is difficult to say exactly how many alternative schools or programs exist in this nation. Several states have now passed enabling legislation designed to encourage the growth of alternatives. California, for example, has mandated that every school district have at least one alternative continuation school.

In a 1977 study conducted for the National Institute of Education, it was reported that the majority of alternatives at the high school level had been developed for disruptive school youth who demonstrated an inability to progress in a normal manner within a traditional school setting. At the postsecondary level, however, many other students are served through alternatives, such as the new student or new client, the handicapped, the senior citizen, dropouts, the underemployed and the unemployed, and others.

This chapter will discuss the following alternatives to traditional schooling:

1. Alternatives that focus on a philosophy of learning
   a. Free schools
   b. Open schools
   c. Vocational schools
   d. Credit by examination
2. Alternatives that focus on a special clientele
   a. Family college
   b. Alternative schools, continuation schools, dropout centers, maternity schools
   c. Adult education
   d. Emeritus institute
3. Alternatives that focus on special resources or facilities
   a. Schools without walls
   b. University without walls
   c. Noncampus college
   d. External degrees
   e. Schools without schools

---

[2]Gould, Samuel B. *Diversity by Design.* Commission of Non-Traditional Study. San Francisco: Jossey-Bass, 1973. p. xv.

4. Alternatives that focus on administration and organization
   a. Schools within schools
   b. Satellite campuses
   c. Weekend college
   d. 24-hour school
   e. Year-round school
5. Alternatives that focus on instructional approaches
   a. Minicourses
   b. Montessori method
   c. Individualized learning programs
   d. Learning centers
   e. Competency-based teacher education

ALTERNATIVES THAT FOCUS ON A PHILOSOPHY OF LEARNING

Alternatives have been formed because of a philosophy of learning that is not in agreement with that of traditional education. One of the most common reasons for starting new schools is a determination to break away from restrictions and pressures for conformity placed on children by conventional school authorities. The Liberation School was organized as a result of the women's liberation movement, and its founders intended it to be a place where role playing was eliminated. Other schools were begun because frustrated parents developed deep dissatisfactions over traditional school practices. Desires for moral and religious training, for better preparation for college, for more humane treatment, and for greater emphasis on vocational training are some of the other reasons.

Free schools. The free school was founded by those who believed practices of conventional schools inhibited creative learning. The free school, often looked upon as a revolt against the practices of conventional education, is an attempt to eliminate compulsory attendance and other governmental controls and to place education back under the control of the people and learning back in the hands of the learners. By placing the functions of planning, execution, and evaluation of learning in the hands of the students, the advocates of free schools propose to develop enough confidence and responsibility in students to enable them to handle their own affairs.

Free schools know no racial or socioeconomic lines. The movement possesses many characteristics of the communal living culture and the practices of certain religious sects.

Most free schools are plagued with financial problems and harassed by governmental and community pressures. A few of them, including six in Berkeley, California, receive community support. The Other Ways School has a contract with the Berkeley Board of Education to carry out its unique program and to train teachers. The voucher system is being given consideration in several areas as a way to bolster the sagging financial structure of parochial and private schools. Its acceptance would be a big boost for alternative schools and would give parents the opportunity to participate in making decisions and choices about the education of their children.

Underlying the free school movement are the ideas of the British Infant Schools, A. S. Neill's Summerhill, and Jean Piaget. Parents observed millions of nonmotivated pupils, particularly among the disadvantaged in urban centers of population. They were concerned about the apparent inhumanity of many schools and the lack of interest and progress of too many children. Students were bored and humiliated, feeling that education was not for them. Some teachers were dissatisfied and frustrated because they could not break out of the traditional system to provide human individual help for children who desperately needed it.

Unfortunately, the lack of structure, an important ingredient of the free school, contributes to problems. Although parents advocate educational settings that enhance student freedom, they differ in their definition of freedom; some even feel that children will naturally learn the things they need to know if left to themselves. Students are not required to attend classes within time frames or to learn amounts of material at the same rate as others in the free school. They may do what they want to do, learn what interests them—all within a relaxed, unrestricted environment.

Parents are often disappointed when they do not see visible evidence that learning is taking place, as they did within a traditional setting. Some parents may break away, organizing a *new* free school that represents a varying instructional system in place of the one believed to have basic weaknesses. In the process, some free school advocates have had to face one of the problems that plagued conventional educators for so long—determining what is the best environment for learning.

Leadership in the free school movement needs to establish objectives that will provide direction to the movement. Utopian ideas and ideals may have to be tempered by the hard realities of the world as it exists. Educators in free schools must guard against developing students who are too inflexible to adjust to a more structured environment, just as educators in public schools must guard against developing students who are too inflexible to adjust to a freer environment.

Open schools. Open schools and schools without walls should not be used synonymously. Open schools is the more comprehensive term, which may or may not refer to physical walls. The central notion is that an open program prevails, developed by teachers and students together and untouched by syllabi, rules, or regulations imposed from the outside. The difference between an open school and a free school is that open schools exist within the public school system while the free school operates independently.

Open schools are highly experimental learning environments. The concept of the open school is associated with Britian's Open University. Most open schools have these characteristics:

1. A flexible learning environment with large open work areas surrounding a resource center and library
2. Informal teaching methods
3. Nongraded procedures
4. Emphasis upon student decision making and responsibility.

Proponents of the open school concept believe that students have more positive attitudes toward themselves, more self-confidence in working difficult problems, and more positive attitudes toward school.

The St. Paul Open School was developed to provide students with competencies needed to live in a complex, changing world, in short, to be highly effective people and responsible citizens. Students possess much freedom to determine their educational program; there are no high school graduation requirements. Learning activities include community-based learning, independent study, exchange programs, and participation in various learning centers located in St. Paul. Students must successfully achieve a minimum performance level on a series of competencies planned between the student and adults associated with the school.

Follow-up studies of graduates of the Open School in St. Paul were compared with a random sample of St. Paul High School graduates, all of whom were attending the University of Minnesota, and show that (1) the open school graduates had significantly higher GPS's, (2) the open school students had significantly wider range of declared majors, (3) there was no significant difference in ACT scores.

Negative factors reported by a majority of students in the open school concerned noise—there were not enough quiet areas in the school in which to study. In general, though, St. Paul Open School students tended to perform as well if not better than their conventional school counterparts in both cognitive and affective areas. These findings are supported by both internal and external evaluation teams using combinations of statistical data and naturalistic inquiry.

Vocational schools. Schools known as vocational-technical schools, vocational-technical colleges, area vocational-technical schools, regional occupational centers, and regional occupational programs meet the needs of students in the area of their vocational interests. Their common bond is a dedication to vocational education.

When first formed, vocational schools were considered by many as an alternative to academic preparation and to the programs leading to a degree. Research studies generally support the idea that vocational students come largely from the lower half of the student population in ability. Today, with an increasing emphasis on career and vocational education, vocational schools are better able to serve the interests of students without the stigma imposed by researchers who compare their achievements with nonvocational students in a conventional learning environment.

Credit by examination. Few people can deny that there are educational benefits resulting from nonschool experiences. Work experience, travel, and leisure activities offer valuable educational experiences.

Various programs have been developed to accommodate students who have acquired knowledge outside the classroom. Three commonly used programs are (1) College-Level Examination Program (CLEP), (2) Advanced Placement Program (APP), and (3) Teacher-Made Tests.

CLEP includes two types of examinations—the General Examinations and the Subject Examinations. The General Examinations test information equal to courses taken by college freshmen and sophomores. The Subject Examinations are similar to final examinations given for particular undergraduate courses. Major businesses in the country have begun to accept satisfactory scores on the CLEP examination in lieu of formal college work.

While CLEP offers recognition of college-level work in nontraditional learning settings, the APP offers high school students college-level work to demonstrate college-level achievement. Basically, the objectives of the APP are the articulation of high school and college study, enrichment of curriculum, and motivation of secondary school students. At present more than 1,000 institutions of higher learning participate in this program.

The teacher-constructed examination is an informal method of awarding experiential learning credit. Teacher-made tests are commonly the basis for the credit-by-examination policies currently used by many colleges and universities. Such policies have been found to encourage potential business students to enroll in college courses. The returning student who has recent work experience, or has completed basic courses in a subject area in high school, is often encouraged to take courses if he/she knows that the lowest level courses need not be taken, that courses may be challenged to determine a beginning point for further study.

Regardless of the format, credit-by-examination is straightforward—credit is awarded on the basis of what or how much one knows or how one can perform rather than on the number of hours he/she has attended school.

ALTERNATIVES THAT FOCUS ON A SPECIAL CLIENTELE

There is a growing list of new student markets that require attention to nontraditional methods of study. There are the traditional adult and transfer students who represent markets that seldom have been cultivated in the past. There are the academically underprepared of all ages and ethnic groups. There are married women; the older, working individuals; and the incarcerated. Knowles states the justification for organizing alternatives to learning for the new student:

> To an adult, his experience is him. He defines who he is, establishing his self-identity, in terms of an accumulation of his experiences. So if you ask an adult who he is, he is likely to identify himself in terms of what his occupation is, where he has worked, where he has traveled, what his training and experiences have equipped him to do, and what his achievements have been. An adult is what he has done. Because an adult defines himself largely by his experience, he has a deep investment in its value. And so when he finds himself in a situation in which his experience is not being used, or its worth is minimized, it is not just his experience that is being rejected—he feels rejected as a person.[3]

Family college. Technological advancements are obvious signs of change. But perhaps more significant changes are occurring in social structure, among these, the family. It is apparent that the concept of the family unit and its role in social structure is changing.

---

[3]Knowles, Malcolm S. *The Modern Practice of Adult Education.* New York: Associated Press, 1970. p. 44.

Both these factors have helped create a need for lifelong learning. The need has been met at Rockland Community College in Suffern, New York, through a family college. It seeks to (1) respond to the needs and interests of a variety of age groups found within a typical family unit, (2) further integrate the traditional family by strengthening relationships between its members, and (3) assist the family in transition through education. If reflects the philosophy of community education and service and supports the fact that community colleges have to accept the responsibility of continually interacting with their environment in responding to community needs and attitudes.

To accommodate whole families, a weekend program of course offerings is available. Adults may pursue college credit courses in business education, or may enroll in graduate courses through a local college leading to a master of business administration degree, or may take credit-free courses (such as How To Buy a Used Car) for pleasure, personal enrichment, recreation or leisure use. For the young child there are courses called Computers for Children and Ecology in Everyday Life. Teenagers may enroll in typewriting or other office skills courses. Recognizing that family unity requires shared experiences, trip and tours are scheduled for the whole family.

Finally, education *for* the family *about* the family is provided with the cooperation of the county Mental Health Association and other agencies. This effort involves learning to adjust in order to meet new life situations. The birth of a child, the loss of a family member, the growth of a child into adolescence, the aging of parents, and breakdown of the family unit—all are critical but normal transition periods requiring adjustment in people's lives. Family college is becoming increasingly involved with the family—first, by providing for the needs and interests of the different age groups in the family; next, for the needs of the family as a single unit; xnd finally, for the needs of the family in transition and change. As concern shifts from preparatory to recurrent education, models such as the family college will become increasingly significant in the search for future forms of lifelong learning.

Alternative high schools. These schools provide educational programs for those students alienated from the regular school program. Alternative high schools take on many aspects: continuation schools, dropout centers, maternity schools, to name a few. The goals of these schools include:

1. Providing educational experiences that will motivate the student to complete an educational objective, such as earning a high school diploma.
2. Fostering a maximum positive change in each student by assisting in the identification of personal and emotional needs. If affective domain problems are not given attention in a personalized and individualized manner, cognitive growth is inhibited substantially and loses its importance in the mind of the student.
3. Providing well-planned orientation programs that include insights into the world of work, personal work responsibilities, and efforts required by the individual for job success.
4. Developing acceptable social behavior through efforts to improve self-esteem, strengthen self-concepts, and increase feelings of individual worth.

5. Establishing relationships with cooperating agencies and parents in order to ensure continued success when the student leaves the alternative school.

A strong, supportive and positive learning environment within these educational settings has resulted in success stories that could not have been achieved under a regimented traditional classroom setting.

Adult education. Adult education serves many purposes in today's society: former dropouts can go back to complete the requirements for a high school diploma, basic educational subjects can be improved, or new citizens can learn to speak English. Adult education can also be a means of individual development and a prolongation of education. For many years it has been the source of recreational courses. With its no college-credit status, adult education reflects the pulse of society. It rides the tide of innovations, technological advances, self-awareness concerns, and economic situations.

Often the offerings of business skills courses in adult education programs are limited to the availability of equipment and facility. Facilities are frequently borrowed or leased from local high schools or vocational-technical schools (regional occupational centers in California).

From an administrative viewpoint, courses for adults can be scheduled with none of the obstacles of the traditional schools; in addition, courses may be removed from the schedule as easily. Although adult education has been treated here as a separate educational entity, the term has also been used to refer to all adults in all institutions taking courses that do not lead to a four-year college degree.

Emeritus institute. In 1900, there were three million people over the age of 65 in this country; there are now approximately 21 million; and between 29 and 33 million are projected for the year 2000 A.D. At a time when birth and mortality rates have decreased dramatically, more people are living to an average age of 70 to 75. Early retirement is becoming more common, and there is reality and promise for active middle and later years.

Education is for all ages, yet many educational programs are not designed to fill the needs and desires of the older adult in our society—this is especially true of some of our business education programs. The emeritus institute concept, therefore, provides for a cooperative effort between the school and the older adult community in addressing this issue.

For business education, the emeritus institute concept means providing vocational training for those desiring new careers, developing retirement planning and preparation programs for those looking forward to this phase of their lives, permitting advanced placement in degree and certificate programs for those wishing to fulfill a long delayed educational goal, and sponsoring special workshops and lecture series for those desiring to maintain contact with current business affairs.

The goal of the emeritus institute is the "re-involvement" of the elderly in the cultural growth of the sponsoring school, college, or university. This goal, if fully realized, should prove invaluable to the imaginative business educator.

ALTERNATIVES THAT FOCUS ON SPECIAL RESOURCES OR FACILITIES

This nontraditional category may be defined figuratively as a program moving beyond the walls of the building or literally as a concept of involving programs offered outside the school. These schools may be an evolution from open space schools to schools with few or no internal walls and finally to schools with no walls, or no schools at all in the physical sense. They focus on a direct response to the knowledge explosion. Course credit is often granted for doing academic study via the media of television, radio, newspaper, the mail, and the telephone. Tutorials with human mentors and mechanically controlled monitors, as well as simple and sophisticated computer terminals, are being utilized as facilitators and enablers in the teaching/learning efforts.

Schools without walls. An early school without walls concept was implemented in the 1967 Parkway Program in Philadelphia, where much instruction was provided by experts in the community. In addition to community courses and home-based courses, the student attended a daily tutorial session dealing wi h peer counseling.

Evaluation of the Parkway Program showed that the student body represented wide range of academic achievement, students had greater satisfaction than those in conventional schools, student self-concepts improved, parental attitudes and involvement increased, and satisfaction with staff improved. An observation made by the evaluation team was that students perceived rules and regulations not as hostile attacks upon their humanity, but as essential ingredients in creative group living.

University without walls. The Union for Experimenting Colleges and Universities, with grants from the United States Office of Education and the Ford Foundation, started a university without walls program at 20 institutions. The University of Minnesota began the program in 1971 as an alternative form of higher education because (1) students were unable to attend classes during the working day and, more importantly, (2) adult learners desired recognition of past and present experience and an individualized system of learning. Some of the features of the university without walls are: offering classes in neighborhood locations, extending registration hours, offering courses to senior citizens at no charge, reducing tuition rates when no credit is given, and changing content to meet adult needs and interests. In 1977 there were 35 university without walls programs in the United States.

Noncampus college. Perhaps one of the largest colleges without a campus is Coastline Community College in Orange County, California. Coastline has 130 addresses for its classes including city halls, libraries, parks, community clubhouses, and a fire station. More than 23,000 students attend over 1,400 courses in one semester. About one-third of the teaching staff comes from business and industry.

Without buildings to help create a bond among students, invisibility and isolation are common problems of the noncampus college. According to Smith:

> There's nothing to shake your fist at when you're angry, there's no place to retreat when you're confused, and there is no physical image in your mind. It's easy to

say that education is a process designed to help students learn, but it's very difficult to maintain yourself personally and professionally in a world of processes.[4]

External degree programs. The most predominant example of the "without walls" concept is the external degree program. Not only do these programs represent universities without walls, but they have liberal admissions policies and residence requirements, relatively flexible time frames, and student-centered curriculums. This nontraditional type of program is designed to complement the student's learning style while fulfilling his/her educational needs and desires. Classes are generally offered at convenient locations and at times suitable for the program's clientele.

Because the programs do not require costly buildings, libraries, full-time teaching staff, supportive services, and the like, the sponsoring institutions are often able to attract and retain the services of recognized leaders and authorities in various area of study. These recognized leaders act as consultants, lecturers, mentors, curriculum developers, and educational planners.

Utilizing competency-based curriculums, a variety of delivery systems, and the expertise of educational leaders, external degree programs demonstrate a nontraditional approach to a quality and viable educational program. This is evidenced by the fact that many of the external degree programs currently in operation throughout the nation are fully accredited by their respective state and regional accrediting associations.

Schools without schools. A dilemma of different proportions faced Columbus (Ohio) School District officials when the prolonged cold wave in the winter of 1977 caused a serious fuel shortage. Schools were closed, but children went right on attending classes held by teachers in banks, bars, hotels, private homes, and other available places. In addition, they made liberal use of television and radio as citywide teaching media. An afternoon newspaper devoted two pages to school lessons, television and radio class schedules, and other school-related information.

Although innovation was accepted because of an emergency, Columbus officials admit that the experience showed them that they shouldn't be so uptight about the rules associated with public schools. Parents, who became tutors and aids to their children's learning overnight, developed a respect for education they had not had prior to the emergency. In order to keep the process of learning intact, the creative talents of teachers, administrators, parents, and the community were unleashed. In fact, many persons were surprised by their own talents and achievements. The experience also proved that a 50-60 minute class can be effectively presented in 15 minutes on television, although not without considerable effort on the part of teachers who learned how to make main points and eliminate unnecessary verbiage.

The emergency lasted a month, but learning continued. The experience has been described in a 200-page manual, *Handbook for Schools Without Schools.*

---

[4]Smith, P. P. "College Without a Campus." *New Directions for Community Colleges* 4: 69-76; Spring 1976.

ALTERNATIVES THAT FOCUS ON ADMINISTRATION
AND ORGANIZATION

Some nontraditional schools are organized within another school for the purpose of accommodating a special clientele or experimenting with teaching methods. These programs may be administered by a separate staff as a separate branch of the larger school.

Schools within schools. Schools and colleges have been developed under the auspices of a conventionally organized faculty. In 1969 the Paracollege opened its doors within St. Olaf College in Northfield, Minnesota. Although the original purpose of Paracollege was to experiment with and improve a variety of teaching methods, it became, because of the clientele that chose to go there, an alternative track to a degree.

Satellite campuses. During the past decade, higher education was primarily concerned with access to education. As mentioned throughout this chapter, institutions across the nation were busy seeing that the "new student" had the opportunity to learn—even if at minimal levels. More recently, however, higher education has begun to focus its efforts on the maximizing of learning and meeting the needs of its more heterogeneous clientele. To this end, many colleges and universities are establishing and operating satellite colleges.

A satellite college may be a scale model of the parent campus offering a skeleton program to individuals living in remote or inaccessible locations. Satellite campuses have also resulted from a college's attempt to utilize local resources. For example, the business department at Los Angeles Trade Tech College (one of the 10 campuses of the vast Los Angeles Community College District) has developed a travel management program at a satellite campus near the Los Angeles International Airport. This program is hailed as being the nation's largest and most comprehensive program of its kind.

An interest in providing in-service training programs for local business and industrial firms has often resulted in a satellite campus operation. Numerous colleges offer specialized and general education programs to employees of large firms before, during, or after working hours as well as to interested individuals from outside the company. These programs often utilize the facilities of local firms.

Clearly the trend is no longer that "people go to college," but that "college goes to the people."

Weekend college. After the traditional programs of the weekend on Friday, some colleges open the doors to their weekend college. Orange Coast College utilizes this concept so that people with busy weekday and weeknight schedules can make use of blocks of time to concentrate on studies. Over 190 courses are offered, including courses in business and secretarial science.

24-hour school. A variation of the schools within schools concept is the 24-hour school were teachers work shifts to accommodate students. In many center city school districts, people know that, regardless of the hours they work in business and industry, business classes are available around the clock.

Year-round school. The year-round school is one answer to overcrowded classrooms and increasing equipment costs. One estimate is that the year-round school becomes economically feasible when investments in hardware and software constitute 50 percent or more of the total school budget.

Mobile schools. Another way to "take the school to the people" is with mobile schools. Although not an inexpensive investment, transportable training programs are effective alternatives to traditional settings. Business education classrooms on wheels take typewriting, machines, and general office classes to the community on a regular basis. Mobile schools can be economically feasible only if extensively utilized, so in extremely cold climates, other methods of reaching the interested public should be pursued.

ALTERNATIVES THAT FOCUS ON INSTRUCTIONAL APPROACHES

The most common alternatives to conventional learning are provided through nontraditional instructional approaches. Business and office education are readily adapted to the innovative methods of learning, and business educators use nontraditional approaches with varying degrees of success.

Although there are innovative instructional approaches from modular scheduling to television, this section will be limited to coverage on minicourses, individualized instruction, learning centers, and competency-based teacher education.

Minicourses. The minicourse offers unusual opportunities for teachers to experiment with a new technique. Large blocks of time are needed instead of the 45-minute class period and the duration of the course should be one to two weeks. A short course carefully planned should be fast moving and highly motivating. Minicourses may be, for some students, an exploratory course. Some minicourses offered are A Look at the Modern Office, The New Role of the Computer, Modern Family Finance, Adjustment After Divorce, and Survival for Young Singles.

Montessori method. The Montessori method is a revival of a program developed by Dr. Maria Montessori in Italy at the beginning of the century. She developed special learning materials and equipment to prevent permanent retardation among poor, deaf, and disadvantaged children.

The Montessori method became the basis for individualized learning. The materials stress sensory-motor learning and provide a way to progress independently in self-initiated activities. With each child progressing at individual rates, the role of the teacher is to diagnose learning difficulties and provide materials appropriate to overcome them.

Individualized learning programs. Individualized systems of learning or individualized programs are usually incorporated in nontraditional educational settings. (See Chapter 4.) The primary difference between individualized learning in the traditional school and individualized learning in nontraditional settings is the lack of restrictions imposed by time and space in the latter. While in a conventional school, credits and grades may be required at the end of quarters or semesters, classes must be attended, and time boundaries are always present, individualization of instruction in the nontraditional setting opens up limitless possibilities. It gives motivated students, typical in the new student markets, a freedom to learn at their own convenience and pleasure. Individualized learning accompanied by counseling and supportive services provides the student who has been alienated by a regular school program an opportunity to experience, examine, and learn at a rate that permits strengthening of the self-concept and coping with personal problems simultaneously.

Learning centers. In an attempt to make business classes more appealing, to take advantage of technological innovations, and to individualize the delivery system, business educators have borrowed the learning center concept from the elementary educators. To most business educators, the term *learning center* brings to mind rows of carrels equipped with typewriters or other business machines and supportive audiovisual hardware and software. The programs are thought of as boxes of slide-tape presentations, stacks of videotapes, and the like. The instruction is believed to be less formal and yet more personal.

Concerned business educators now realize that there are options to the learning center concept. Such individuals recognize that the true "learning center" is the institution itself, and what we in business education operate are actually "learning absistance centers."

A learning assistance center is nothing more than an environment that makes the learning process as easy, convenient, and attractive as possible. Such a center need not be expensive, not need it tie up vast amounts of district resources. A business learning assistance center may be a specialized center— offering typewriting or shorthand programs only—or a general center offering assistance to students enrolled in a myriad of business subjects. No matter what design it takes, the learning assistance center is looked upon as a place where students can get feedback as to progress and receive assignments based on the diagnosis of performance and needs.

Competency-based teacher education. Often written about and discussed, competency-based teacher education still remains a nontraditional design. A program of teacher education that is completely competency-based, such as that developed and implemented at Wayne State University in Michigan, is rare.

The first step in developing a competency-based teacher education program is to state the competencies that students must demonstrate in order to be qualified to become teachers. Students must learn to break down course material into learning components and write objectives that clearly define each learning component. They must develop learning activities that will take the learners from their present levels to the desired level of competency. They must become comfortable with varying instructional methods so that they will not approach the classroom with only one developed approach—the lecture.

Next, students must plan, with the teacher educator's assistance, how they will develop the competencies needed to become a teacher. Intermediate objectives or steps should be set so that students may progress toward the final goal.

Finally, students will demonstrate their competencies to the teacher educator and classmates or others. The teaching demonstration may be videotaped for future reference by the student in order to make an evaluation of the performance and determine methods of improvement.

In order to instill the concept of competency-based education effectively, teacher educators must implement the concept in their instructional methodologies, not merely talk about it to students. Because future teachers will teach in the same manner as they are taught, attention should be given to alternative methods of instruction.

EVALUATION

Nontraditional business education programs are not always welcomed with open arms by traditional faculty, administrators, school board members, and state officials. Sometimes these programs are tolerated, sometimes promoted, sometimes terminated, and sometimes mandated upon reluctant instructors, chairpersons, or institutions.

An innovative procedure to evaluate the total educational process, including business education, is completed annually at Mt. San Jacinto College in California through an educational audit. The educational auditor provides an assurance to the public that a statistically reliable selection of program objectives has been achieved as reported. The educational auditor may suggest better methods of setting objectives and measuring educational output. The institution publishes an objectives report that must accurately reflect the accomplishments of the educational services rendered.

The educational auditor employed to conduct the audit must possess a strong background in management systems and all phases of the educational process. Ideally, this auditor should be: a new professional—a "Certified Educational Auditor"—trained in educational philosophy, psychology, curriculum development, methodology, statistics, and systems; experienced in the operation of an educational system at the levels of instructor and manager; and thoroughly committed to objectivity in observing, reporting, and making recommendations.

SUMMARY

There is something stimulating, exciting, and rewarding in developing and implementing nontraditional methods to accomplish educational objectives. Innovative ideas, when conceived, designed, and implemented, require imagination, resourcefulness, and productivity with unswerving persistence. Yet sooner or later, all nontraditional forms of education stop being nontraditional; they are either abandoned or they become traditional. The various approaches discussed in this chapter have been tried, evaluated, and challenged. They have not yet passed the "traditional" test, but many have withstood the test of time and, as a result, are growing stronger.

Part II

CHAPTER 4

Individualizing Business Education Instruction

The first chapter of Part II concerns individualized instruction and individual learning in secondary education, two-year colleges, and four-year colleges, and comparisons are made with traditional instruction. This provides a basis for discussing alternatives. All three sections of the chapter clearly recognize that the teacher, and the teacher's preparation, becomes the generator for the adoption of alternatives through utilizing individualized instruction.

Section A: At the Secondary School Level

LOUIS CHACON, JR., and TOBY D. JALOWSKY
Arizona State Department of Education, Phoenix

To meet the diverse needs of public schools that are becoming more and more heterogeneous, business education instructors seem to be turning to new instructional approaches. One approach is relating instruction in various areas of business and office education to the background, interest, needs, and abilities of the individual student. This approach is recognized as individualized instruction.

Individualized instruction falls into two categories—informal and formal. In the informal category, the teacher is aware that some learners need more time to learn or master a particular skill, while others need less. The teacher, then, provides additional challenges to reduce boredom for the fast learners and gives extra practice or drill or allows more time for the slower ones. The teacher may also try a different method of teaching or extra homework assignments.

In the formal system of individualization, the intent is to provide an individual program for each student after diagnosing, prescribing, and evaluating. The diagnosis phase pretests to determine what the student knows or can do in a specific learning area. Next follows the prescription, the selection of an instructional program for the student. The teacher then provides the student with the materials for the selected or assigned program, and the student completes that work. The evaluation consists of a posttest administered to measure what has been learned, and if the student has achieved a certain level of mastery, he/she moves on to the next level of learning.

"Individualized instruction consists of any steps taken in planning and conducting programs of studies and lessons that suit them to the individual student's learning needs, learning readiness, and learner characteristics or 'learning style,' " according to Glen Heathers.[1] To this working definition we can relate various approaches to individualization such as *self-paced* instruction. In this approach students with different learning abilities are exposed to the same materials and permitted to work at their own rate of speed, some faster and some slower than others. The value of this is quite obvious; those students that are able to master the subject quickly are not held back, while those that have some degree of difficulty are not forced to move at an uncomfortable pace.

Another method is the *personalized approach,* which could be defined as that which relates the subject being studied to the personal background, interest, needs, and abilities of the student.[2] Through this method the students not only proceed at their own rate/speed, using materials suitable for their individual abilities, but they derive some immediate practical value from the procedure.

Another individualized instructional approach is *mastery learning.* In this approach, it is assumed that all students can master a great deal of what they are taught in school "if the institution is approached systematically, if students are helped when and where they have learning difficulties, and if they are given sufficient time to achieve mastery, and if there is some clear criterion of what constitutes mastery."[3] This type of instruction can be designed for use in a typical group-based classroom situation.

There are many other approaches to individualized instruction mentioned by various authors in periodicals and textbooks. Those discussed here are used only to help define the overall concept of individualized instruction.

Individualized instruction employs various modes to provide for the needs, readiness, and learning styles of students such as:

1. Individual students, at any level of schooling, can work on different learning tasks toward different goals.
2. Individual students can use different learning materials or equipment in working toward the same learning goal.
3. Individual students can study a given task in different types of individual or group settings—individual seat work, pupil-team arrangement, subgroups.
4. Individual students can work on a given learning task with use of different methods of teaching/learning. This method can be lecture, group discussion, tutorial assistance, or independent study.
5. Individual students can be assigned to different teachers to produce effective student/teacher match-ups. The personality and teaching style of the teacher is important in determining how well a given student progresses.

---

[1]Heathers, Glen. "A Working Definition of Individualized Instruction." *Educational Leadership* 34:342; February 1977.

[2]*Personalizing Instruction in Business, Economics and Related Subjects.* Saratoga Springs, NY: Center for Business and Economics Education, Empire State College, 1976. pp. 4, 5.

[3]Bloom, Benjamin S. "An Introduction to Mastery Learning Theory." *Schools, Society and Mastery Learning.* (Edited by James H. Block.) New York: Holt Rinehart and Winston, 1974, p. 6.

6. Individual students can be allowed different amounts of time as needed to complete a learning task. This mode is a central feature in all modes of individualization.

No specific system or approach developed can or should be advocated for all types of learners; however, educators must experiment, research, and implement those approaches that will improve the teaching/learning process, and individualization is one that deserves serious consideration.

CONSIDERATIONS FOR INDIVIDUALIZED INSTRUCTION

Individualized instruction is much more than changing methodology, and it must be more than a token change to get significant results. Educators must comprehend students as individuals and provide for individual effort and achievement.

No specific system or approach ever invented can possibly be advocated for all types of learners, although eclectic systems that combine numerous, diverse approaches seem likelier to succeed than systems of limited variety. We are only now beginning to understand the terrible price we have paid for our over-long addiction to one-dimensional formats, particularly whole-class lecture instruction. Greater understanding is necessary, and it needs to be paired with a readiness to act.

In part, the efforts of educators to individualize instruction have resulted from the increasing recognition that each student is unique and learns differently, but providing for these differences has been a slow process. One facet of individualized instruction is the proposition that students should be given the opportunity to select some of their learning goals. Programs must be developed that are flexible enough for the student to decide, at times, what he/she is to learn.[4]

Among the types of individualization are programmed learning, instructional packages, contracts, work-study experiences, and community experiences.[5] Grouping in some form is another accepted principle of individualized instruction. There are several grouping plans available, and the one used should be the one that most nearly fits the needs of the students at that specific time. Students interact a great deal and learn about cooperative efforts in their groups. They can voice their opinions about the curriculum and have the opportunity to play different roles in the group—director, facilitator, secretary, etc. Decision making can be emphasized.

Materials prepared for individualized instruction vary in reading rate and interest and are often at a high cognitive level. Different learning styles are respected, and greater care must be taken in developing the sequence of topics and the variety of sequences used.

The amount of time the teacher spends with each student is approximately the same. More time is spent with small groups of individuals; however, lecture and lecture discussion are still used when necessary. There

---

[4]Wright, C. Dan. "Five Important Considerations for Planning Individualized Instruction." *High School Journal* 60:111-12; December 1976.

[5]Dunn, Rita S. "Individualizing Instruction: Questions and Answers." *National Association of Secondary School Principals Bulletin* 59:32; April 1975.

may be greater opportunity for the teacher to work with students who have special needs and to diagnose their learning difficulties. Those learning needs can be discovered formally and informally through teacher-made or standardized tests.

Students are encouraged to take on a greater responsibility for their own learning. They know that within defined limits they can opt for certain materials, a pace that suits them, and a particular learning style.

Spontaneous interaction and planned interaction are promoted, but students work alone when it is important to the learning process. The emphasis is to balance independent work, group work, and whole-class work as it suits the needs of the students and is within the competence and supervisory ability of the teacher. The goal is not individualization as an end in itself but to achieve the degree necessary to maximize student learning.

CONCERNS WITH INDIVIDUALIZED INSTRUCTION

While there are a great number of advantages that go along with individualization of instruction, there are also some disadvantages or problems:

1. In comparison with whole-class instruction, the amount of time the teacher spends in contact with a pupil may be reduced. As an example, if a teacher has a class of 30 students, a 50-minute period of *whole*-class instruction gives a student 50 minutes of contact with a teacher—less the time the student's attention wanders. If the class of 30 were individualized, with each student working alone and the teacher going around the room providing assistance, the average contact between student and teacher would be 1.6 minutes. As indicated earlier in the chapter, those teachers involved with individualized instruction would probably argue that they now are able to spend more time with those individual students that need assistance.

2. With individualization the amount of paperwork for instructors increases tremendously. There must be a record of each student's progress and assignments, which includes testing, completion of objectives, and skills achieved. In rebuttal to this concern, instructors involved with individualization would state that the use of student aides and/or clerical help would solve the paperwork problems.

3. Students must be kept productive at their assigned tasks. Does the student understand the skill he/she is to learn? Will the student follow through and do the assignment rather than daydream or bother someone else? Some students lack the self-discipline and the maturity to work on their own.

4. Individualization is not the most desirable situation for learning because it neglects the social development of the student. There seems to be little opportunity for student interaction and meaningful interchange. It is also felt that individualized learning may promote loneliness, alienation, and boredom.

5. Students may develop undesirable work habits and become easily distracted.

6. The individualized approach would probably not be considered organizationally or financially feasible in the public school system.

7. Schools of higher learning, presently, do not seem to be preparing teachers with the necessary teaching skills of diagnosis, evaluation, individual consulting, and counseling methods that are quite essential to individualization.

57

SYSTEMS APPROACH TO INDIVIDUALIZE

A systems approach to instruction is defined as a systematic way of identifying, developing, and evaluating instructional materials and strategies which are designed to accomplish a particular educational goal.[6] A systems approach is a logical way of solving a problem. Because of the creative processes involved in designing individualized instruction, the systems model presented in Figure I should be considered as a guide and not a rigid set of procedures.[7]

FIGURE I.

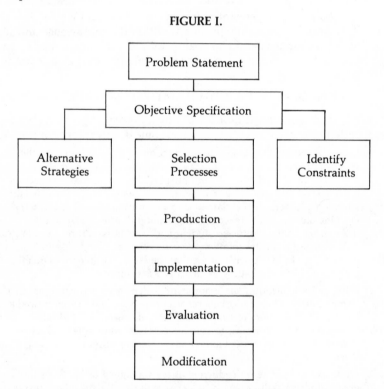

The term "systems approach" is likened to a road map. The student is identified with having specific attitudes and knowledges and desires to prepare for an initial job by the most efficient and direct means possible. The challenge for the teacher is to create an atmosphere for learning, allow the student to move comfortably and function within that atmosphere, as well as to make available all the resources necessary. Thus, an itinerary (courses of instruction) with each student's objective in mind must be planned. The performance-based objectives are classified in three categories: cognitive,

[6]Twelker, Paul A.; Urbach, Floyd D.; and Buck, James F. *The Systematic Development of Instruction: An Overview and Basic Guide to the Literature.* Corvallis: United States International University in Oregon, 1972.

[7]Atkinson, Francis D. "A Systems Approach to the Design and Implementation of Mediated Individualized Instruction." *High School Journal* 60:125; December 1976.

affective, or psychomotor. Cognitive deals with the intellectual processes such as remembering, understanding, problem-solving; affective involves feelings and attitudes; psychomotor concerns muscular coordination and response. These objectives help communicate to the student what is to be achieved. The objective should include the outcomes, conditions of learning, and a criterion of accepted performance with careful specification of instructional objectives. Two elements must be resolved: the discrepancy between what is known and what must be learned and the characteristics of the target population.

The most creative part in the system's approach is alternative strategies. Many individuals should be involved in the process of identifying various strategies—students, administrators, paraprofessionals, parents, etc. Teachers will participate in materials development and adaptation of commercially prepared materials.

Since all students do not respond to any one method and learning styles differ, various alternatives must be provided through instructional packages selected to meet each student's particular needs. A variety of instructional resources will be offered to enhance student learning. For example, the student may be required to do one or all of the following sample activities related to a specific objective: (1) listen to an audiotape recording, (2) read specific materials, (3) view a related film, (4) complete programmed materials, (5) participate in a simulation game, (6) interview several business people, and (7) produce a videotape program illustrating the specific learning objective. Constraints of money, time, space, personnel, and availability of audiovisual equipment must be considered, as indicated earlier in the chapter. How much planning time and training will teachers need and what will it cost? How many students can be accommodated? How can the faculty be motivated? How much clerical assistance, supplies, equipment will be needed? Is there additional paperwork? A complete list of limitations should be prepared in advance, each one of them then carefully evaluated to decide if it can be surmounted. The alternative strategies must be compared with the identified limitations to decide the best method to follow. What strategy will best fit the stated instructional objectives?

Selection of media is a difficult task, and the conditions to consider include objectives, content, responses required, feedback to be given, and sequence and pace in which instruction is to occur. Environmental considerations are time available for instruction, location where instruction takes place, and availability of equipment and skills required for using the equipment.[8] Integrating media and materials into the learning process is a major element in a systemized approach to individualized instruction.

Considerations for the classroom teacher. Ultimate success for implementing the system rests with the teacher, who must know the target audience, review curriculum materials, understand exactly what the student will be doing and learning, and be responsible for the operation of the individualized program. An essential component of the management system is the kind of reinforcement and motivation provided to the student. Individualized

---

[8]Locates, Craig, N., and Atkinson, Francis D. "Media Selection." *Educational Technology* 16:19-21; August 1976.

instruction focuses on the needs of each student. The teacher becomes a manager and works with other managers, paraprofessionals, and aides in a team-type fashion. Managers become accountable and are responsible for preparing materials, learning packages, giving diagnostic tests, and helping with remedial problems.

Through preservice and in-service education, the classroom teacher should learn to implement individualized instructional programs. The next step is preparing students for individualized instruction. Frequently individualized instruction changes the responsibilities students must assume. They will be learning more independently and will assume responsibility for a greater part of the evaluation through pre- and posttests which will be self-scored.

The systems approach is useful in designing instructional activities or adopting existing materials and activities for individualized instruction. The importance of utilizing many strategies is emphasized in order for the student to become comfortable with the new method of learning. Teachers need a variety of resources to design and implement individualized instruction.

Teachers aren't experienced writers and should not necessarily attempt to write new instructional materials. Instead, text material already prepared can be adapted for use in individualized programs by reviewing the available existing materials, preparing performance objectives for it, writing individualized instruction directions, and preparing pre- and posttests.

All the data and materials in the beginning stages must be reviewed and evaluated. Evaluation procedures need to be planned in the early stages of implementation. Constant revision and modifications are built into the process in order for objectives to be attained.

IMPLICATIONS FOR THE FUTURE

Changes in curriculum, facilities, equipment, course content, and styles of learning can be a frightening thing. Are there pitfalls? Absolutely.

Students are accepting change, even demanding it. Machines are providing for change. In fact, the only thing we can depend on in this world is change. One of the most significant things to consider in meeting change in the school is flexibility—flexibility in programs and in scheduling.

It is appropriate that one chapter of this Yearbook is focusing on individualized instruction. The U.S. Office of Education and the National Association of Secondary School Principals have affirmed that ". . . the primary purpose of American Secondary Education is (or should be) to enable the individual to live, to function, and to participate advantageously to himself or herself and to the societies in which the individual will find himself or herself."[9]

Many secondary school business educators accept the concepts of individualizing curriculum and instruction, yet few business teachers practice

[9]Chaffee, John, Jr., editor. *New Dimensions for Educating Youth. A Bicentennial Report on America's Secondary Schools.* U.S. Department of Health, Education and Welfare and the National Association of Secondary School Principals. Washington, D.C.: Government Printing Office, 1976.

individualizing for many good reasons. There are not as yet sufficient guidelines for integrating theory and practice.

The university teacher education program to a great extent influences the business teacher, who then determines the quality of the program in which he/she teaches. If prospective teachers had the opportunity to enroll in university classes utilizing individualized instruction strategies, the personal experience with it would most likely encourage them to try the techniques in their classes.

A great deal of literature about individualizing instruction is available, and a wide variety of software and hardware can be purchased. Money and time are necessary ingredients to plan and implement individualized instruction strategies, but probably the most important ingredients are the support of administrators and the creativity and initiative of classroom teachers.

The concept of individualization will experience considerable growth in the future and will be instrumental in meeting public demands about producing competent learners and workers. The rate of this expansion depends primarily upon the willingness and ability of our teachers, administrators, and teacher educators to assert leadership in educational change.

It might well be that we have held on to tradition too long and have ignored the ingenuity of students. We have provided them with unrealistic competition, have standardized the range and depth of our curriculum, and have provided a limited choice of learning experience. A school is more or less individualized depending on the degree of autonomy given the students.

If business educators are to provide quality education for each individual, then new, experimentally sound institutional approaches must be developed. The individualized approach in the teaching of business and office education seems to be feasible and desirable. As educators, we must attempt to improve our curriculum and methodology. We must stretch our imaginations, study current and proposed practices, *experiment*, and then make some bold decisions. We must accept new ideas and new techniques, not just for the sake of change, but because of our concern to increase our teaching effectiveness.

Section B: At the Two-Year College Level

GLORIA R. LITTLE
Scottsdale Community College, Scottsdale, Arizona

The elementary and secondary schools of our country are fully committed to serving American youth from diverse social origins. During the decade of the sixties, an awakened social conscience brought a national commitment to extending postsecondary educational opportunities to everyone. This commitment was reinforced by a special report to the Carnegie Commission on Higher Education (1970), which recommended that a public community college be established within commuting distance of every potential student by 1980.

Providing educational opportunity to all persons, without regard to their previous educational experience or accomplishments, carries with it the obligation to provide suitable methods of instruction in order to ensure maximum success. Traditional instruction characterized by the lecture method in a fixed 50-minute class period, three times per week for 16 weeks, is no longer appropriate for all the youth of the country nor for the adults who are unemployed, underemployed, or seeking personal growth through the education process.

INDIVIDUALIZED INSTRUCTION AN ALTERNATIVE

The two-year colleges have proudly proclaimed a special commitment to teaching—a commitment unlike that of other higher education institutions that include research as well as teaching. Community colleges have taken great pains to stress that teaching staffs are not intensely involved in the research-and-publish activity so prevalent in four-year institutions. It is claimed that teaching personnel in the two-year colleges devote full time to teaching.

In the past when community colleges dealt primarily with students who planned to transfer to four-year institutions, their instructional methods closely resembled those found in any college or university. Now community college teaching techniques are beginning to show greater diversity as these colleges assume the responsibility for educating more and more nontraditional students—students whose abilities, goals, and interests require special treatment if student failure is to be prevented and student success assured. Community colleges are pioneering in the development of individualized instructional materials and strategies to better accommodate the student where he is, rather than at some arbitrary point. Financial efficiency, too, has provided an impetus to experimenting with instructional procedures as the accelerating costs of operating a community college become a reality.

The community college has been called by some the "people's college." Having opened their doors to all, they are now faced with providing not minimal education but developing the talents of all to maximum effectiveness, as well as the obligation to offer all students the opportunity for high-level achievement. Attaining this goal requires reshaping the curriculum and improving instruction.

THE NUISANCE OF INDIVIDUAL DIFFERENCES

The scientific study of human behavior has clearly demonstrated individual differences, but the practitioners often work with groups of students who are doing the same thing at the same time in as much the same manner as possible as though no such evidence was available. Individuals are taught as though they were a homogeneous group. Teachers have met classes faithfully three times per week, given the same assignments to every student, and treated each student exactly the same in the hope that the nuisance of individual differences would disappear.

The large number of students of diverse backgrounds enrolled in community colleges has upset the traditional ways of thinking about education. In traditional education, the instructor permits the level of attainment to vary while time is perceived as constant. In individualized programs of instruction, mastery learning permits all students to learn to the same high level of achievement regardless of the amount of time required. In traditional settings we turn out some students who are educated and some who are not. We attest only to the fact that they have all spent the same amount of time in a particular class or program. In individualized programs of instruction we assert that anyone can learn a subject to mastery if given adequate time and instruction and provide for individual differences by holding attainment constant and letting time vary.

BASIC PRINCIPLES OF INDIVIDUALIZED INSTRUCTION

Essential ingredients for effective learning upon which all methods of individualized education are based include:

1. The student is at the center of the learning process where he is active rather than passive. The student is involved mentally and often is engaged in physical manipulation of learning materials as well. The instructor assumes the role of manager preparing materials, diagnosing, prescribing, motivating, and generally serving as a resource for the student. The shift is from learning to teaching.

2. The goals of learning are clearly and explicitly communicated to the student in order to seek the student's active involvement in the learning process. The use of specific instructional or behavioral objectives has become fairly widespread. The objective states what the student will be able to (or tend to) do at the end of the instructional sequence, the conditions surrounding the activity, and the degree of proficiency achieved.

3. The work covered in a semester or a quarter is divided into small units (learning modules) in which objectives can be specified and immediate reinforcement of correct learning behavior assured.

4. The small learning units and frequent testing provide a means of recognizing and rewarding correct responses so that the student does not proceed with an inadequate or incorrect understanding of the concepts involved.

5. The learner may control the pace of the presentation recognizing that not only do individuals differ from one another in rate of learning but often differ from time to time and from task to task in their learning efficiency.

THE NEW LEARNING

Programmed instruction. S. L. Pressey, the inventor of a rather primitive type of teaching machine, applied the "laws of learning" to teaching and is credited with the initial idea of applying behavioristic concepts to education. Programmed instruction consists of a series of "frames" that are carefully arranged to successively "shape" the desired behavior. Test questions in the program provide the immediate reinforcement and feedback. The rate of learning is controlled by the learner, but the creator of the program has complete control over what will be learned, how it will be learned, and when mastery has been attained.

There is fairly consistent evidence in the research that students learn the facts and skills presented by programmed instruction in less time than is required by other means. The research also suggests that programmed materials are most effective in disciplines where learning tasks are sequential and can be presented in small units which can be reinforced by the "right" answer. Courses such as accounting, business mathematics, shorthand, typewriting, and business English, in which highly structured, directive, concrete tasks are presented, have found programmed texts very helpful to students. Programmed texts, however, should be used as supplements and not as replacements for other forms of instruction. The use of programmed instruction to teach facts and skills should relieve the teacher of routine tasks, making it possible for the teacher to spend more time with the special problems of individual students.

Computer-assisted instruction (CAI). In CAI programs the computer is used to interact tutorially with the student through a self-paced program or course of instruction. The student and the computer communicate through a teletypewriter; the computer types instructions, diagnostic questions, and feedback messages, and the student responds via the keyboard. Using sound, sight, and touch, the computer is able to present words to be spelled, sounds to be made, and instructions to be followed. The computer is able to present images and symbols to be responded to by touch. It is able to evaluate student performance and direct the student in all directions for appropriate learning activity. The computer, however, possesses no magical ability to transform poor instruction into quality instruction. Once the motivation based on the mechanical gadgetry of the computer is exhausted, skillfully prepared programs must provide the motivation. Critics of CAI point out that the learner simply responds to whatever appears on the screen in front of him or her, and they question how "active" the student's mind really is in this process. Although costs have been reduced markedly in recent years, the expense involved in CAI has limited its use in many colleges. In addition many faculty members have resisted learning computer language and resent being forced into computer-logical ways of thinking about their subject matter. Nevertheless, there is evidence that short periods of instruction on the use of computers can motivate faculty to use the computer for instructional purposes and that this procedure shows great potential in the area of business. Courses in filing, business communication, business mathematics, statistics, and accounting have been successfully taught with computer assistance.

Computer-managed instruction (CMI). In CMI the computer is used to manage individualization through diagnostic testing and assignments designed to meet individual needs. In typical programs, the computer is used to score tests, diagnose learning problems, prescribe appropriate assignments, and report results on an individual and cumulative basis. If self-paced learning is effective, students soon become so diverse that a single instructor will find it difficult to handle their individual needs, and the attempt to individualize instruction will break down. CMI provides the assistance needed to accompany individualized instruction for it can present to the student alternate goals and subgoals, diagnose and store information about the learner, make appropriate assignments of methods of study, and provide continuous monitoring and assessment of information on how much practice a student requires, how well the student retains information, and what kinds of instructional alternatives the student chooses or does well with. CMI has great potential for managing the complexities of individualized instruction.

MASTERY LEARNING UNDERLIES SELF-PACED LEARNING

A learning module is a self-contained unit with clearly defined objectives, usually consisting of learning materials, a sequence of activities, and provisions for evaluation. Students may use the modules independently at their own rate—and at times of their own choosing—to replace or supplement the more traditional lectures, laboratories, and discussions.

Mastery learning is the concept that learning must be thorough—one unit must be learned to a high level of competency before the next unit in the sequence is attempted. Grades and semesters become almost meaningless when mastery learning is implemented since all students ideally would earn A grades, but would take as much time as necessary to accomplish this mastery.

In the 1920's two programs which incorporated the concept of mastery learning, the Winnetka plan and the Morrison plan, were launched in elementary schools in Illinois. The major features of the plans were: educational objectives were specified, instruction was organized into learning units, diagnostic progress tests were administered after each unit, and mastery on one unit was required before the student could proceed to the next unit. Perhaps because of the lack of technology needed to sustain the plans, they disappeared only to reappear again in the 1960's as corollaries of programmed instruction. Two programs of learning, the audio-tutorial approach and the Keller plan or PSI (Personalized System of Instruction), have emerged from self-paced modules and mastery learning.

Audio-tutorial (A-T). The tape, which gives audio-tutorial its name, serves as a programming device. The method has three distinguishing components: independent study sessions, the general assembly, and integrated quiz sessions.

The independent study session takes place in a learning center that is open throughout the day and evening. The center provides learning stations or carrels equipped with various media. The student entering the center may pick up a printed sheet of behavioral objectives and go directly to a booth, which may be equipped with physical objects such as specimens, equipment, and models; printed materials such as texts, study guides, journal articles; slides, movies, filmstrip and audio tapes. Through earphones, the student listens to the voice of the instructor suggesting a variety of learning activities.

The general assembly meets once a week and is used for activities best done in a large group—guest lectures, special films, major examinations. Attendance is not required except for special occasions.

The integrated quiz session takes place in small groups consisting of 6 to 10 students and an instructor meeting once a week. Each student prepares for the session an explanation of each of the items in the study unit. This procedure helps students integrate their knowledge by being required to teach it to others; it provides for interaction among the members of the discussion group; it provides information for the continuing evaluation of course materials; and it gives instructors knowledge about the learning problems and strengths of individual students.

Although not without some limitations, A-T and variations thereof appear to have enormous potential for use with business students. Because students differ in their responsiveness to various media, the multimedia approach makes provision for individual preferences for different kinds of activities and for the use of different sensory modalities such as reading, listening, and the manipulation of concrete objects.

Personalized system of instruction (PSI). Typically, in the PSI or Keller plan, the course is broken down into 15 or 20 self-paced learning modules, with learning objectives clearly spelled out by the instructor in a study guide. Using the guide and textbooks, articles, and other printed materials, the student masters each learning unit at his or her own rate, studying wherever and whenever convenient. When the student feels prepared, he or she presents himself/herself to a student proctor for testing. The test is a 15- to 20-minute short-answer quiz which the student must pass at a high level of competency. It is graded immediately and if the student fails, the proctor may quiz him/her further to determine areas of difficulty, help with special problems, or refer the student for further study. There is no penalty for failing to pass the mastery tests, but the learner may proceed to the next unit only after demonstrating mastery of prior units. Lectures and demonstrations are not required, but are used to inspire and motivate. Emphasis is on the written word. Other media, although sometimes used, are not of fundamental importance. Mastery learning is essential, and self-pacing is an obvious and necessary accompaniment. The time for learning will vary to compensate for the individual differences in learning rate. Lectures are used for motivation rather than for the dissemination of information. Lectures were used to provide information to groups of learners before the invention of the printing press, custom continues to demand that the professors demonstrate knowledge through the lecture. The role model of the scholar may be of some benefit to the students. PSI is not without its problems—student withdrawals, grading, boredom of students, the difficulty of defining "mastery," etc., but its advantages suggest that as a system of individualized instruction it should be explored and creative energy invested to determine its effectiveness in teaching business subjects.

IMPLICATIONS FOR BUSINESS EDUCATION

The use of individualized instruction in the private business colleges (with new students arriving almost daily) as a means of integrating new students into the mainstream of the particular course being taught has been well known for decades. Faced with the challenges of a new and diverse student body, the individualization of instruction is rapidly becoming commonplace in public postsecondary business classrooms across the country. Learning laboratories, learning centers, packaged programmed materials from publishers, programmed materials prepared by instructors, the availability of technological media, and faculty acceptance have all contributed to the recognition of individualized learning as a viable means of effective learning. Business students are observed using time clocks to record the time spent in the learning center using tapes and earphones to direct their learning activities in shorthand, typewriting, accounting, and other business subjects. They are being permitted, even encouraged, to enter and leave a program or course when they wish and are given the opportunity to learn at a pace that is consistent with their individual learning capacity. Business teachers are being freed from the routine tasks of teaching facts and skills and are available for diagnosing, motivating, and providing appropriate instructional sequences to meet the varying abilities of students. Maximum teacher-student contact is provided in the hope of developing in the student a positive attitude toward learning. Students are not only learning facts and skills but are learning to allocate time and to accept responsibility for their own educational advancement.

Despite trends toward behavioral objectives, audio-tutorial instruction, and computer-assisted learning, it seems clear that no one method is effective for all students. More research is needed to help business teachers identify the learning styles of individual students so that the question of which methods work best for which students can be answered. Since we all have characteristic ways of using our minds, we need more research to help us gain insight into teaching and learning styles. No one method can be regarded as a panacea for all students in all subjects.

It is imperative, therefore, that in our search for innovative teaching strategies we implement programs only after we have given considerable thought to the systematic collection of data for evaluation purposes. The end result will be that we will have concrete information on which to introduce improvement and change in the teaching-learning process.

As business teachers we should be committed to placing the student at the center of the learning process by increasing learning activity options and providing ópportunities for students to design portions of the curriculum; we should be committed to recognizing and responding to individual differences in skills, values, and learning styles through a flexible curriculum which permits learning at different rates and in different ways; we should relate to students with openness and respect and provide a supportive climate for learning; we should provide students with positive reinforcement and opportunities for success; and we must make the community as extension of the classroom. It is time that we measure our teaching success in terms of the learning success of our students.

Section C: At the Four-Year College Level

DONALD C. CLARK, SALLY N. CLARK, and VIOLET S. THOMAS
University of Arizona, Tucson

Business educators at all levels must be committed to providing each student maximum opportunities to attain an education and become a productive member of society. Individualization of instruction, with its emphasis on meeting the needs of all students with their varying abilities, backgrounds, and aptitudes, provides a challenging way to increase the options that are available in providing the best possible learning environment for all students. Basically, individualized instruction can best be described as a process for accommodating each student's needs through the provision of a variety of alternative ways to learn at a rate of speed that is comfortable. It is a concept that is workable at any level of education, including the four-year college or university.

The concept of individualization of instruction is certainly not new. It has been discussed by educators for many years, and attempts at devising instructional programs to meet individual needs were introduced over 50 years ago at Winnetka, Illinois, and Dalton, Massachusetts.

In recent years the renewed interest in individualized instruction can be attributed to a combination of factors. Included in these would be the accountability movement with its primary emphasis on learning outcomes, the general dissatisfaction of the public with the overall quality of education from kindergarten through higher education, the increased emphasis on the need to provide for the needs of the handicapped and of the culturally disadvantaged students, and demands made on the schools as a result of increasing pressures associated with federal funding, legislation, and Department of Health, Education, and Welfare guidelines.

Business educators have taken a strong stand in support of individualized instruction. In a statement developed by the Policies Commission for Business and Economic Education entitled "This We Believe About Implementing Individualization of Instruction in Business Education," the following points were made:

We believe that:

1. Individualization of instruction is psychologically sound and educationally valid.

2. Individualization of instruction has merit for all subject areas in the curriculum.

3. The success of efforts to individualize instruction depends upon the commitment and interaction of administrators and supervisors, teachers, teacher educators, students, and parents.[1]

Very little information is available to indicate the degree of acceptance and implementation of individualization of instruction at the college/uni-

---

[1]Policies Commission for Business and Economic Education. "This We Believe About Implementing Individualization of Instruction in Business Education." *Business Education Forum* 28:18-19; May 1974.

versity level. It can be said, however, that change at this level occurs slowly. In the public schools the tendency has often been "to expect too much too soon" as, for example, attempting to individualize by changing an entire school to a system of modular scheduling with little time for in-service preparation. The opposite is often true in higher education as it is seldom a question of changing too rapidly. The charge from the public and from its clients (in this case, prospective teachers) is more often the failure to try innovations and to be responsive to the changing conditions and the existing needs of society and the business community. Change at this level has more often been forced by legislative action, government funding, accreditation standards, or by certification requirements rather than by a true commitment to providing a more effective program.

If, then, substantive change is going to be made in the direction of individualized instruction, educators must become aware of some of the roadblocks. First of all, there is some question as to whether or not it is a concept that is valued by college/university faculties. Even while recognizing the existence of individual student learning needs, the idea of building programs to accommodate these needs may be perceived as impossible or at least not important in higher education. Tyler believes there are conditions that militate against individualized programs at this level. These include the interest of many faculty members in knowledge for its own sake and little concern for its meaning and value to the nonspecialist, the fact that higher education has been more of a sorting process than an educating process, and efforts at curriculum reform have been simplistic in nature (i.e., largely confined to the development of new courses, or reorganization of existing courses, solely on the basis of content).[2]

Perhaps as a result of these conditions, the classical approach of lecture-study-recite-test still appears to be firmly entrenched as the preferred instructional method, There have, however, been some attempts to develop programs that focus more on the individual needs of students. Some of these programs include programmed instruction, individual study programs (honors), computer-assisted instruction, peer tutoring and counseling, work study programs, learning activity packages, simulations and games, student contracts, and multimedia activities. In addition to these, several comprehensive systems have been devised and implemented at colleges and universities. These include the audio-tutorial system developed by Postlethwait, Bloom's mastery learning program and programs based on mastery learning, the Keller plan (personalized system of instruction or PSI), and competency-based or performance-based teacher education (CBTE or PBTE).

The audio-tutorial system of S. N. Postlethwait of Purdue University was developed to maximize educational opportunities for students of diverse backgrounds, levels of abilities, and skills. The system, which includes independent study sessions, general assembly sessions, and integrated quiz sessions, is organized so that students can proceed at their own pace, filling in the gaps in their background information and omitting portions which have been covered previously.

---

[2]Tyler, Ralph W. "Historical Efforts To Develop Learning on a Competency Base." *A CBC Primer*. Atlanta: SREB, 1975.

Mastery learning as proposed by Benjamin Bloom holds to the principle that most students in any given situation can learn thoroughly all the important concepts provided (1) students are given clear guidance on what is to be learned and the criteria for determining when mastery has been attained; (2) adequate learning resources are available and the resources are appropriate to the varied backgrounds, abilities, and learning styles; and (3) the rate of learning is varied to accommodate the learner's ability to assimilate the material. Mastery learning differs from traditional programs in that instead of holding time constant and accepting a wide range of achievement, it provides for variation of learning styles and time and stresses a uniformly high level of achievement for all.

Based on Bloom's concepts, the Keller plan (PSI) is an individually paced system that incorporates a combination of mastery learning, student self-pacing, modules, peer tutors/proctors, emphasis on written materials, and the use of lectures as motivational devices rather than as sources of information. PSI is most adaptable to courses that are highly structured and have relatively stable content. Pascarella also found that:

> . . . the most dramatic differences in both achievement and course attitudes were indicated at the relatively highest levels of motivation, indicating, perhaps, that the greatest benefits of PSI in mathematics instruction may accrue to the most highly motivated students.[3]

Competency- or performance-based programs have been the most common approach to the individualization of instruction in teacher preparation programs. In describing the implementation of its CBTE program at the University of Georgia, Calhoun writes:

> . . . the Business Education Department at the University of Georgia has identified and validated competencies that should be demonstrated by vocational business teachers; are developing, modifying, and assembling multimedia instructional materials for a variety of classes; are organizing and implementing our courses around the mastery of competencies rather than completion of a specified number of hours in class . . .[4]

Performance-based education is built on the premise that the learning process is facilitated if teachers know what they want students to learn and if the learners are aware of exactly what is expected of them. PBTE or CBTE is the application of the principles and practices of performance-based instruction to the teacher preparation program. It is structured to provide a variety of learning activities to assist the prospective teacher in the acquisition of predetermined teaching competencies.

In the following sections the concerns and problems unique to teacher education programs will be discussed, and a systems model for individualizing business teacher preparation programs will be presented.

---

[3]Pascarella, Ernest T. "Student Motivation as a Differential Predictor of Course Outcomes in Personalized System of Instruction and Conventional Instructional Methods." *Journal of Educational Research* 71:24; September/October 1977.

[4]Calhoun, Calfrey C. "Georgia Model for Competency-Based Business Teacher Education and Certification." *Business Education Forum* 32:49-50; November 1977.

CHALLENGES AND CONCERNS IN BUSINESS TEACHER EDUCATION

Business education takes on different emphasis at different levels. Secondary schools generally attempt to provide students with both broad economic understandings and preparation for initial employment in business. The primary focus in vocational schools and junior colleges tends to be job preparation. The four-year college or university undertakes a variety of roles. These include instruction in basic skill areas, development of administrative and managerial competencies, and the preparation of teachers in the business subjects. As the individualization of instruction in the skills and general business areas at the high school and junior college levels have been discussed in the previous sections of this chapter, the focus of this section will be on individualizing the business teacher preparation program.

The Rockefeller Report states that no educational system can be better than its teachers.[5] The quality of our schools is largely dependent upon the quality of the teachers who staff them; and carrying it a step further, we may say that the teachers strongly reflect the strengths and weaknesses of the college and university programs which prepare them for initial certification. Teacher preparation programs have for years been accused of producing poorly qualified teachers. Fast-paced changes in the educational profession have made new demands upon the whole process of preservice and in-service teacher education. Beginning teachers frequently find themselves unable to meet the challenging tasks and demands to which they are asked to respond in present-day schools. In spite of this, many of the nation's colleges and universities continue to prepare the majority of future teachers in traditional programs in conventional school systems.

There are many concerns that must be taken into consideration when discussing any teacher preparation program, whether traditional, individualized, or some other alternative program. Business educators in the teacher preparation program are faced with the difficulties involved when dealing with course content that is not clearly defined. The basic orientation for many business educators has been in the skills area where specific levels of competency are easier to define. Business educators have been proud of their long association with business and industry in a cooperative determination of skill needs and competencies required for success in the business world. An important factor contributing to the unclear definition of course content in the teacher preparation program is the acknowledged lack of agreement on the part of the teaching profession and the general public as to the characteristics of an effective teacher.

The ultimate criterion for judging a teacher preparation program is whether it produces competent graduates who can enter the teaching profession and perform effectively. The question must then be asked: What makes an effective teacher? There is a lack of an adequate research base as to what specific teacher behaviors positively affect student outcomes. Systematic research and evaluation in the field of teacher education are seriously lacking. Dickson and others state: "It is one thing to plan a course

[5]Ehlers, Henry, and Lee, Gordon C., editors. *Critical Issues in Education*. New York: Holt, Rinehart and Winston, 1964. p. 360.

of training for teachers but quite another to determine how future teachers will behave once they are responsible for their own teaching."[6] Mott writes: "Competency-based business teacher education requires that a student's (teacher) exit performance satisfy established minimum standards. Therefore, an important first step is deciding the nature of these (minimum) competencies."[7] The selection of competencies expected as an end result is thus crucial to the successful implementation of any individualized program, but we must continue to ask what competencies does a prospective teacher need to successfully enter the teaching profession. It should be pointed out that this concern is as much a part of the traditional teacher preparation program as it is of an individualized program. It must also be emphasized that the teacher preparation program is concerned with determining competencies essential to the beginning teacher entering the classroom as a professional for the first time. An undergraduate teacher education program cannot prepare a teacher who can fully demonstrate professional competence in all the various situations and with the different types of students the professional situation may demand.

No single program can possibly be advocated as meeting the needs of all learners. Individualized instruction is not just a method or procedure or a way of organization. It is a philosophy of teaching based on responding to the needs of individual students. Some students learn best through individualized instruction while others may learn best through the traditional method of classroom instruction. Who learns best with what procedures may also change with time and with course content. Some course content needs to be handled through individualized approaches; other course content lends itself to alternative approaches. In some cases, various forms of individualization result in more efficient use of time. In other cases, group enthusiasm and competition among students with similar backgrounds and goals may bring about quicker achievement of the goals desired. An individualized program must have as an integral part the inclusion of options or alternatives, and therefore, it can best be defined as the provision of alternative learning strategies that fit each student's needs and interests so as to facilitate maximum learning and development. In teacher education programs individualization of instruction varies in degrees from total implementation of a program to the individualization of isolated concepts within a typical, traditional instructional system.

An important concern that has too often been neglected is acknowledgment of the fact that just as students are unique individuals, so are teachers. When implementation of individualized instruction is seen as a single program, all teachers are forced into the same mold. One teacher may be able to use a particular approach very effectively, while another teacher may accomplish the same goals by effectively using a completely different procedure. Teachers must be helped to evaluate their own abilities and select

---

[6]Dickson, George E., and others. *Partners for Education Reform and Renewal.* Berkeley, Calif.: McCutchan Publishing Co., 1973. p. 23.

[7]Mott, Dennis L. "A Rationale for Competency-Based Business Teacher Education." *Business Education Forum* 32:45; November 1977.

those procedures that enable them to operate most effectively while at the same time meeting the varying needs of students. There should be as many options available to teachers as to students.

Any new program makes demands on teachers and requires that they develop new competencies. Lambrecht states: "It is continually apparent to those who work most closely with the individualized instructional mode that as the options broaden from which students and teachers may choose, their responsibilities and challenges increase—they do not diminish."[8] The challenge is to help prospective teachers learn a variety of instructional roles and evaluation procedures. Stone and Ivarie point out:

> . . . he or she must manage profitable social interaction and group learning activities; arrange and develop activities providing open and structured support, time use, and materials; relate curriculum development to the needs of the culture; and organize and present interesting and vital stimulus materials.[9]

In an individualized program the teacher must facilitate learning by assuming the roles of counselor, diagnostician, and prescriber. He or she no longer can be primarily a disseminator of information (although this role must not be abandoned and should still be included among the alternatives).

How can the prospective teacher be helped in acquiring the appropriate role? Every university or college class in the professional sequence should provide not only a model of good teaching but opportunities for students to actually experience personalized learning by:

1. Seeing college instructors utilizing individualized instructional procedures
2. Experiencing personal learning through the use of individualized instructional techniques
3. Meeting objectives by personal selection from a variety of learning experiences
4. Exercising responsibility in the attainment of learning objectives
5. Viewing and participating in a variety of successful field-based individualized instructional programs.

Further justification for individualization in higher education, particularly in the area of business education, comes from the profession itself. The Policies Commission for Business and Economic Education recently prepared a statement of beliefs and policies regarding individualized instructional programs. In the section designated *Teacher Educators* the following statement is made:

> As teachers of teachers, teacher educators have a continuing responsibility in helping prospective and experienced teachers develop appropriate concepts of individualized instruction as well as methods by which individualization can be achieved. In order to achieve this goal, teacher educators must become involved in working directly with school administrators, teachers, and students in the local school system.[10]

---

[8]Lambrecht, Judith J. "Choices for Teachers Too—When They Individualize." *Journal of Business Education* 50:238; March 1975.

[9]Stone, David R., and Ivarie, Ted. "A Learning Skills Model for Competency-Based Teacher Education." *Business Education Forum* 32:47; November 1977.

[10]Policies Commission for Business and Economic Education, *op. cit.*, p. 18.

Research conducted at the University of Arizona and other institutions indicates that students consider their student teaching experience or internship the most valuable part of their training program.[11] Although it is generally agreed that the prospective teacher must acquire an appropriate classroom role, relatively little systematic thought has been given to the problem of how such a role can be acquired. Hazard states:

> Teachers in classrooms represent the single most influential force in shaping new teachers' professional behavior. The socialization of preservice and pretenure teachers turns on the classroom teacher's performance as supervisor, model, shaper, and molder of young teachers. Some teachers are prepared for this responsibility; most are not.[12]

Travers and Dillon point out additional problems:

> The most common training technique related to the achievement of that particular objective has been to expose the student to experienced teachers, who supposedly manifest the desired role. In recent years, suitable live-role examples have become more and more difficult to obtain because of the large number of candidates entering the teaching profession and the scarcity of teachers willing to demonstrate their skills. The result of this situation has often been that any teacher willing to demonstrate his performance has been presented as the model to be followed.[13]

Meeting the individual needs of students must include more opportunities and options in preservice observation and participation. Studies at the University of Arizona support other findings in which new and prospective teachers cite a need for more opportunities for field-based experiences.[14] This cannot be accomplished without better school-university cooperation.

Traditionally, teacher education in America has been planned and managed almost unilaterally by colleges and universities. The secondary schools have had a negligible role, and their participation usually has been limited to student teaching and field work programs. While public schools have thus long participated physically in preparation of teachers by accepting student teachers or interns, they have shared little in the decision-making aspects of the program. Until recently the impetus for cooperation came mainly from the colleges. Now, however, school faculties and teacher organizations are expressing the desire to have a greater voice in the training and certification of teachers. This will require the universities to relinquish some of their traditional and cherished autonomy and share responsibility with the public schools.

Agreements between universities and the public schools must be predicated on a clear understanding of the resources and expertise each party can contribute to the undertaking. Power struggles between and among

[11]Clark, Sally N. "Perceptions of the Secondary Teacher Preparation Program of the University of Arizona." Doctor's thesis. Tucson: University of Arizona. 1977.

[12]Hazard, William R. "Negotiation and the Education of Teachers." *Teacher Education: Future Directions*. (Edited by Margaret Lindsey.) Washington, D.C.: Association of Teacher Educators, 1970. p. 117.

[13]Travers, Robert M. W., and Dillon, Jacqueline. *The Making of a Teacher*. New York: Macmillan Publishing Co., 1975. p. 24.

[14]Thomas, Violet S. "The Secondary Teacher Education Program as Perceived by Selected Graduates of The University of Arizona." Doctor's thesis. Tucson: University of Arizona, 1969. Clark, *op. cit.*

professional education's several constituencies will doubtless continue, but strife and duplication of services can be avoided at the outset by an explicit identification of the roles and responsibilities to be undertaken by each constituent group. Any program of mutual cooperation must assume that the secondary schools and the colleges and universities have a mutual concern in the preparation of teachers and that each can bring a wealth of experience and personnel to teacher education.

A SYSTEM FOR TEACHER PREPARATION PROGRAMS IN BUSINESS EDUCATION

The philosophical approach in the development of any type of instructional program, especially one emphasizing individualization, is that the instructional process should be viewed as a dynamic, open system, and therefore, the planning program should utilize some of the basic concepts of systems analysis. Systems analysis requires that the total system be identified and carefully defined. Once this has been done, the system's inputs and subsystems can be delineated and their desired outputs considered. A common method for conceptualizing systems entails representation of elements in a model such as a basic information-transformation-output model shown in Figure I.[15]

FIGURE I. Basic Information-Transformation-Output Model

This model implies that the system under study has a set of inputs that are acted upon by some transformation process to yield some form of outputs. If a business teacher education program can be defined as consisting of two major subsystems, an instructional subsystem and a managerial subsystem, the program can be cast into the input-transformation-output model as presented in Figure II.

FIGURE II. An Individualized Teacher Education Program as an Input-Transformation-Output System

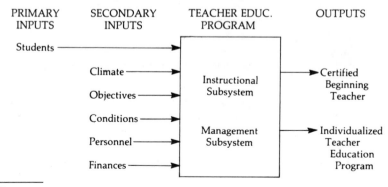

---

[15]Chase, Richard B., and Clark, Donald C. "Long Range Planning in School Districts." *Educational Technology* 15:33; October 1974.

The components of each of the system elements in the model are defined as follows:

PRIMARY INPUTS: Students preparing to become business education teachers are viewed as the primary inputs into the program. Through the process of interaction with and among the instructional and management subsystems, these students are transformed or developed into qualified, certified beginning teachers.

SECONDARY INPUTS: Significant influence is exerted upon the planning, organization, and operation of the subsystems by these inputs. Included are: (1) climate (attitudes and values of the community, school, and college/university); (2) objectives (skills, competencies, knowledges as identified by the profession, student goals); (3) conditions (philosophies, programs, and availability of schools and teachers for field experiences); (4) personnel (skills, attitudes, knowledge, flexibility, and availability of college/university instructors); (5) finances (resources for media, equipment, facilities, personnel, etc.).

PROGRAM SUBSYSTEMS: The *instructional* subsystem deals directly with the prospective teacher in the transformation process. This subsystem is divided into four instructional modules. These include:

1. Business skills and principles
   Basic knowledge and skills commonly required of a business teacher
   Principles of business (economics, accounting, marketing, etc.)
   Principles of business education

2. Educational principles
   Philosophy and foundations of education
   Educational psychology and learning theory
   Child/adolescent growth and development
   Organization and operation of the secondary school
   Introduction to teaching

3. Instructional methods and evaluation
   Developing and sequencing learning experiences (content organization, unit and lesson planning)
   Alternative methods of instruction
   Evaluative methods and procedures
   Specific methods of teaching business subjects

4. Applied field experiences
   Early observation
   Participation (tutoring; small group instruction; mini-lessons)
   Student teaching

Major operational components of each instructional module include (1) goals and objectives, (2) content/subject matter, (3) time/group size (schedule), (4) staff utilization, (5) methods, (6) resources, and (7) evaluation.

The *management* subsystem is concerned with the smooth functioning of the instructional subsystem. In its coordinating function it deals primarily with scheduling, staffing, student placement, field coordination, record-keeping, and evaluation.

OUTPUTS: As mentioned previously, the primary output of this system is a student who has been "transformed" into a "qualified," certified beginning teacher. A by-product or secondary output of the system may be an individualized teacher education program that could be used by other colleges and universities.

Rationale for individualization. It is important to recognize that the basic information-transformation-output model that was used to present the teacher preparation in business education system has its derivation in product development. As a result, the model makes the assumption that when fixed inputs are transformed by a fixed process or treatment a fixed product or output will emerge. This is represented in Figure III.

FIGURE III. Basic Input-Transformation-Output Model with Fixed Elements

This model insures uniformity in the quality of product or output. Educators, unlike manufacturers, are not dealing with products nor can they exercise control over the quality or variety of inputs (students). Although most educators recognize that students enter the instructional system with varying abilities, backgrounds, interests and skills, they fail to understand that application of a fixed treatment to a variable input will produce an output having variability closely reflecting the input variability.

FIGURE IV. Basic Input-Transformation-Output Model with Variable Inputs and Variable Outputs

Figure IV represents traditional teacher preparation programs where all students, regardless of background, are placed in the same program and progress through the sequence until they have accumulated the necessary required units for graduation. As a result of this process that sets standards on a quantitative basis, there is no real control on quality of teachers prepared. If teacher educators are going to prepare teachers who have some uniform basic skills or minimum competencies (fixed outputs), then modifications are going to have to be made in the instructional program (subsystems) that will accommodate individual needs. Fixed outputs should not be misconstrued as the production of beginning teachers who are all the same, but rather should be interpreted to mean that all beginning teachers should have certain basic skills and competencies. Figure V shows a model of such programs.

FIGURE V. Basic Input-Transformation-Output Model with Variable Inputs, Variable Transformation Process, and Fixed Outputs

Figure V represents the basic elements of an individualized instruction program for the preparation of business teachers. It points out the need for the development of more options/alternatives in the instructional subsystem. Building individualized programs requires reexamination of the operational components—(1) goals and objectives, (2) content/subject matter, (3) time/group size (schedule), (4) staff utilization, (5) methods, (6) resources, and (7) evaluation—of the instructional subsystem and restructuring them to fit the following criteria:

Flexibility of time to accommodate individual learning rates
Variety of group sizes to accommodate a variety of learning situations
Specific content objectives sequenced logically, but flexible enough to accommodate individual needs
Flexible use of professional and paraprofessional staff
Alternative instructional approaches that include provision for teacher to student(s) interaction, student to student communication, and media to student learning
Assessment procedures that include diagnosis, prescription, and criteria referenced evaluation

Program alternatives. Most instructional programs that are currently available to students in business teacher education can be classified as traditional, continuous progress-mastery learning, open, or alternative. These programs, which are briefly described, will be compared based on their structure for each of the operational components.

1. The Traditional Subject Specialization Program (still the most common program found in American schools today). At the college/university level this program places great value on subject specialization. Instruction is basically lecture in nature within the frame of rigid time blocks.

2. The Continuous Progress-Mastery Learning Program. This program allows students to progress at their own rate through the curriculum sequence. Emphasis is placed on individual growth and in providing successful learning experiences for each student. The development of performance objectives, content sequencing, diagnostic and prescriptive techniques, criterion-referenced evaluation procedures, and a variety of resources are necessary in this program.

3. The Open Program. Based on the concept that students need the opportunity to learn concepts and material that are of interest to them, the open program tries to provide an environment conducive to problem solving and interaction. Students are involved in the development of personal objectives and are given a great amount of freedom in the selection of learning activities (courses).

4. The Alternatives Program. Based on the premise that there are an infinite number of learning styles and needs, this program attempts to provide a variety of avenues toward the accomplishment of objectives. Each of the three previous programs described could be incorporated into the alternatives program.

Each of these four instructional programs will now be examined and compared. The extent to which any of these programs are individualized is largely dependent on the degree to which they meet the criteria previously elaborated.

Traditional Subject Specialization	Continuous Progress-Mastery Learning	Open	Alternative
GOALS Based on traditional knowledge General statements of instructional intent Developed by professionals—researchers, instructors	GOALS Broadly based on student and professional need Emphasis on the individual and various rates of learning Considerable student and professional input	GOALS Broadly based but primary focus is on student needs and interest Emphasizes student development and selection of goals	GOALS Broadly based on student and professional needs and interests Emphasis on the total student—learning styles and rate, interests, strengths and weaknesses Total involvement in setting basic goals (students and professionals)
OBJECTIVES Taken from textbooks Tend to be specific Developed by subject matter specialists Almost exclusively cognitive in focus	OBJECTIVES Tend to be specific Stated in terms of performance Developed by instructors based on input from professionals and students More cognitive than affective in focus	OBJECTIVES Vary—specific or general as determined by student need or interest Determined by student with assistance from a professional Affective in emphasis	OBJECTIVES Basic specific skills and competencies for all students Variety of alternatives for accomplishing objectives Emphasis on both cognitive and affective
CONTENT/SUBJECT MATTER Traditional in nature Organized in courses (English I, Ed., Psych., etc.) Content determined by instructors, researchers, textbooks, and commercial courses of study All students are required to take a certain core of basic courses Students meet other requirements by selecting from acceptable courses	CONTENT/SUBJECT MATTER Tends to be less traditional Organized into modules and sequenced so students can progress at their own rate Not all students have same sequence Content determined by instructors with input from students and professionals Mastery or competency is demonstrated before a student can move to the next module Requirements are met by demonstrating mastery of predetermined objectives	CONTENT/SUBJECT MATTER Not traditional Required content is determined by student needs and interests in consultation with the instructor Contracting	CONTENT/SUBJECT MATTER Not traditional Minimum basic competencies determined by students and professionals Requirements are met by demonstrating mastery in predetermined content areas Alternative sequences and methods are available to students in working toward mastery

Traditional Subject Specialization	Continuous Progress-Mastery Learning	Open	Alternative
TIME/SCHEDULE Schedule is rigid Length of period usually fixed Academic week of 15-18 class hours	**TIME/SCHEDULE** Schedule is flexible Time needed dependent upon individual student learning rate Determined by professional judgment for group activities	**TIME/SCHEDULE** Schedule is totally flexible Determined by student in consultation with instructor	**TIME/SCHEDULE** Schedule is rigid or flexible depending on individual and professional needs and interests
GROUP SIZE Usually rigid Lecture classes may be 100 or more Seminars may be 15 or less Predetermined at time of registration	**GROUP SIZE** Flexible Based on objective, students, and preferred methodology	**GROUP SIZE** Flexible Based on day-to-day needs of individuals or small groups	**GROUP SIZE** Flexible Based on the various individual and group needs
STAFF Rigid One instructor per classroom	**STAFF** Flexible Some use of team teaching Instructional aides Tutors	**STAFF** Flexible Teaching teams Instructional aides Tutors Volunteers	**STAFF** Flexible Depends on learning needs and interests and alternatives selected
METHODS Lecture Question/answer (recite) Read; write Test	**METHODS** Limited lecture Small group instruction Independent study Learning centers Tutorials Games/Simulation Learning packages Media packages	**METHODS** Small group instruction Inquiry/problem solving Independent study Learning centers Tutorials Games/Simulation	**METHODS** Small group instruction Lecture Outside speakers Inquiry/problem solving Learning centers Tutorials Games/Simulation Learning packages Media packages
MEDIA Textbooks Supplementary books Films for whole class viewing Records/tapes	**MEDIA** Supplementary books Materials for group and individual study Records Tapes Learning packages Filmstrips/slides/ loops Video cassettes Simulations	**MEDIA** Supplementary books Materials for group and individual study Learning centers	**MEDIA** Depends on the alternatives Supplementary books Materials for group and individual study Learning centers

Traditional Subject Specialization	Continuous Progress-Mastery Learning	Open	Alternative
FACILITY	FACILITY	FACILITY	FACILITY
Rigid, single-purpose rooms (lecture halls, classrooms with stationary desks)	Flexible in function with provision for large group instruction, small group work, and individual study	Flexible in function	Flexible in function
EQUIPMENT	EQUIPMENT	EQUIPMENT	EQUIPMENT
Desks (fixed)	Tables and chairs	Tables and chairs	Depends on the alternatives chosen
Record player	Record player	Record player	
Tape recorder	Tape recorder	Tape recorder	
Projectors 16mm Slide/filmstrip	Individual slide/tape/ filmstrip viewers	Individual slide/tape/ filmstrip viewers	
	Listening centers	Listening centers	
COGNITIVE EVALUATION	COGNITIVE EVALUATION	COGNITIVE EVALUATION	COGNITIVE EVALUATION
Achievement tests	Teacher-made tests	Observation	Demonstration of basic skills and competencies
Teacher-made tests	Performance of tasks	Self-evaluation (with instructor) based on accomplishment of previously developed student goals	Nature of evaluation dependent on learning alternatives
Reports and papers	Demonstration of skill		
	Criterion referenced assessment		
		Processes in problem solving and social interaction	
AFFECTIVE EVALUATION	AFFECTIVE EVALUATION	AFFECTIVE EVALUATION	AFFECTIVE EVALUATION
Generally not primarily concerned with attitudes	Observation	Self-concept	Self-concept
	Scales and surveys	Observations of attitudes, participation, successes and failures	Observation of attitudes, participation, successes, and failures
	Attendance		
	Student time management		Student time management

SUMMARY

The introduction of any new program, particularly one involving individualized instruction, will pose challenging management problems. It demands new ways of looking at organizational patterns and instructional techniques. The tendency is for those administering a new program based on the principles of individualized instruction to underestimate the expertise required for program development. As a result, problems arise which affect goal accomplishment, demoralize the staff, and frustrate the students.

Management of individualized programs must be viewed from two levels: the program level and the instructional level. At the program level, provision must be made for scheduling, facilities, curriculum development and sequencing, identification of program goals and objectives, staff utilization and development, production of media resources, coordination of field activities, and administration of program evaluation components. Of great importance is the recognition that the development and implementation of many of these items, especially the writing of goals, objectives, and instructional units and materials, is extremely time consuming and expensive.

At the instructional level, management of daily student schedules, individual sequences, appropriate instructional alternatives, assessment and recordkeeping procedures, and media resources are important functions of the instructor. A learning or resource center properly planned and managed can contribute greatly to program success. Also, at the instructional level, consideration should be given to the provision for the training, effective use, and coordination of ancillary personnel such as aides, media technicians, clerks, readers, and student assistants.

Another area of concern to those wishing to develop and administer individualized instruction is the assumption that college students are adults and therefore can automatically benefit from an individualized program. Even at the university level, some (perhaps many) students are not sufficiently motivated or self-disciplined to make effective use of individualized instruction. Individualized programs place heavy responsibility on the student for self-discipline and self-direction and knowing when and how to most advantageously use resource persons. Provision must be made in the program for those students who are not able to handle this responsibility.

Finally, provision must be made for a comprehensive, viable evaluation program. This program must assess on a continuous basis the effectiveness of each system component and provide feedback for revision. Without evaluation, any effective individualized system is in danger of becoming unresponsive to individual needs, unmotivating, and out of date. A systematic and continuous review will ensure timeliness of content, relevancy to students, and will avoid the common pitfall of many individualized programs—becoming an institutionalized sequence of learning packages and independent study.

CHAPTER 5

Simulation in Business Classes

Simulation is not new to most experienced business educators. While the term may be new, the business education teacher has always been a classroom innovator who seeks new ways to present realistic situations. These range from demonstration lessons in methods, to sales presentations in marketing classes, to practice sets in office practice and bookkeeping/accounting. Our writers take a look at what is being done currently at all three levels of education. They present a number of practical suggestions for the business teacher to bring about new and better classroom simulations.

Section A: At the Secondary School Level

ELSIE DONNEL

University of Northern Colorado, Greeley

A variety of simulations ranging from very simple to complex can be found in virtually all business classes in today's high schools. Although the concept of simulations can be traced back several centuries, their wide use as a teaching method in American education has developed in just the past three decades. This method of instruction provides the student with an effective means of learning through experiences taken from actual work situations in a controlled environment. Greater employability, marketable skills, and improved work attitudes have encouraged more and more teachers to incorporate simulated learning activities in their teaching. Although there are numerous commercially prepared simulations available, many teachers prefer to develop their own in order to meet the specific needs of their students and communities, and teacher-prepared simulations are usually considerably more economical. An overview of the basic criteria, the "how" of developing simulations, is provided in this section for those business teachers who are considering this method of teaching.

BACKGROUND

Simulations take many forms and are known by a variety of terms. The main purpose of using a simulation is to bring as much reality into the classroom situation as possible. They can be used to effectively teach basic concepts such as human relations, economic principles, decision-making skills, and problem solving. Classroom content and the business world are linked through simulation activities, and because of this, they are a motivational change of pace for the students in the classroom.

There are three basic kinds of simulations used in business classes today utilizing physical, social, or economic concepts: educational games, task simulations, and job simulations. Of the three, educational games are used more often because they can be used readily with large or small groups, may be completed in one or two class periods (although some extend for two or more weeks), can be adapted easily to other content areas, are highly motivational, and can be purchased or prepared quite inexpensively.

Factors to be considered in the development of educational simulation games include the following:

1. Determine the concept to be learned and the length of time the class will need to fully understand the principle.
2. State the objectives of the simulation.
3. Identify the student activities and procedures. Students may have choices or decision-making activities related to the purpose of the simulation.
4. Give the directions in easily understood terms. It is imperative that students have a clear understanding of the purpose of the simulation and the procedure to be followed in the interaction of the activity.
5. Follow the simulation with discussion or a summary of the learning activities that relate back to the objectives of the simulation. Students should have the opportunity to evaluate their experiences.

Educational game simulations may involve a variety of resources. Many are pencil and paper activities. Role-playing, computer use, game boards, or other devices may be used, depending upon the resources available.

The second type of simulation, the task-oriented one, is usually prepared by the teacher to meet the needs of specific students. They become a means of reinforcing or teaching new concepts in a motivational way. Task simulations are small units usually designed to be completed in a short period of time. They relate to one segment or concept of the student's learning, or they may be a part of a sequence of activities related to a concept. Frequently, the task simulation is done by the individual without group interaction or participation. Because they are relatively simple to prepare, they lend themselves readily to classes such as consumer economics, business law, business English, or recordkeeping, in addition to the clerical and secretarial classes. Elements to be included in the planning are as follows:

1. Relate the learning activity to a real situation. Use a local firm name or forms if available.
2. Describe the activity or job students are to complete, using objectives.
3. Prepare instructions for the students along with any materials they may need.
4. Plan some form of evaluation.

Task simulations will fit any class. They may be used for reinforcement of a concept or the learning of a new activity. Students like the variation from text materials. The expense of supplies and the amount of time involved in the project are small.

The third type of simulation job is the job simulation which is designed to extend for a length of time ranging from several weeks to one year. The class time involved may be one period a day or a blocked time of two or more periods. Ideally, the blocked time permits students to spend more time on the project which is more realistic for them. The job simulations usually involve a group of students ranging from 15 to 25. Some simulations are designed for fewer students; however, in such instances, the simulation should run for a shorter period of time rather than a semester or year. If the group size is between 15 and 25, the work for four or five stations could be incorporated.

Job simulations normally involve knowledge learned in several classes and an integrated approach is used to provide a practical office situation. Critical incidents are woven within the tasks to give a realistic setting to the activities. Students usually rotate on the various jobs included in the simulation in order to gain insight about job roles, workflow, and interaction among the individuals holding the various positions. Teacher-made simulations can include the content of the other business courses offered in that school to expose the students to as many positions as possible or take an interdisciplinary approach and include other departments in the school in addition to the business department. The interdisciplinary approach would necessitate the cooperation of the staff members in those departments.

JUSTIFICATION FOR SIMULATION

Realistic work experiences provided within the school environment give the students an opportunity to face challenges as close as possible to those they will meet on the job when they leave school. Among the advantages for using this method of teaching are the following:

1. Students have the opportunity to experience human relations. Team work and cooperation are necessary.

2. Students have an opportunity to not only use skills previously learned but also refine them to be marketable skills. New skills can also be learned during the simulation, or the student may do remedial work.

3. Students with all ranges of ability and skills can work together successfully. The pretests and job interviews help to determine the positions they will fill.

4. The materials used in a simulation provide the student with the variety frequently found in a real environment. Actual forms of the company the simulation is based upon may be used.

5. Simulations give the students firsthand career planning information. Rotation schedules expose them to as many positions as are built into the activity.

6. The value of team work must not be overlooked. Students learn what happens when employees are absent or neglect their obligations. The importance of working together and the continuance of the workflow are emphasized.

7. The responsibility of caring for the equipment is part of the process. When there is a breakdown of equipment, the normal workflow is interrupted.

8. Simulations provide the student with the opportunity to tie the knowledge gained from the text with job-related experiences. Individuals

have the chance to demonstrate knowledge, skills, and attitudes necessary to get and keep a job.

9. Social skills are developed as a part of the office interaction.

10. Communications skills are refined. Students compose and type mailable letters. Oral communications also improve as the individuals learn to give and understand directions, clarify tasks, and share in problem-solving activities.

11. Simulations are designed for particular learning experiences. The teacher can build into the program whatever is going to meet the needs of those particular students.

12. Individual performance evaluations can be more beneficial for each student's needs. Should remedial training be necessary, the teacher has the opportunity to include these experiences. The simulation should be flexible.

13. The simulation is a bridge for the student that links the individual with actual office experiences in the security of a controlled environment. The adjustment to work experience after completing high school is considerably easier.

14. The simulation can be used as a culminating or capstone experience in schools where a cooperative work program is not feasible. In many schools students have a quarter or semester of simulation as juniors and enter the cooperative program as seniors. A combination of simulation and directed work experience outside of school has also proven successful.

15. Students are motivated with the opportunity to demonstrate their abilities in an environment different from the traditional classroom setting. Not all students will have the same degree of readiness; however, each student's responsibilities can be geared or designed to those specific skills the person already possesses or is ready to acquire. Individual needs and progress can be taken into consideration throughout the simulation activities.

Although simulations do provide many advantages for students, they also require considerable time to develop and perfect. Teachers who plan to prepare their own should begin the year before they plan to implement it. It is also necessary for the teacher to be familiar with this method of instruction. Many universities or colleges offer a workshop in the techniques. If it is not possible to attend one of these, visit a school that is using a simulation and observe the activities and talk with the staff. Some state department of education offices have guidelines available to teachers. Use several resources to assist in the planning and development of sequences.

PLANNING THE JOB SIMULATION

The first consideration in planning a simulation is the needs of the students. Review the objectives used in the business classes and determine the kinds of activities lacking or needed to provide them with the basic occupational skills for successful employment. Do students have the qualifications for local employment after graduation? The integration of skills, knowledge, and attitudes is a necessity if the students are to be prepared to cope successfully with the work environment after high school. The goals of simulation should incorporate most of these needs as major objectives.

The decision of whether or not to simulate should be discussed with the other members of the department and the advisory committee. There should be agreement upon the needs of the students and an expressed willingness to cooperate with the planning and development of the simulation materials.

The second major consideration is the administration. Once the decision to simulate has been made and the general objectives outlined, the administrator should be contacted. Expect a number of concerns. One will be whether or not additional equipment will have to be purchased. If so, is there a state plan for reimbursement? Will the simulation require major changes in scheduling? For example, implementing a block program could be a major concern. Is there adequate physical space without large expenditures in capital outlay for the remodeling of classrooms? Sometimes simulations can be handled in rooms that are used by other classes during the other hours of the day with only minor changes. Will one or more teachers need released time to develop classroom materials? Has a community survey been taken to assess the needs of the area? Have those needs been taken into consideration in the objectives of the simulation? How many additional dollars will be needed to prepare office forms and supplies? Does the vocational department of the state have guidelines for simulations or curriculum available for school use? Have advisory committee members been involved in the decision? Will the simulation involve one or two areas of the business department or the whole department? These and similar questions are to be expected. It will be necessary to plan a strategy for selling the simulation to the administration and board of education. Be well prepared.

Once the needs have been determined and administrative approval obtained, the next step is to decide what to simulate. From having taken a community survey or from work experience, select a firm to serve as the model for the simulation. After obtaining consent from the business to pattern the simulation after it, spend at least one week in the offices of the firm to gather firsthand information about the various positions, forms, work-flow, and equipment. Lay the ground work for developing a simulation that will provide a good systematic program for the students. A member of the firm may be willing to serve as a consultant for the simulation.

With the materials at hand from the visit, plan the operation of the simulation. Delineate the scope of the program, state goals and objectives, and set a time table for the entire simulation. Consider such factors as how many students are to be involved, the type of simulation needed, how many positions will be necessary, and the number of stations. The prerequisites for enrolling in the course will determine to some degree the depth to which the simulation will parallel the actual firm's operations.

The simulation must be viewed as a part of the total vocational program. Whether the simulation is the capstone experience for seniors or a preparatory course offered for juniors who will enter the cooperative work experience program their last year will make a difference in the number and kinds of experiences to be included. Even if the simulation is to run a year, presimulation learning activities and review will be necessary. Depending upon the prerequisites for enrollment, this period may last up to six weeks.

The prerequisite criteria for enrolling should be considered. In some schools there is no prerequisite other than an interest in the program, while in others, a specific level of proficiency is required in typewriting or shorthand. The prerequisite may be courses rather than skill proficiencies. For example, one or two semesters of typewriting or a completion of core courses may be the minimum for enrollment. The simulation may be limited to seniors only. Regardless of the prerequisites, simulations are usually restricted to second semester juniors or seniors.

DEVELOPING A JOB SIMULATION

After the approval has been given and the basic priority items established such as available space, equipment, length of time, and number of class periods, define the limits of the simulation based upon these items and potential class enrollment as well as community needs. Prepare flowcharts of the responsibilities and duties of each position. The following outline provides basic items to be considered in the overall planning:

I. *Initial planning*
   Scope of the simulation
   Company product or service
   Limits of the simulation (time periods, size of class, skills)
   Positions to be filled
   Student selection criteria
   Publicity for the program (students, faculty, public)
   Funds for materials, supplies, equipment

II. *Preparation of the simulation*
   Introduction
   General objectives
   Behavioral objectives
   Description of each position
   Basic script
   Units of transactions and critical issues
   Evaluation procedures
   Remedial units or special projects
   Pretests, posttests, keys

III. *Materials for the students*
   Orientation
      Folders for each position with inventory sheets, job applications
      Duties of each position
      Facilities and equipment
      Supplies
      Flowcharts
   Job description manuals for each position
   Procedures manual for the office
   Special projects and materials
   Rotation schedule

Evaluation of students
  Team members
  Ability to follow directions
  Solve problems
  Performance (work habits, use of supplies, neatness, use of time)
  Absences
  Posttests
  Evaluation by office manager

IV. *Test simulation before student use*
  Determine if stated objectives have been met
  Work through the units of transactions to determine that job activities
    are properly integrated
  Directions clear
  Interaction
  Realistic activities without too much repetition
  Opportunities to set priorities
  Assess evaluation, pretests and posttests

Testing the simulation to be sure that activities are compatible and fit the workflow is important. Other members of the department may assist with the testing, or employees of the firm after which the simulation is designed may help. If a large number of positions are developed and additional help is needed, members of the advisory committee may be asked.

IMPLEMENTATION

After the materials are developed and the program is ready to operate, the students should be selected. Those interested in the program should complete a personal inventory sheet that will indicate the skills and knowledge they already have. After a brief overview of the simulation, students should complete application forms for the positions they are qualified to fill. An interview for that position should follow. Videotaping is an effective device for teaching job interview techniques. Pretests for each position need to be given. Students are then selected to fill the various positions, and the rotation schedule can be determined at this time.

Once the students are selected and have enrolled, there should be an orientation session with them. They should be made aware of the objectives of the course, the facilities and materials available, the methods of evaluation, and the rotation schedule. For each position there should be a job description and training plan.

Prior to full simulation, there should be a simulation tryout. This will provide students with the opportunity for questions about their positions, workflow, materials, or whatever. Once everyone feels comfortable with the process, the full simulation should be undertaken.

Periodic meetings should be planned so that the students have an opportunity to discuss the activities. Any adjustments needed can then be made. The opportunity to summarize activities is important.

Evaluation should be planned throughout the activities. The criteria set forth earlier for student evaluations should be used. In addition, there should be evaluation of the simulation by students and faculty. This information can be used later for revisions. Finally, a follow-up of students who have gone through the program should be planned. A first year and third or fifth year follow-up should provide sufficient data to determine the value of the simulation.

LEARNING PLANS

For each student in the simulation, there should be a learning plan that indicates that individual's skills, interests, courses taken, and career goals. In the presimulation activities, the student may review or learn new skills based on needs. There are broad areas that should probably be covered with the class as a whole because of the importance of interaction. These areas should also be included on the learning plans. Some of the broad areas to be considered for the learning plans are as follows:

I. *Orientation*
Objectives and purposes of a simulation
Explanation of how a simulation works
Student responsibilities
Overview of flowchart, facilities, equipment, supplies
Job description manuals
Special projects
Rotation schedule

II. *Occupation exploration*
Opportunities—vertically and laterally
Aptitudes and interests toward career objectives
Occupational trends

III. *Personal development*
Appearance
Speech
Attitudes
Grooming and hygiene
Manners
Personality inventory
Responsibility development

IV. *Human relations*
Co-worker relations
Employer-employee relations
Social and civic responsibilities
Human wants and needs
Business ethics

VII. *Job application and interview*
Data sheets
Applications
Interview preparation
Job interview
Employment tests
Payroll forms
Employee's manual

VIII. *Leadership*
Student activities
Parliamentary procedure
Problem-solving techniques
Decision making
Accepting responsibility and delegating authority
Building self-confidence
Types and techniques of leadership

IX. *Units of the simulation*
Telephone usage
Filing
Financial forms
Correspondence
Skills for typing and shorthand
Duplicating equipment
Communications
Business machines
Management
Accounting procedures
Records

Pretests should be utilized where possible. Learning activity packets, either teacher-prepared or purchased, should be available for individual use. The areas just mentioned are suggested guidelines, and some of them would probably be included in classes preceding the simulation. It is important, however, that there be a learning or training plan for the educational needs of each student. The student's plan should be used for counseling and planning course work.

CONCLUSION

As educators become more concerned with the needs of individuals and the employability of students, the use of simulations will continue to grow. Even though teacher-made simulations require considerable work to develop, in many cases they more closely meet the needs of the particular students involved. A number of the commercially prepared simulations are available from major publishing companies, and most of them can be readily adapted to fit the class size. Colleges and universities, state departments of education, and vocational education divisions offer workshops or in-service programs to aid in the development of curriculum materials. Innovative teachers will use these means to prepare materials for simulations. The trend is for more realistic activities in the classroom, and simulations are a viable method of teaching to meet student needs.

Section B: At the Two-Year College Level

WILLIAM H. CURLOTT

Colorado State Board of Community Colleges and
Occupational Education, Denver

It is important at the outset that the relevance of relating the objectives of any particular curriculum technique with the objectives of the delivery system responsible for providing the learning experiences be realized. Today, it is generally agreed that two-year postsecondary business programs are provided for students with varied learning abilities and experiences complicated by a profusion of career goals. Also it must be recognized that postsecondary schools have to take into consideration mobility, transferability, occupational and career training, and local community manpower needs as well as personal or career guidance and counseling.

The objectives are usually reflected in the philosophy of the institution such as those at Otero Junior College, La Junta, Colorado:

1. Developing personal and social awareness
2. Developing occupational skills
3. Offering lower division college education
4. Developing basic educational skills
5. Providing special services
6. Offering programs of interest to the community as well as to the students
7. Providing continuing education.

Realizing the varied learning abilities and experiences of its students, the catalog further states, "It is the college's philosophy that the college must meet these needs regardless of the age or academic background of the community member."

The technique employed by simulation as a teaching-learning strategy is to place students in a reproduced, real-life situation for a period of time necessary to complete the tasks required to reach specific goals. During this time, students are involved in such learning experiences as decision making, worker interaction, work flow quantity and quality standards, and other activities leading to the acquisition of skills and a positive self-image. These will be extremely important accomplishments due to the broad range of student abilities, experiences, and goals mentioned earlier.

The objectives of any simulation program will vary with the individual program but will have some basic similarities. Broad objectives may be inferred from Virginia Barger's statement that the many problem-solving situations presented through office simulation challenge students to:

1. Develop tact and still accomplish whatever must be accomplished.
2. Be objective regarding their work and interpersonal relationships.
3. Accept failure and success gracefully.
4. Accept their individual shortcomings and assets and to work with them.

5. Work effectively with fellow employees.

6. Work with a supervisor.

7. Developing screening techniques.

8. Develop the ability to organize office work, meeting deadlines for bank deposits, issuance of statements, and other deadlines.[1]

Two-year college curriculum considerations. Now that the institutional and teaching-learning strategy objectives have been broadly presented it is well that specific challenges encountered at the two-year college level be addressed. Some basic business curriculum considerations are: (1) the nature of the student, (2) curriculum offerings, and (3) administrative acceptance. These are three broad areas of challenge that set the two-year colleges off from the secondary or university levels.

Nature of the student. The student body of any two-year college is by its very nature atypical. There are many unique situations as a result of its community commitment and open-entry, open-exit philosophy. A good example is the situation during the sixties when a segment of the postsecondary population was represented by those who enrolled in school as an alternative to entering the armed forces. This circumstance presented a definite challenge to the institutional philosophy in such areas as motivation, career goals, self-image, and other objectives. Also there are countless federally supported programs that make use of the community college facilities and resources to accomplish their goals. There is also the age disparity mentioned earlier in the adult programs, the programs for upgrading skills, and support for those students who return to school later in life to acquire skills with the intention of returning to the world of work. All of these circumstances and more contribute to the heterogeneity of the two-year college student body.

Curriculum offerings. Because of the unique role assigned the junior or community college in today's society, a business curriculum on the postsecondary level must be prepared to serve three types of students: vocational, transfer, and continuing education students.

The vocational curriculum should have as its primary goal the development of skills, knowledges, and attitudes of the vocational student needed to succeed in business and office occupations. The trend is to award an associate of applied science degree to the students successfully completing a vocational degree business curriculum. The vocational curriculum typically services the career or terminal student preparing for the world of work who desires to enter the job market upon completion of the two-year program of studies.

There are students who must be served at the postsecondary level, however, who intend to further their education beyond the associate of applied science degree level. These are the students who would like to begin their postsecondary education near home for various reasons and then transfer to a four-year college or university and apply their credits towards a baccalaureate degree. In the development of curriculums for transfer students the program of articulation enters the picture, and complicated arrangements

---

[1]Barger, Virginia. "Office Simulation, An Effective Technique." *Balance Sheet,* February 1970.

have to be made and agreements reached so that the credits of the two-year institution will be accepted by the four-year institutions.

Another group of students who have to be considered by the business curriculum designers are those who desire to enroll in continuing or adult education courses. These are generally representatives from the younger and older segments of the population who have no degree aspirations but instead are looking for retraining for employment or avocational, self-improvement type offerings.

Administrative acceptance. Most of the two-year vocational business programs are subject to some type of reimbursement formulas arrived at by the state in which they reside. In order to be eligible for the funding the programs have to meet certain requirements and standards also usually established by the vocational divisions at the state level. It follows then, in order for innovative programs to be considered by the local administration, proof will be required that the programs will not only provide worthwhile learning experiences for the students but will also meet those guidelines established by the various vocational state departments. Therefore, it is important that whoever is directly responsible for vocational instructional techniques, such as office simulation, have an understanding of what the state requirements are in order to sell the proposal to their administration, who in turn can convince their respective boards. Too often an attempt is made to update and innovate teaching techniques, especially in vocational areas, without an understanding of what is required further up the administrative hierarchy, causing the initiators to be unsuccessful in their attempts.

Office simulation models in two-year business classes. One of the program areas where simulation has proven most successful and effective at the postsecondary level is office practice. In this area students not only develop skills, knowledges, and attitudes but are able to provide office services to the community.

An example of one of the more successful office simulation programs began in 1972 at Lane Community College, Eugene, Oregon, and is now being offered in other colleges and high schools in the United States and Canada.[2] Each simulation employs from 4 to 36 individuals in these three areas: Main Office, Training Division, and Supportive Services (which represent the bank and other business contacts outside the organization). In larger schools four simulations are operated concurrently: Branch A, Monday, Wednesday, Friday morning; Branch B, Monday, Wednesday, Friday afternoon; Branch C, Tuesday, Thursday afternoon.

In a medium-sized simulation, the Main Office employs an accounting clerk, a mail/file clerk, payroll clerk, receptionist/librarian, secretary, supply clerk I, supply clerk II, and typist/billing clerk. The Training Division employs a training clerk and typist/clerical trainees. Supportive Services include the liaison officer I, who functions as creditors, utility companies, and customers; and the liaison officer II, who functions as the bank.

In small offices, positions are combined; in large offices, the manager may employ more than one secretary, accounting clerk, payroll clerk, and

[2]Lynn, Helen. "Office Simulation Brings Stimulation and Enthusiasm." *Business Education Forum* 30: 24-25; May 1976.

billing clerk. Any of these optional positions may also be added: assistant manager, administrative assistant, equipment clerk, machine operator (duplicating/reprographics), stenographer, and utility clerk (pivot person).

Daily operations include these primary activities: (1) training, (2) producing office work for customers, and (3) performing office duties required by the work flow. Through a rotation plan, each employee participates in all three of the above primary activities and holds as many of the positions as simulation time permits.

Individualized, hands-on, self-paced training units provide realistic, stimulating simulations of on-the-job performance in tasks common to business offices. Some of the units are similar to portions of the Main Office positions; others represent tasks from other types of businesses. The training units are used for career exploration and development in the following ways:

1. As preparation for the assumption of a position in the simulated organization
2. As preparation for a student's specific career goal in the real world
3. As a method of determining aptitudes for various types of work
4. As a means of testing interests and skills
5. As a tool for teaching work organization in logical sequence and correct hand motions.

While an employee is in the Training Division, he/she also produces customers' jobs. The manager has several options for this input: he/she may accept work from the community, from the school, or from another instructor in the department; or use a combination of these.

The jobs, from a variety of fields, provide a full cycle of work flow, beginning with the initial request for service, continuing through the completion, recording, invoicing, and posting operations to the payments made by and received from the customers, the depositing of these payments, and the bank reconciliation at the end of the month.

The simulation is divided into two phases: orientation and simulation. The simulation phase is further divided into rotations and closing operations.

On the first day, the students receive a Working File Manual (employee's handbook), and the manager explains the format, calling special attention to the section on orientation and to the glossary of terms in the appendix. During the first week, students prepare applications for employment, listen to an explanation of the operations and the organizational structure, tour the office, become familiar with the equipment and machines, and receive general information about company policies and procedures, including working hours, pay scales, fringe benefits, and promotional opportunities.

Each applicant then decides which position he prefers from those in the staffing pattern the manager has selected. Each applicant is encouraged to list his first three choices in rank order. He is assured, however, that the choices are not binding and that he may change his mind later. At this point, the importance of learning how to match oneself to a real position is stressed.

As soon as the application has been completed in an acceptable manner, the employee is hired. The manager screens the applications, interviews the applicants if time permits, makes selections, and announces the appointments. Each appointment is for three weeks.

Witholding Allowance Exemption Certificates are then completed along with certain other induction papers. The Working File Manual contains explicit instructions for completing and routing each of these forms, thus freeing the employees to work at their own pace and also freeing the manager to circulate and interact with the employees.

At the beginning of the second week, employees receive procedure manuals for their respective positions and take them to their assigned work stations. Employees in related positions are asked to work together to assure that all work is completed; thus a more skilled employee may help a less skilled one. However, employees are usually so highly motivated that each prefers to complete the work independently.

The papers that were prepared during the orientation phase are given to the mail clerk to distribute to the appropriate persons for further processing as part of the opening duties in the simulation phase.

Each manual contains preliminary matter that explains the purpose of the manuals, their general content, and guidelines for using them. The four major sections of each manual are Job Description, Opening Duties, Regular Duties, and Supplies/Equipment. A fifth section, General Information, is provided for the addition of employees' notes and other supplemental material that may assist employees in performing their duties.

The Opening Duties section of the manual guides the employee step by step through the tasks necessary to obtain supplies, activate records, and either set up the work station or inspect it for proper organization. Within a week the office begins to hum. As one student put it, "Everything is done with such seriousness that one forgets it's a simulation."

Employees receive and deposit their paychecks twice a month. Superior performance is rewarded through recognition as employee of the week or of the month, through pay raises, and through promotions. The most popular rewards have been checks for $1, a fresh carnation, and chocolates.

Employees rotate to new positions every three weeks. The employee's stated preferences, real-life goals, present skills, and those which need developing or polishing, as well as the organization's needs, are considered in making appointments to positions. Grades are based on five factors which are measured from available data: (1) dependability, (2) cooperation, (3) knowledge of job, (4) quality of work, and (5) quantity of work.

In conjunction with the simulation, to assure that the student does in effect have a worthwhile learning experience, it is a good idea to meet with each student and prepare a learning plan—a plan geared to each student's needs in career preparation. The plan should be designed to allow for generalized and specialized learning in a specific occupation or cluster which the student has identified as a career objective. The learning plan is useful in preparation for employment. It should be designed so that a student can proceed from simple to complex tasks during the preparation period. Individualized instruction as well as simulation is one of the strengths of the learning plan concept.

Another approach that has been used successfully with simulation is to conclude the learning experience with an internship period. One of the more popular methods is to have the class meet two hours daily on campus during the fall and winter quarters, during which time students can earn credits for each quarter's work. The third or final quarter the students spend on the job. This period of time spent on the job is referred to as an internship period, and during this period, credits can be prorated according to the number of hours spent on the job. This method can also be applied to a semester schedule.

During this experience students can direct their program by completing a training plan as opposed to a learning plan. The training plan is an integral part of the cooperative education method but could be adapted to an internship. As in the cooperative education method the training plan should be used as a guide for the training sponsor, student, and teacher who also acts as a coordinator. The plan is used for assignment of job activities, for the evaluation of student progress, and for future training.

One of the important accomplishments of a training plan is to get the student to declare a career objective. Once this is done the training plan becomes an essential component in the student's business program. The training plan can help provide up-to-date and practical learning experiences sequentially planned for students in preparation for entry-level employment.

To really assure that the right student is assigned to the right job the businesses that are going to provide the work stations should be contacted to furnish job descriptions indicating the duties and responsibilities. In response to that information the students will be able to direct their resume information and final training for a specific job.

Simulation in other business program areas. Simulation can be used effectively in other business program areas on the postsecondary level. Subject areas such as marketing, management, and introduction to business can be simulated with the use of games and computers. A common approach is to program the game so it is error free. Classes can be divided into teams representing companies in competition. The "companies" can in turn elect officers, identify goals, and assign specific responsibilities with appropriate titles. Each group then makes its decisions, analyzes the strategies, and with the aid of the computer to simulate time, can determine the results. At the conclusion of the simulation the students submit a written report in which the overall results of the decisions made are addressed.

While using simulation in other program areas, a variation of the simulation technique can be applied. Simulation can be used very effectively with the cooperation of other business classes. A basic office simulation class can cooperate with bookkeeping and accounting classes for the services they offer or a law class for the benefits of their expertise. There can be a cooperative effort for mutual benefit between the stenography, the business machines class, and the office simulation class. The combinations and variations are endless and dependent upon the local situation. This cooperative approach can be expanded to include other departments within the school or, interscholastically, to include other schools within or outside of the system.

Business simulation in adult classes. Since it has already been established that adult education is partly the responsibility of postsecondary education, a presentation of simulation in adult business classes is in order. As was mentioned earlier, members of the adult education classes usually are representatives of the older segment of the community's population. Naturally, adult students would require different considerations in the emphasis and utilization of teaching methodologies. Some of the important points to remember concerning adult learners are the following:

1. Adults who have been away from systematic education for some time may underestimate their ability to learn, and this lack of confidence may prevent them from applying themselves wholly.

2. Methods of teaching have changed since many adults were in school, so that most of them have to go through a period of adjustment to "strange, new conditions."

3. Various physiological changes occur in the process of aging, such as decline in visual acuity, reduction in reaction speed, and lowering of energy levels. These changes may operate as barriers to learning unless devices to produce louder sound and larger print are used, for example.

4. Adults respond less readily to external pressures for learning, such as grades.[3]

In a paper presented by Lawrence M. Knolle and Robert F. Nicely, Jr., at the annual meeting of the American Educational Research Association in Chicago, April 1972, various simulations designed for adult learning experiences were described. The basis of the approach was dictated by the definition of simulation which states "an operating model that displays processes over time and thus may develop dynamically." It is stated in the report that this definition implies that the teacher can design a simulation that can be managed and then can be increased in its complexity.

There were three methods of simulation used in the adult class. The first simulation focused on providing students with realistic experiences in dealing with varying kinds of office communications. A second simulation was of a detailed office procedure for processing a letter from its initial development to mailing. The third simulation involved the formation of two small companies which were in competition with each other. The teacher reported that the "office" simulations seemed very easy to design and implement. The students were all actively involved in their learning and in making some decisions about the content of their learning. Individualization was accomplished in the simulations via student self-evaluation and self-selection from a variety of office tasks.

Follow-up and evaluation. The importance of a follow-up of a practical real-life training program such as simulation cannot be minimized. It is extremely important to determine whether the students are employed in the job for which they are trained, whether the training was adequate, and if the jobs are fulfilling their job aspirations. There are several techniques that can be applied for an effective follow-up with strengths and weaknesses involved in all of them. The initial factor to consider is the time involved to

---

[3]Allen, Thomas R., Jr. "Preparing Teachers for Adult Distributive Education." *Business Education Forum* 30:27-29; May 1976.

accomplish the project effectively. It is generally agreed that the best method is a one-on-one situation with the teacher and the student employees and their employers. The obvious weakness with this technique is the time involved and student mobility—the fact that in some cases the students will not be geographically available. Any type of mail follow-up such as letters, questionnaires, post cards, and other forms of survey instruments traditionally have a poor return percentage and often place parameters on the information being gathered. However, any of these methods would be better than no follow-up at all.

Evaluation should be constant and consistent throughout the existence of the program. Teaching techniques, teaching materials, testing methods and materials, community resources used, every aspect of the program should undergo continuous evaluation.

One of the most reliable and dependable sources of evaluation is the students themselves. Keith J. Edwards at the Johns Hopkins University Center for the Study of Social Organization of Schools reported on students' evaluations of a business simulation game as a learning experience. His report investigated this technique in terms of specific claims which have been made for this kind of teaching. Ninety-nine junior college students in introductory business courses answered a questionnaire after playing the game as an ongoing, semester-long activity. The results support the claims that games are self-judging, increase student motivation, and increase students' understanding in areas related to the game, but not the claim that games have special value for low-achieving students. The students consider the game experience most valuable for learning relationships and for getting a feel for the real situation. In general, the students' evaluation supported the instructor's reason for using the game. Also, acceptance of the game as self-judging was associated with low tolerance for ambiguity, and reported increases in business understanding were related to the students' course grades and their understanding of the game.

The most rewarding evaluations by students a program can receive are such spontaneous evaluations as those quoted by the students at Lane Community College, "This is the only class I have ever had that I have attended every day," or "This is the best class the school could offer to train students for going out in the business world," or "This is the only class I can get up for."

Section C: At the Four-Year College Level

OWEN FIELDS
Longwood College, Farmville, Virginia

Four-year colleges have long been considered havens of the lecture method—the telling method with its groups of passive listeners busily taking volumes of notes as professors in their real or imaginary academic regalia share their wisdom with their students. The lecture method has been handed down over the years from professors to students who become professors who hand it down to their students who become professors, ad infinitum. Professors, for the most part, tend to teach in the way they were taught; and the popularity of the lecture method has continued to the present day. However, the stronghold of the lecture method has begun to diminish somewhat in four-year college classes, although there are still situations and times when the lecture method is undoubtedly the best method to use.

Probably nowhere in four-year colleges has the stronghold of the lecture method diminished more than in schools of business, as innovative teachers have searched for ways to make the learning experiences of their students more meaningful, more realistic, and more lasting. Technology has added greatly to the number of ways teachers have found to approach the many subject areas found in schools of business, and many teachers have eagerly adopted the newer methods. Programmed learning with computer feedback, individualized instruction, multi-media presentations, educational television, video recording, simulations—all have been utilized by teachers in their quests to improve their instructional techniques.

While many of the new techniques have proven to be viable in many ways, the simulation approach appears to be one of the most successful and one of the most widely used of the newer methods of teaching business subjects. Yet, the simulation approach is new in name only, as simulation-type activities have been frequently utilized in four-year college business classes for many years.

The term *simulation* has been given many definitions, and they all have a common theme. A simulation is a piece of reality, a model of a real-life situation, a step in the direction of realism in which students act out roles and often interact socially with other students to experience the problems encountered and the decision-making skills required in the various positions and careers which they may later take up as graduates of four-year college business programs.

Simulations take many forms, although role-playing activities appear to be the predominant form used in four-year college business classes at the present time. The following paragraphs deal with specific courses or subject areas found in schools of business and describe some of the ways in which the simulation approach is applied.

BUSINESS EDUCATION

Role-playing is one of the most popular forms of simulation in business teacher education methodology classes, and the ultimate simulation for most preservice business teachers is probably the demonstration lesson. Demonstration lessons are extremely familiar to most business educators, for very few have not trembled as they assumed the role of "teacher for the day" to a class of hypothetical high school students—their own classmates. Very few have not had doubts about their selection of objectives from among the many possible ones, and their selection of teaching methods from among the many

100

about which they have learned. And, very few have not wondered whether they have actually taught anything to the class in their demonstration lesson. Thus, the preservice business teachers have assumed the roles of practicing business teachers and have had many of the actual experiences that in-service business teachers have each and every day. The demonstration teachers prepare lesson plans, prepare teaching aids, present lessons, and obtain feedback in one form or another—feedback needed to determine the relative success of their "lessons." Demonstration lessons are often recorded on videotape for later self-critiques by the demonstration teachers. This form of feedback is perhaps the most valuable, for the playback of video recording provides the opportunity for students to see themselves as others see them.

OFFICE MANAGEMENT

A simulation used by many teachers of office management courses is also of a role-playing nature and is often the culminating project of the office management course. After an in-depth study of the many areas included in the course and armed with the knowledges and insights they have acquired, office management students assume the roles of office analysts. Each student "analyzes" a different office by studying the office building and its surroundings, the office floorplan, the arrangement of furnishings and equipment, the records management system, the colors and decor, and by interviewing executives, secretaries, and clerks.

Students prepare a meaningful report based upon their observations and present realistic, considered suggestions for improvement in the office observed. Feedback may be obtained from instructors, peers, and personnel of the office which has been analyzed. Good suggestions for improvement by office management students may be incorporated by offices, and impractical suggestions delineated through discussions with instructors, classmates, and office personnel with the reasons specified and clarified for the report writers.

OFFICE PROCEDURES

Instructors of office procedures classes in four-year colleges rely upon simulations to enhance their students' understanding of course content as well as to increase their ability to perform the many duties required of secretaries in today's business world. Simulations are also used extensively to develop the decision-making skills often required in executive-level secretarial positions to which graduates of four-year colleges aspire.

Role-playing is the principal type of simulation used in office procedures classes, and it has various degrees of complexity. The simplest roles are probably those that emphasize telephone techniques and receptionist activities. Scripts may be utilized to present correct procedures early in the study of the subject matter; and spontaneous, unrehearsed situations may be used at later intervals as students refine their skills.

The familiar "in-basket" exercise is also popular and effective. This activity challenges students to define their priorities in terms of which tasks must be accomplished and in what order on a given day. Students are presented with various pieces of data in the form of letters, memorandums, telephone message notes, business forms, business reports, etc. They must first decide upon the order in which the tasks will be performed and then do the required work. "In-basket" decisions are based upon knowledges developed by the students through reading textbooks and journals, discussing alternatives, and analyzing the merits of the many sequences in which the work could be done.

Familiar secretarial or clerical practice sets are still used in many office procedures classrooms. Because business teachers are so familiar with practice sets, they will only be discussed briefly here. Practice sets are true simulations as they require students to perform the many duties and tasks required of a secretarial or clerical worker in a particular position or type of business. The term *practice set* is slowly but surely giving way to the term *single-station simulation* or *single-position simulation*.

Model office simulations in which students may assume various roles from time to time and in which a flow-of-work pattern must be established do not appear to be as popular in four-year college programs as they are in community college and high school programs. Model office simulations, though, seem to have the potential for providing the best introduction to office routines and for defining the importance of accuracy and timeliness, as the accomplishment of one student's work may often depend upon work received from another student. Model office setups will undoubtedly be seen in increasing numbers in four-year college business programs.

One example of a recent innovation in office procedures used by many instructors in various types of office procedures classes, including general secretarial, medical secretarial, and legal secretarial is a text by Lee and Brower.[1] This simulation might be called an "on-going" simulation, as it begins on day one and continues, building upon each new learning, throughout the entire course. The "on-going" simulation is a role-playing activity and is of the single-position variety, as no one student's work affects the work of another in any way. The simulation is adaptable to self-paced instructional programs or to more formal classroom settings. It works as follows:

1. Students study texts and receive input from their instructor.

2. Projects related to each topic are completed, and students are instructed to file the projects for use at a later time.

3. Simulations are introduced. These simulations put students in an office situation which involves many areas of secretarial work. Instructions students receive during the simulations come from many different sources. Written data includes incoming mail, reports, etc., as well as materials prepared earlier as project work. Dictation, directions, and telephone calls are provided via tape recordings. Rough-draft copy or transcribing machine recordings may be provided for nonshorthand students.

4. Students work while the tape recording sets the pace. Student secretaries have simulated direct contact (by way of the recordings, of course) with

---

[1]Lee, Dorothy E., and Brower, Walter A. *Secretarial Office Procedures.* New York: McGraw-Hill Book Co., 1976.

employers, fellow employees, and office visitors. Musical interludes of "work time" are provided, and interruptions (telephone calls, visitors, etc.) occur frequently. Thus the often hectic atmosphere of an actual office is simulated. Work must be organized, priorities must be set, interruptions must be handled, and tasks must be accomplished.

Such simulations may occur several times during a given office procedures course and are cumulative; that is, each simulation builds upon all learnings that precede it. This includes all project work completed and all prior simulations accomplished. The final simulation represents a review as well as an application of all course learnings. Users of this type of simulation prepare students to make their transitions from college to offices much more easily than would otherwise be the case.

BUSINESS COMMUNICATIONS

It has often been noted that communication abilities (oral and written), problem-solving abilities, and human relations abilities are among the most important qualities a business person can possess. It has also often been noted that these qualities represent the areas addressed (or which should be addressed) in business communications classes. Yet, though most business communications instructors attempt to include all three areas in their courses, few are able to interrelate all three in a typical one-semester survey-type business communications course. The use of simulation provides one solution to the dilemma.

Wunsch describes a business communications simulation that he feels is highly successful in accomplishing its objectives.[2] The simulation is available commercially and is designed to include oral and written communications, problem solving, and interpersonal relations.[3]

In the simulation, which may last from three to four weeks or longer, students work at various management-level assignments in a simulated company that manufactures audiovisual tutorial study carrels. As "managers," students must write letters and memorandums, complete forms, make telephone calls, attend meetings, and make personal visits. Students must work together to complete their assignments, and office procedures or transcription classes may be utilized to accomplish the dictation and transcription work.

Wunsch feels the BUCOMCO simulation described briefly here is a worthy addition to business communications courses. He says, "Students are exposed to situations in a simulation which cannot be experienced in a traditional classroom setting—situations which they will ultimately face in the world of work."[4]

In business communications classes almost all letters, memorandums, and reports are forms of simulations; for in almost every instance, the students must project themselves into the positions of others and view facts

[2]Wunsch, Alan P. "Simulation—A Realistic Approach to Business Communications." *ABCA Bulletin* 39:25-26; March 1976.

[3]Melrose, John. *BUCOMCO, A Business Communications Simulation*. Chicago: Science Research Associates, 1977.

[4]Wunsch, *op. cit.*, p. 26.

and figures and problems from perspectives other than their own in order to complete assignments. Of course, some business communications projects are extremely realistic. The letters of application with corresponding personal data sheets written by most business communications students are examples of "real" projects as are many business reports undertaken by students, reports which relate directly to problems encountered in other business courses, or problems relating to currently held full- or part-time business positions.

ECONOMICS

The often vague concepts encountered by students in economics classes can often be made less abstract through the use of simulations. A number of possibilities exist for the use of simulations in the many types of courses in economics found in four-year colleges.

One example of an economics simulation is a forecasting simulation for a basic economics course as reported by Clayton and Hoyt.[5] These authors describe their simulation model as a simple Keynesian expression with nine equations and a built-in, Phillips-type relationship in which students play the role of economic policymakers. The students' goal is that of achieving satisfactory levels of inflation and unemployment by manipulating variables such as money supply, government spending, taxes, and transfer payments. Computer technology aids students to manipulate the variables as they strive to balance inflation and unemployment over a hypothetical, simulated 10-year period. Clayton and Hoyt report that students' responses to a questionnaire relating to their use of the simulation were generally favorable, that most students increased their self-confidence in using computers, and that most students recommended the continuation of the simulation in subsequent basic economics courses.

The opportunities for the use of simulated real-life activities abound in the area of economics. Interested economics instructors need only search the literature for examples and then put their imaginations to the task.

ACCOUNTING

Although practice sets, or single-position simulations, are available to complement many college-level accounting textbooks, particularly textbooks for introductory accounting courses, the use of these types of simulations appears to be limited at the four-year college level. Accounting instructors in four-year colleges generally tend to utilize accounting problems of varying lengths to give their students practice in accounting techniques, and they use case studies to help their students develop decision-making skills.

Case studies, according to Horn,[6] present descriptions of situations occurring in the real world which are then focused around particular

---

[5]Clayton, Gary E., and Hoyt, Daniel R. "A Forecasting Simulation for a Basic Economics Course." *Collegiate News and Views* 31:5-9; Winter 1977-78.

[6]Horn, Robert E., editor. *The Guide to Simulations/Games for Education and Training, Volume 2—Business.* Third edition. Lexington, Mass: Information Resources, 1977, p. 4.

problems. Students are asked to analyze the problems and come up with solutions. Case studies require students to project themselves beyond the classroom walls and scrutinize problems from an assumed perspective—that of the person or firm that has actually encountered the particular problems involved. Case studies are indeed simulations; they represent another form of role-playing.

Simulations certainly are not a brand new idea in accounting classes as indicated by a 1964 book by Churchill, Miller, and Trueblood.[7] These authors describe in great detail how they reinforced their graduate accounting students' knowledges in and understanding of auditing concepts by having the students act out the roles of auditing teams charged with auditing the financial records of other teams in a game that was being conducted by upper-level graduate students of management. The authors present evidence of the extensive, realistic work accomplished by the student auditing teams. They also relate that the auditing teams had many good effects upon the work of the management teams. While this particular simulation was played out by graduate accounting students and while it was elaborately conceived and executed, the same concepts and practices could well be adapted and modified for use by undergraduate students at various stages of their accounting studies.

BUSINESS ADMINISTRATION AND MANAGEMENT

Business and industry have long been using simulation techniques to help management personnel develop the leadership abilities and managerial skills needed to deal with the diverse problems that are encountered daily with subordinates, peers, superiors, customers, and suppliers. Likewise, the instructors of business management-type courses in four-year colleges have adopted simulations to enhance the development of their students. Role-playing activities and case studies are the most popular types of simulations used in the various types of administration and management classes found in schools of business.

Fox states that cases used early in business courses should acquaint students with business situations and guide them to the areas needing special attention. At later stages of case usage, the purposes should shift from the development of solutions to the recognition of problems. The ability to find the appropriate questions is itself a needed skill; therefore, cases without given questions should be used at times. Fox says, "When learners face a case without questions, it challenges them to project themselves into realistic conditions of uncertainty and pressures so that they can formulate a sound course of action without prompting."[8]

Business case studies are usually based upon or adapted from real business situations, and instructors will neither have nor give solutions since many different solutions might be appropriate for a given case. Instructors, of

---

[7]Churchill, Neil C.; Miller, Merton H.; and Trueblood, Robert M. *Auditing, Management Games, and Accounting Education.* Homewood, Ill.: Richard D. Irwin, 1964.

[8]Fox, Harold W. "Two Dozen Ways of Handling Cases." *Collegiate News and Views* 26:17-20; Spring 1973.

course, should critique the work of their students and, through discussions, help them refine their abilities to see problem areas, to analyze problems, and to present appropriate, realistic, and considered solutions. Case-study problems may be simple or complex. They may involve only a single happening or they may involve the operations of entire companies or industries. They may be handled by individual students or by student teams. Case studies are viable forms of simulations; they have been used in both business and educational settings for many years.

Many extremely complex simulations are frequently used in business administration classes, particularly in upper-level classes. These simulations are forms of case studies, and they many times involve the use of competition among management teams within classes or among classes within schools or even among schools. Most such simulations require computers for the manipulation of a complex set of variables and to provide rapid knowledge of the consequences of simulated decisions. These so called "management games" are discussed more thoroughly in Chapter 6, which relates to gaming and games.

The case for the use of role-playing simulations in business classes is succinctly stated by Silver, who lists the following advantages: increased student interaction and participation, less static classroom environment, fun in learning, attitudinal changes, involvement of quiet and shy students, and utilization of current subject matter.[9] Add to this listing the realistic situations encountered and the enhancement of learning which is possible, and one may easily conclude that the route of simulation may be the only way to go.

BUSINESS LAW

Lectures and assigned readings combined with two forms of simulation, case studies and mock trials, have for many years been the principal teaching strategies used by professors for teaching courses in business law. The simulations provide for the application of gained knowledges while the lectures and assigned readings provide for gaining that knowledge.

Case studies are used most often in business law classes, and the many "cases" provided in business law textbooks and the many available supplemental books of "cases" will attest to this fact. Case studies as used in business law classes at the four-year college level are similar to those used in other areas of the business curriculum, except that principles of law rather than principles of management or accounting must be applied to the cases. Students must project themselves into the positions of others who have legal problems with which to deal, apply basic principles of law, and arrive at considered "verdicts." Class discussions are useful for the purpose of clarifying which principles of law are involved and for considering possible alternatives. As in any other area of business study, cases in business law may be simple, one-student exercises, or they may be complex situations which

---

[9]Silver, Gerald A. "Role Playing—An Effective Teaching Method in Introductory Business." *Journal of Business Education* 48:242-44; March 1973.

require the input of teams of students. Case studies in business law may also be debated with team competition and perhaps panels of judges.

Mock trials appear to be used less often than case studies in four-year college business law classes primarily because of the demands mock trials make on instructors and students in preparation time and the often limited number of legal principles which may be emphasized. Yet, the mock trial may be the highlight of a business law course for four-year college business students and might be well worth the extra effort required.

Mock trials demand a knowledge of courtroom procedures and of the roles played by the various participants in a trial—defendants, plaintiffs, judges, clerks, recorders, bailiffs, jury, witnesses. For this reason procedures must be studied, and a class visit to an actual trial is recommended.

Whole classes may participate in mock trials, and outside experts may even be incorporated into the proceedings. A real judge, for instance, will certainly add to the mock trial presentation, and his presence will certainly create interest among class members and nonmembers alike.

Two articles on mock trial presentations are recommended: Baulch[10] and Wade.[11] Both articles deal with secondary school settings, but innovative, interested four-year college teachers of business law will find the articles to be excellent starting points for their own mock trials.

SUMMARY

The many ways in which simulations may be utilized in four-year college business classes have hardly been exhausted in this brief report. As innovative business teachers combine their creative talents with the technicians who are capable of designing new equipment, simulations in four-year college business classes will probably become more and more realistic. Perhaps one day a business education simulator will exist that will represent to schools of business what the space capsule simulator represents to the nation's space program.

---

[10]Baulch, Janet. "Simulation in Secondary School Business Law." *Journal of Business Education* 51:366-68; May 1976.

[11]Wade, Eugene Howard. "Development of a Mock Trial." *Journal of Business Education* 45:339-40; May 1970.

CHAPTER 6

Gaming and Games in Business Education

Games and gaming are an outgrowth of the case or problem approach to learning. Business teachers have used practice sets, which may also be classified as simulation activities, for many years. Games and gaming add a new dimension to the process by helping to develop the competitive spirit, which is a strong factor in the day-to-day living of most of our population, especially in the business world. The use of games and gaming is growing at all levels in business education, and the possibilities are limited only by the imagination of the teacher.

Section A: At the Secondary School Level

TOMMIE BUTLER
Arkansas State Department of Education, Little Rock

GEORGIA M. HALE
Arkansas State University, State University

Business teachers, as well as other educators, have long recognized the need to motivate students and have sought methods to create a change of pace that would add interest to their instructional programs. The use of educational games and simulations has captured the imagination and enthusiasm of many innovative teachers. Because of various viewpoints regarding what constitutes an educational exercise in gaming, these definitions provided by Lewis, Wentworth, Reinke, and Baker will be used for further discussion:

> A learning *game* is a model of student interaction which usually involves a "winner," and the winner is a person who has learned enough content to win the game. The game essentially provides a competitive setting for the learning of subject matter content.
>
> *Simulations* are an attempt to model a portion of reality in an artificial situation. They reproduce the social, economic, or political process of particular systems of social interactions. Students assume roles in the system and try to understand how the system operates by participating in it as a member, not as an observer.
>
> A *simulation game* is a combination of these models which tries to use the role-playing, modeling features of simulation for learning how a system operates and the competitive nature of games to encourage student motivation. Most exercises available have both of these characteristics.[1]

---

[1]Lewis, Darrell R., and others. *Educational Games and Simulations in Economics.* Third edition. New York: Joint Council on Economic Education, 1974. pp. 1-2.

It is recognized that the topic of simulation was discussed in the previous chapter; however, the assumption was made that the writers would use the "flow-of-work" simulation concept rather than the gaming concept. Should there be similarities of ideas expressed, perhaps different approaches to the subject will reduce the probability of redundancy.

HISTORICAL PERSPECTIVE OF GAMING

The games of children do not change much through the years. Single games played with song or repeated rhyme are much the same the world over. Marbles is one of the oldest games of skill and was played in ancient Egypt and Greece. Because of their competitive nature, games of skill become more popular as children grow older. Some persons like sporting games which give them more exercise; others prefer games which make them think.

Some of the most popular games are played on boards marked off in squares or other kinds of divisions. Probably the oldest board game is chess, a form of which has been played in China for more than three thousand years, and in Europe, for over a thousand years. Most authorities agree that chess has proven to be one of the most difficult of all games to master. Playing cards are as old as the history of civilized people, and it is believed that more games can be played with cards than with other types of equipment. During the twentieth century, the manufacture of game equipment has become a multimillion dollar industry both in the United States and various other countries.

Business education literature indicates that business games were introduced to business students around the middle of the twentieth century. Evolving from early studies of the theory of games of chance by the Swiss mathematician Daniel Bernovlli (1700-1782), the game theory was first formally applied to business decision making through mathematical analysis by Morgenstern and von Neumann in 1944.[2] Since that time business games have been widely used in management courses in schools of business throughout the country. Since games were introduced in high school classrooms in the middle 1960's, their creation and use, and the discussion of their educational worth, has increased geometrically each year. This public and professional attention and the resulting new games make any publication on the subject quickly outdated.

Perhaps no other business subject area has developed so fast or had as much effort devoted to gaming as a motivational technique for teaching as the area of economics. This emphasis has been enhanced by the thrust of the Joint Council of Economic Education. For the study and evaluation of games involving the use of economic behavior, goals and/or concepts, the University of Minnesota has been designated by the JCEE as the national repository of economic games. Recognizing its responsibility to provide educators with updated information on all facets of economic education, the JCEE decided to revise and expand its earlier bibliographies of games and simulations to

---

[2]Morgenstern, Oskar, and von Neumann, John. *Theory of Games and Economic Behavior*. Princeton, N.J.: Princeton University Press, 1944.

include as many of the new developments as were publicly available. The result is a comprehensive publication serving as an invaluable resource document that includes these features:

1. A section on constructing, selecting, and using educational games and simulations in economics

2. A review of findings and annotations of the current research on instructional games and simulations

3. An annotated listing of all currently available simulations and games for the teaching of economic and related topics which fit their criteria for inclusion

4. A listing of other published games and simulations bibliographies and of journals currently addressing themselves to this area.

RATIONALE AND GAMING OBJECTIVES

Ernest C. Arbuckle, Chairman of the Board of Wells Fargo Bank, speaking at the 1976 NBEA Convention in San Francisco, challenged business educators to provide their students with a knowledge and understanding of the function of business in our society, how it operates, and how it performs. Mr. Arbuckle asked that students be prepared to think objectively and knowledgeably about the business institutions in which their skills will be applied, that they understand the all-important subject of what creates jobs and how profits are used. This challenge is just one example illustrating the need for exciting ways to teach economic concepts to high school students. Mr. Arbuckle further stated that a pervasive ignorance of basic economics and of the structure and functioning of the private enterprise system is the greatest threat to the system. Thomas B. Duff, director of the Center of Economic Education at the University of Minnesota, Duluth, adds further documentation of the negative attitudes of Americans toward the business community and the inaccurate concepts held regarding the amount and purpose of profit in our economic system, which is evidenced by polls conducted by Gallup and Opinion Research Corporation. In addition, Dr. Duff explains that a recent study of 21,000 high school students conducted by the Joint Council on Economic Education indicated that more than 50 percent of these students could not distinguish between capitalism and socialism nor did they know that the U.S. economic system was based on free enterprise.[3]

Because of the lack of more relevant training in the teaching of economics, most business educators will readily admit their feelings of inadequacy regarding this subject matter. Thus, the need for techniques and games to assist in teaching economic concepts has been recognized and responded to by various councils, organizations, and companies. Because of this need and response, it is not surprising to find the forerunner in the business gaming area to be in the subject matter of economics.

These observations are not meant to imply that teachers do not desire and need motivational materials in other subject areas as well. Teachers are continually searching for ways to create a more effective learning environ-

---

[3]Duff, Thomas B. "Now Is the Time for Basic Business." *Business Education Forum* 31:24-25; May 1977.

ment. Many variations of games have been successfully introduced in the business education classrooms. Because of a desire to provide exciting activities for students, many teachers have developed their own games, some have found commercially prepared games that provide the exercises needed, and others have accepted invitations to participate in team competition involving two or more schools.

Basically, two types of games are used: one that simulates problem-solving and decision-making activities which go on in business, and the other composed of competitive interaction which incorporates review and recall exercises regarding cognitive learning.

The major thrust of the games simulating transactions that occur in various businesses is to provide the student with an opportunity to apply classroom knowledge to realistic situations. Therefore, students have the opportunity to test their ability to cope with situations in a simulated game before meeting them in real life. Resource use and opportunity cost take on real meaning beyond the theoretical when students grapple with game decisions involving these concepts. Eight objectives of simulation games have been identified by Gerald R. Smith:

1. Simulations require the student to make decisions that cross over typical functional lines thus requiring a broader viewpoint.

2. Simulations provide an opportunity for student interaction in organizational teamwork.

3. Simulations improve the student's communication, leadership, and interpersonal relation skills.

4. Simulations aid the development of logical and rational decision-making skills in the student.

5. Simulations sharpen the student's ability to cope with and react to change.

6. Simulations demonstrate the importance of other business skills such as budgeting, forecasting, planning, organizing, and the like.

7. Simulations get the student involved in the learning process and increase his/her level of motivation.

8. Simulations demonstrate to the motivated student the need to learn other related business topics.[4]

The recall/review games incorporate many of the same objectives as the simulation games. These include the motivational factors and maximum student involvement as well as communication, leadership, and interpersonal skill development. In addition to these characteristics that are inherent in most classroom gaming activities, the recall/review activities serve yet another purpose. If a more interesting technique can be devised to encourage students to review for examinations, why shouldn't the learning process be designed to include them? Competition or striving with others for recognition or profit is a motivational factor that involves both young and older individuals in sports, the classroom, or the competitive marketplace. These recall/review activities are designed to have these factors as well as the

---

[4]Smith, Jerald R. "The Novice's Guide to Classroom Gaming." *Business Education Forum* 30:28; February 1976.

objectives for encouragement of cognitive learning of subject matter materials. The components not included in the recall/review games are the problem-solving and decision-making activities. Most of these games utilize short periods of time that make them easier to work into classroom schedules.

VARIATIONS OF GAMES PLAYED

A survey of the current literature regarding gaming has produced at least three distinct variations that are now utilized in high school business education classrooms. These are:

1. Computerized business games with competitive teams in the classroom or among schools
2. Commercially packaged games that teach economic concepts, usually in a competitive setting
3. Recall/review game activities which may be prepared by the teacher or purchased in game books.

Each of these variations will be discussed, examples will be given, and similarities noted. References will be listed for the convenience of teachers who wish to investigate the possibility of using some of the games.

COMPUTERIZED BUSINESS GAMES

A survey of the literature revealed that an article describing the use of computerized business games on the high school level was published as early as 1971. It was also discovered that high school business teachers in at least three states—Illinois, Minnesota, and Arkansas—were excited about the use of this teaching technique in their classrooms. In February 1978, an inquiry regarding the Arkansas games was received from S. J. Dunster, a business teacher in Coquitlam, British Columbia, who indicated that the Canadian program was similar. The programs discussed here are selected from those used in Illinois, Minnesota, and Arkansas.

Allen Johnson, a high school business teacher in Flossmore, Illinois, stated his interest in business games as follows:

> Enthusiasm in the classroom, an honest but elusive goal for any teacher, has recently become the daily norm for my business law and management classes. With the aid of a computer, a modest supply of funds, and a touch of fantasy, classes of normally blase and coolly sophisticated seniors have been "turned on" to management. The object of interest has been a computer-directed game where as many as sixteen companies, each run by a small group of students, compete for the imaginary market of a single, homogeneous product.[5]

Mr. Johnson described how he organized his classroom into companies of three or four students. Each company group sold the same hypothetical product, selected the name of its company, and began with the same assets: $10,000 cash, two standard factories worth $5,000 each, four raw material

---

[5]Johnson, Alan. "Turn-On to Management." *Balance Sheet* 52:22; December 1970.

units worth $500 each, and two finished inventory units worth $2,500. The decisions made by the students included: number of units of raw materials to purchase, number for production, selling price, capital expansion, whether to borrow money, and whether to issue stock or dividends. A unique and realistic feature of the Illinois simulation that was not evident in the other games was the "special situations" that were built into the computer program. At random, but no more than twice, the companies could experience an event such as a fire, a 10 percent cost reduction because of research and development (R&D), transportation strike, special assessment tax, or a strike threat. The students made decisions once a week, and these decisions were punched in port-a-punch cards (requiring no keypunch equipment) and mailed to the supplier for processing. Feedback was in the form of computer printouts each week showing comparative rankings of the companies in each of several categories.

A similar simulation game was developed by Thomas B. Duff while teaching at Richfield Senior High School in Richfield, Minnesota. This game was played on an experimental basis in three of the eight basic business classes in the school, with each class having two groups of three teams each. These three classes became so popular that students in the other five basic business classes asked to be included in the high-level, decision-making activities. An exciting feature not utilized in other simulations was the input of decisions into a computer through a teletype terminal located in the classroom and connected to the computer by telephone. After all decisions involving each group, in competition with the others, were typed into the computer, a printout was available in seven minutes. The game was played for eight consecutive school days, with the first day for orientation and a trial run. The following recommendations and observations by Dr. Duff are noteworthy:

> After using this management simulation game with eight sections of students, the basic business teachers at Richfield Senior High School strongly recommend that simulation games be made a part of the basic business curriculum wherever feasible. Besides meeting the major objective of enabling the participating students to gain an appreciation of the complexity of operating a business in our contemporary society, there appeared to be a number of spin-off benefits, which would also be present in other simulation games utilized in the basic business courses. First, the low-ability or nonacademic student developed a certain pride from the fact that he too was able to utilize one of the so-called "academic" pieces of equipment in the school—the teletype had been used primarily by college-bound and accelerated mathematics students. Second, the concept of time sharing, which is currently very popular with small and middle-sized businesses, was illustrated every day during the exercise. Finally, the students were forced to operate in a group decision-making process just as they will be forced to do more and more as they mature and enter our modern society. And as one student so aptly stated: "Well, at least no one has slept in class for the last eight days!"[6]

[6]Duff, Thomas B. "Simulation Games — A Basic Business Natural." *Business Education Forum* 26:66; March 1972.

The Arkansas computerized business games are unique in that the games are played with teams formed from various high schools around the state. Twenty-one high schools participated in the 1977-78 games and were divided into three industries according to school size. (The variance in school size was from 100 to 1,500 students.) Teams were selected at the discretion of the business teachers in each school, and they varied in size from a selected few who met after school to entire classes where the games became a part of the instructional program. One teacher used five accounting classes, allowing each to make its decisions. Two students from each class were elected to a Board of Directors which, in turn, had to combine the five sets of decisions into one set to be fed into the computer. In selecting company objectives, the following factors were emphasized:

Responsibility to customers—Customers expect a stable and reasonable price for a quality product. Quality is improved through research and development.

Responsibility to workers—Workers expect good pay and good working conditions. These goals can best be accomplished by having stable production with a minimum of dramatic changes in production levels.

Responsibility to stockholders—Stockholders typically expect steady or rising dividend rates and/or steady growth of the firm. The firm must have steady or rising profits to accomplish these goals. Wide fluctuations cause stockholder discontent which can be disastrous.

Responsibility to community—The firms have a responsibility to pay taxes and provide employment to members of the community. To accomplish this, the firm must make steady profits, which are taxable, while maintaining wages and employment for workers.[7]

In the business world, conditions of risk and uncertainty create the need for decision making, and the decisions are often based on various degrees of knowledge which are usually less than perfect. The computerized game introduces decision making with limited knowledge and uncertain conditions. Decisions and their outcomes are dependent upon the actions of competitors. Because of the various strategies employed by the teams, different outcomes are possible for a given decision. Individual teams make such decisions as product price, level of production, allocation of funds to marketing, research and development, maintenance, purchase of raw materials, plant expansion, and dividends.

Evaluations of the gaming activities are an important concern to the business teachers. The evaluation methods used in the Arkansas games include all areas of the gaming activities:

Two methods are used to evaluate each team. Method I is an evaluation of the discounted rate of return on initial owner's equity. A discounted rate of return is computed for each firm and serves as an objective evaluation of management's performance. This evaluation is made at the end of each fiscal year and provides information regarding the standing of each team, permitting each team to analyze and revise its strategy. Evaluation at the end of the second fiscal year is based on the rate of return for the two-year period and affects the final position of the

[7]Butler, Tommie; Henry, Mavis; Musick, Joseph A. "A Secondary School Adventure in the Free Enterprise System." *Business Education Forum* 32:22; November 1977.

team. Once game play is finished and each team's rate of return is decided, the team's biennial report to stockholders must be prepared. Charts, graphs, pictures of the company's officers, and advertising campaigns are among the items included in the written report. By this time, the company has become so real to the team members that the teacher and other observers are amazed at the expertise and terminology used by the students as they prepare their written report and practice for the oral presentation.

Method II consists of evaluating the written and oral reports in which all teams make a presentation to a panel of business personnel. This presentation is approximately 15 minutes of discussion relative to objectives, achievement of objectives, defense of strategy, future outlook, and expansion plans. The first-, second-, and third-place winners of each industry are selected on a scale of 40 percent for rate of return, 40 percent for oral presentations, and 20 percent for the biennial report. The important factor is not whether the team wins or loses, but how much awareness of the American business enterprise system has been acquired by secondary students.[8]

The Arkansas Power and Light Company has developed an informational packet that describes the games in more detail and has agreed to mail a copy to interested people in other states. The games are now a cooperative effort by Arkansas Power and Light Company, University of Arkansas at Monticello, and the Arkansas State Department of Education.

Similarities and uniqueness of the three computerized business games have been noted. They should be evaluated each year and improvements implemented to maximize the learning experience for the students. One of the most important evaluative components is a debriefing session to discuss which strategies worked or didn't work, and why. One of the most important concepts for students to learn is that businesses must make a profit to remain in business, but at the same time fulfill their responsibilities to customers, workers, stockholders, and the community.

COMMERCIALLY PACKAGED GAMES

Teachers may use games for a variety of purposes; therefore, the choice of a commercially packaged game for classroom use will depend entirely upon the teacher's objectives and the concepts that would be relevant to a particular class. Some important questions a teacher should ask in determining the right game for the learning activity will include:

1. Do the activities meet the educational objectives previously determined?

2. Does the game have a sound knowledge base?

3. What concepts can be learned by playing the game?

4. Are the activities presented in an organized sequential order?

5. Is the complexity of the game appropriate to challenge the students, yet not beyond their learning ability?

6. Will there be enough class time available to effectively play the game?

7. Will the game be a fun activity as well as educational?

---

[8]*Ibid.*, pp. 22-23.

As stressed with the computerized business games, the debriefing sessions are crucial to the effectiveness of the activities. These sessions provide time for the students to reflect upon and draw conclusions from their experiences. Although the use of commercially packaged games is relatively common, some teachers still are uncertain when to use them or how to expect a class of students to react while participating in the exercise. To help teachers understand their role, Lewis, Wentworth, Reinke, and Becker have these suggestions:

> In order to gain maximum benefit from the use of simulation-games in the classroom, teachers must realize that games and simulations require as much or more teacher preparation time as most other classroom techniques, a change in the teacher's classroom role, careful organization, well-stated instructional objectives, and supporting curriculum. These exercises cannot be effective in isolation. They must be used in conjunction with other activities in a carefully planned unit in order to be most effective.

> Teacher preparation is probably the most important element influencing the success of a game or simulation exercise. The teacher must have enough understanding of the exercise's objective, its system, its pressure and problems, and the frustrations encountered in the experience to operate effectively as umpire, coach, provoker, sympathizer, leader and final authority. The teacher must move in and out of different roles with flexibility and insight to keep the experience self-sustaining . . .

> Student orientation should familiarize the participants with the demands that will be placed upon them by participating in the exercise . . . The best way to understand an exercise is to play it and work out problems as they arise. After the first round or two participants should grasp the concept of the game and play without difficulty.

> Throughout the exercise the teacher should circulate among the students. The teacher should observe, listen to negotiations, offer suggestions where they seem appropriate and provide reassuring comments to those participants who seem to be doing well.[9]

A list of commercially packaged games that meet a certain criteria for inclusion can be obtained in the publication, *Education Games and Simulations in Economics*, published by the Joint Council on Economic Education, 1212 Avenue of the Americas, New York, New York 10036. Many of the games are excellent for teaching concepts about the American business enterprise system. To intrigue business teachers and encourage them to investigate the use of these games, a description of three games follows:

1. Game: BEAT THE MARKET
   Source: South-Western Publishing Company
   Subject: Economic price determination
   Grade level: Junior-senior high school
   Playing time: 1 hour each game
   No. of participants: Up tp 42 each game
   Cost: $53, set of five

This set of five simulation games on economic price determination stimulates student interest and builds economic understanding. Students simulate the

---

[9]Lewis, Darrell R., and others, *op. cit.*, pp. 46-48.

116

actions of consumers, representing "demand," and of producers, representing "supply." Their interactions as players result in price determination in a variety of limited and competitive markets. Each game may be played independently and provides for team competition, individual competition, or a combination of both. The series of games include:

GAME 1: Limited Market
GAME 2: Limited Competitive Market
GAME 3: Competitive Exchange Market
GAME 4: Competition or Subsidy?
GAME 5: Competition or Control?

2. Game: MR. BANKER
   Source: Federal Reserve Bank of Minneapolis
   Subject: Commercial banking and Federal Reserve policy
   Grade level: Junior-senior high school
   Playing time: Four 40-minute sessions
   No. of participants: 6-30
   Cost: $15

This simulation acquaints participants with the money and credit system of our nation and how it affects and is affected by changes in economic conditions. Its major objective is the deposit-money creation function of commercial banks and the need for a central monetary authority—the Federal Reserve System— to change the rate of growth of the money supply and the cost and availability of credit.

3. Game: LIFE CAREER
   Source: Bobbs Merrill Educational Publishing
   Subject: Career choice and opportunity costs
   Grade level: Junior-senior high school
   Playing time: 2-6 hours
   No. of participants: 4-20
   Cost: $35

Life Career contains certain features of the "labor market," the "education market," and the "marriage market" as they now operate in the United States and as projections indicate they will operate in the future. Participants work with the profile of a fictitious person, allotting time and activities among school, studying, a job, family responsibilities, and leisure time. Each team represents a teenager planning and then living through about eight years of life. The objective is to plan a life which gives specific rewards to the person whose role is assumed by the participants. It is intended to give participants some advance experience in planning for their own future.

RECALL/REVIEW GAMES

In addition to the simulation games used to help develop problem-solving and decision-making abilities, recall and review exercises are used in the business classrooms. Many of these games have been developed by teachers and patterned after television quiz shows. Anne Scott Daughtrey discussed the use of these games for basic business classes as follows:

These games are best used for changing the pace of instruction; for shortened class periods, such as assembly days or pep rally days; or for end-of-week or end-of-unit review facts or vocabulary. They are usually good techniques for slow learners whose attention span is short and for whom the game atmosphere provides relief from more demanding learning techniques. Judiciously used, however, some review and recall games can be stimulating for students of better ability also. Care should be taken to see that these games are not overused for students at any level of ability. Using a crossword puzzle each week, for example, would soon defeat the purpose of the game and its power to motivate. Tendency for overuse is the greatest pitfall the teacher faces in employing these games in basic business classes. The game usually can be classified as either vocabulary building and review or recall of facts, concepts, or business leaders and their contributions. Spelling may sometimes be included in the games, though this is usually a secondary aim . . . .[10]

She classified some of the games used in basic business classes in two categories. Under "Games for Vocabulary Building and Review," she lists:

Crossword Puzzle: May be student and/or teacher made; also available from published sources for basic business subjects

Scrabble: The commercial game, but using only business words

Definition Bee: Variation of the spelling bee

Concentration: Adaptation of TV game, but matching word to definition. Magnetized chalkboard, bulletin board, or flannel board can be used

Definition Cards: Printed sets of terms and definition cards available for many subjects including economics, marketing, business law

Tic-Tac-Toe: May be a live game in which student moves to squares when he gives correct term or definition; or it may be the usual paper game with two players; or a chalkboard game with class divided into two teams

"Games for Recall of Facts, Concepts, or Business Leaders and Their Contributions" would include:

What's My Line?: Through questioning, identify business/industry leaders and their fields

Tic-Tac-Toe: As shown above, but using concept category

Twenty Questions: Identify leaders or concepts through a set of twenty questions in difficult-to-easy order

Charades: Questioning and pantomime to illustrate careers, concepts, leaders, laws, etc.

You Were There: Act out in pantomime or with lines a significant event in the history of business or industry

GAMES FOR THE SKILLS AREA

Review/recall games are used for motivation not only in basic business classes but also in the skills area. June Dostal, an enterprising business teacher who has published a book of games, stated her enthusiasm for the use of these games.

---

[10]Daughtrey, Anne S. *Methods of Basic Business and Economic Education.* Second edition. Cincinnati: South-Western Publishing Co., 1974. pp. 183-84.

118

Every teacher knows that motivation is one of the key factors which influence learning, and games are one motivational and learning device which can be useful in stimulating interest in any class. Certainly the majority of time in any class should be devoted to learning the basic skills and knowledge of that course. However, an occasional deviation from the usual routine is desired on special occasions such as the last day before a holiday or as a reward for behavior modification. Games can make the class fun and are an excellent way for reluctant learners to sit up and take interest. Games can also be used to advantage as a different learning device to review for chapter, unit, or semester exams. Games provide a welcome relief from classroom routine.[11]

Some teachers incorporate already established games into their business classes as motivational activities. A good example was designed by Toni Bartolotti at Rome Catholic High School, Rome, New York. Monopoly was used to teach accounting! Students were not allowed to use the paper money, but had to set up individual "T" accounts. After a set period of time (possibly two classes), players figured out their proprietorship: P=A-L. The player with the largest proprietorship is the winner. Clever instructions were used, such as: Player lands on Park Place and decides to buy: debit Park Place; credit cash.[12]

A brief sampling of games that have been used successfully in the various skill areas follows. With only slight modification, many can be transposed into a similar activity for another subject and/or purpose. For example, bingo can be used for almost any subject—typewriting, shorthand, office practice, etc.

Typing bingo. Student receive a card similar to regular bingo except it has symbols, numbers, or other items as answers to questions which are asked. Students must know the answer to the question asked before covering the space. This may be played for horizontal, vertical, diagonal, or black-out bingo. It is a good test review game.

Typing speed and accuracy sheets. Students receive a duplicated sheet of paragraphs starting at 20 words per minute and increasing by five words a paragraph up to 75 words per minute. During a one-minute timing, students strive to complete the paragraph without errors. When this is done (sometimes after several attempts), the date is placed beside that paragraph and the student goes to the next paragraph. Each student's speed is posted on a progress chart for comparison with other students.

Progress game in typing. Mainly an accuracy drill, this game can also encourage speed when students compete in order to finish first. Rules: Students progress one step when they type the following without error (if an error is made, the student goes back to #1):

1. The sentence on the chalkboard
2. The alphabet
3. Their name, address, telephone number, and social security number
4. The months of the year

---

[11]Dostal, June. *150 Activities for Business Education Classes.* Portland, Oreg.: J. Weston Walch, 1975. p. 1.

[12]Bartolotti, Toni. "They're Playing WHAT in Bookkeeping!!!" *Balance Sheet,* March 1977. p. 144.

5. A list of 15 objects in the room
6. The titles of eight songs
7. The names of eight birds
8. Five parts of the typewriter
9. Fifteen of the United States
10. A set of progressive drills or paragraphs.

This game could be shortened or lengthened as desired; for instance, the teacher could take a timed writing with the students and raise one letter grade for those who make fewer errors than the instructor.

Typing football fun. Decorate a bulletin board to resemble a football field, marking off yards. Make up small paper footballs with students' names (or an assigned number) written on them. All students begin at the goal line and advance forward as they reach certain yards on timed writings. For instance, a one-minute timed writing advances the student's football to the yard of his/her speed. Students may only advance, however, if no more than one error is made on the timed writing. This game lasts throughout the football season, and it is exciting for the students to see how their classmates' speeds compare with their own and how they have improved over the weeks. At the end of the game, grades can be given on the teacher's own scale. The same bulletin board can be used for two or three typing classes.

Shorthand password. Divide the class into two teams. One from each team comes to the chalkboard and is given the same password (written on a card) by the teacher. One student writes the shorthand outline of a possible clue to that word. His/her team tries to guess the word from the clue. If the first team misses, the other team has a chance to guess, and so on back and forth until a team guesses the password. The winning team gets one point.

This same format can also be used for guessing famous quotations. Words from the quotation are written in shorthand outline in turn until one team states the complete quotation accurately. Turns at the chalkboard must be taken individually from each team, and the team with the most points wins.

Shorthand—cities and states. Write in shorthand outline the names of cities and states on two sets of 3 x 5 index cards. Select captains, and divide the students into two teams. The captain of each team holds the cards. If team one misses the shorthand outline, the card is given to team two. If team one guesses the outline, they keep the card. At the end of the game, the team with the most cards wins.

Shorthand BREFO. This game can help motivate and teach students the various brief forms. The procedures and rules are those used in playing bingo; in fact, the back of any bingo card can be used to make the cards used in BREFO. Five rows and five columns can be divided on the card with 25 different brief forms written in the squares. Brief forms may be repeated on different cards, but never on the same card. They should also be written in different rows and columns on the various cards, not in the same square on each card. This will require the students to search for the brief form when playing and prevent memorization of where a particular one is located. One free square may be allowed anywhere on the card if desired. The object of the game is to cover (bingo covers can be used) all of the brief forms in a particular row or column—either vertically, horizontally, or diagonally. The first student to do so is the winner. (Any variation used in bingo may also be used in this game—some may wish to cover the entire card instead of just rows.) Use the shorthand book or develop a "kitty" of brief forms cut out and written on small pieces of cardboard for the caller, who may be either the teacher or a student.

Dictation from popular musical records. This game or exercise can be used in any shorthand class. Students bring their favorite records to class, and while listening to the records, they write the lyrics in shorthand. This encourages the use of new-matter dictation, and also provides a change for the students who are accustomed only to the teacher's style of dictation. The shorthand teacher can join in with this activity; students will usually work harder if they have a chance to compete with their teacher.

Accounting crossword puzzles. The objective of the game is to test the student's ability to recall accounting terminology. Design a crossword puzzle with clues that can be solved only in accounting terms. It will take some effort to fit the answers appropriately in the vertical and horizontal spaces; but after that is completed, simply fill in the unused spaces with a black magic marker and number the clues to fit the correct answer across and down. The game is played the same way as a conventional crossword puzzle. The puzzle can either be solved by two-student teams competing against time or by students competing against each other on an individual basis. Creative students may even want to make up their own puzzles.

CONCLUSION

A survey of the professional literature will produce many more articles and examples of games that have been created by innovative business teachers. The use of instructional games and simulations has gained a more popular acceptance than many other new teaching techniques.

Donald Wentworth and Darrell Lewis reviewed current research studies devoted to this subject, summarized the findings, and suggested some directions for future research. Their conclusion was that more research with a broader, more imaginative perspective is needed. Research identifying behavioral variables and using more careful controls and more sensitive instruments must be conducted and replicated before the field of games and simulation research can move out of its infancy stage.[13]

Even though more research is needed, the certainty remains that teachers who use games in their business education classrooms are excited about the activities. They seem to be convinced that the games create an effective learning environment providing additional opportunities for the growth and development of their students. Keeping this in mind, it seems safe to say that gaming and games in high school business education are here to stay!

---

[13]Lewis, Darrell R., and others, *op. cit.*, p. 73.

Section B: At the Postsecondary Level

JOHN S. HOAGLAND
State University of New York at Albany, Albany

MURPHY A. SEWALL
University of Connecticut, Storrs

The purpose of this chapter is to review business gaming with major emphasis on applications in the curriculum of business schools at four-year colleges and universities. While business gaming has a history of little more than 20 years, the number of different types of teaching tools in this area, to say nothing of the number of specific materials, has grown at an astonishing rate.

For our purposes, "gaming" is a structured method for treating decisions by participants so that processed outputs can be assessed by students as well as the instructor. The term "game" is widely accepted in business and government to describe decision making in a simulated environment. Although students may refer to "playing" a game, the phrase does not have the usual meaning. Hardly anyone has been known to play a business decision game for relaxation.

Business games are designed to help prepare students for careers in the field. The lessons are intended to be applied to later life. This intent differentiates business gaming from leisure-time games such as bridge, checkers, or Startrek (a popular computerized game that has "invaded" virtually every large computer system in the nation).

A BRIEF HISTORY

Most authors attribute the origin of gaming for business instruction to the game created by the American Management Association in 1956, which was probably also the first game processed on a computer.[1] A manually computed game also appeared in 1956,[2] and at that early stage of computer development and availability, such games proved more feasible for widespread use.

The rapid expansion of computer technology over the past 20 years has all but made the manually scored game extinct. While the authors do not have any documentation, it is hard to imagine a business school today that does not have access to a computer for processing the calculations required for a game. Most computer-based games are normally processed in a "batch" mode. Students' decisions are punched on cards and read into the computer. Occasionally, the game program is read in at the same time. More often, the program for the game is stored in the computer's library. More sophisticated games and processing procedures also maintain in the computer a "history" of previous plays of the game by the same participants.

---

[1]Beach, Dale S. *Personnel: The Management of People at Work*. Third edition. New York: MacMillan Publishing Co., 1975.

[2]Andlinger, G. R. "Business Games — Play One." *Harvard Business Review* 36:115-25; March-April 1958.

In recent years, some games have been developed that permit remote terminal-based input of decisions. A few of these also provide terminal-based, "on-line" output of the results. Generally, on-line games are able to deal with only low levels of games, as defined below.

One of the more exciting recent developments in game technology is the concept of program modules that can be inserted in programmable hand calculators. Thus, each student in a class, with an appropriate calculator and program module, could input decisions and receive on-line responses.

It is virtually impossible to document the number of games that now exist. Although catalogs of games are published by several groups and individuals, the rate at which new games are developed continues to outpace the ability of bibliographers to collect them. During the time it takes to compile, print, and distribute a catalog, a substantial number of new games are developed.

As a final note on the historical coverage of game development, it is significant to note that some scholars are becoming concerned with the development of a "theory" of game use (not to be confused with the Theory of Games first developed by Morgenstern and von Neumann.[3] Burns and Gentry propose that the major variables of such a theory include:

a. The business concepts being taught,

b. The nature of the game task,

c. Game conduct,

d. Student or participant attributes, and

e. The instructor.[4]

The following analysis of business gaming will concentrate on the first two of these categories, with some comments on the third.

CONCEPTS TAUGHT

Probably the most useful place to begin an analysis of the state of business gaming is in terms of the scope of the game. Here we would identify four basic levels of scope.

Knowledge of techniques. Conceptually, the simplest form of game has the purpose of providing knowledge about a given technique or tool through the use of a special-purpose, simulated environment. One example would be PERTSIM, which is designed to familiarize the participants with the process of production network analysis.[5] The objective of this exercise is to achieve profit maximization in the management of a project. Another example, developed by one of the authors of this paper, is aimed at developing an understanding of the research technique, multidimensional scaling.[6]

[3]Morgenstern, Oskar, and von Neumann, John. *Theory of Games and Economic Behavior.* Princeton, N.J.: Princeton University Press, 1944.

[4]Burns, Alvin C., and Gentry, James W. "Some Thoughts on a 'Theory' of the Use of Games and Experiential Exercises." *1977 Proceedings of the Association for Business Simulation and Experiential Learning.* pp. 187-94.

[5]Swanson, L. A., and Pazer, Harold L. *PERTSIM.* Scranton, Pa.: International Textbook Co., 1969.

[6]Sewall, Murphy A. "An Experimental Exercise in Multidimensional Scaling." *1976 Proceedings of the Association for Business Simulation and Experiential Learning.* pp. 97-111.

Subfunctional analysis. A number of games have been developed to deal with various segments of any given business function. Those in the area of marketing appear to dominate this category followed by specific activities associated with the production function.[7]

In a subfunction game, the basis of the exercise is found in the process of a major set of activities that might be placed under the jurisdiction of some manager on a continuing basis. Inventory management, advertising strategy, commodity trading, and manpower planning are examples of such subfunction processes in several business functions which have all been adapted to gaming.

Intrafunctional analysis. Almost every functional area of business has at least one game available that attempts to integrate several subfunctions applicable to the area. The purpose of these games is to demonstrate the complex interrelationships that link these processes. Many functional games attempt to represent the totality of the function.

One of the earliest functional games was developed in the early 1960's by Ralph Day.[8] The Marketing Action Game, now in its third edition, still enjoys widespread use. The majority of the modifications that have been made in the original game are intended to take advantage of progress in computing technology; conceptually, this game retains its original character.

Functional interdependence. A very limited set of games have an explicit purpose of linking two normally distinct business functions, such as production and personnel management.[9] One is tempted to hypothesize that such developments, and subsequent usage, depend to a large extent on an interpersonal setting that facilitates interaction between faculty members across functional lines. It is obvious to those with experience in university teaching that such settings are in the minority.

Overall management strategy. Although "general management" games appear at the top of this hierarchy, they have the longest history of any of the levels. In addition to being the most prevalent of the commercially published games, these tend to be more complex than those at the lower levels of this analysis. There is, however, a great deal of variability along this dimension. Probably the most widely adopted of these games at the university level is the international management game, INTOP.[10] Other widely used games include The Executive Game,[11] The Executive Simulation,[12] and IMAGINIT.[13]

---

[7]Day, Ralph L. "Marketing in Action in Collegiate Education." *1974 Proceedings of the Association for Business Simulation and Experiential Learning.* pp. 8-14.

[8]Day, Ralph L., and Ness, Thomas E. *Marketing in Action: A Dynamic Business Decision Game.* Third edition. Homewood, Ill.: Richard D. Irwin, 1973.

[9]Hoagland, John S., and Pazer, Harold L. "Enrichment of a Multi-Functional Game Through Dynamic Overlays and Intensive Decision Analysis." *1974 Proceedings of the Association for Business Simulation and Experiential Learning.* pp. 93-99.

[10]Thorelli, Hans B., and Graves, Robert L. *International Operations Simulation with Comments on Design and Use of Management Games.* New York: Free Press, 1964.

[11]Henshaw, Richard C., and Jackson, James R. *The Executive Game.* Revised edition. Homewood, Ill,: Richard D. Irwin, 1972.

[12]Keys, Bernard, and Leftwich, Howard. *The Executive Simulation.* Second edition. Dubuque, Iowa: Kendall/Hunt Publishing Co., 1977.

[13]Barton, Richard F. *The IMAGINIT Management Game.* Lubbock, Tex.: Action Learning, 1973.

THE NATURE OF THE GAMING TASK

At the extremes, gaming may be used in the context of a single assignment on the one hand to a self-contained, complete course of instruction on the other. One obvious dimension of the nature of gaming in a course or a curriculum is the duration of play.

Games can be used as a "one-shot" assignment. Generally, one-shot games are intended to illustrate the use of a specific technique or, possibly, some facets of specific subfunctional interactions. More complex games may require new sets of decisions over several interactions of the game program in order to demonstrate fully some of the interdependencies of the process being modeled or to allow for the unfolding of a strategy.

The duration of games can also be sorted out in terms of their relationship to other segments of the business curriculum. At the narrowest level of gaming usage are games used to facilitate understanding as a supplement to other pedagogical techniques such as lectures or cases.[14] Even in this usage, a game may involve a significant portion of the total time allocated to the course in which it is embedded. For example, business policy courses often employ a general management game which may absorb one-third of the student's time in the course, both in and out of the classroom.

In some instances, gaming may be the dominant element in a total course. Usually, such game courses are taken over a full semester or quarter as part of a regular course load. However, in at least one school of business, the game is allocated a two-and-one-half-week period in the middle of a semester during which there are no other academic activities or assignments. This configuration provides opportunities to engage in other innovative types of arrangements. For instance, the different decisions used in an overall management strategy game can be differentiated into finance, marketing, production, and personnel functions, which must be integrated for even modest success in the game. General instructions about the game can be given to all participants, but detailed instruction about each functional area can be limited to only those participants responsible for that class of decision. The participants for each functional area in a "corporation" (team) can then be physically separated to locations requiring interaction by telephone or in writing to achieve the necessary coordination; that is, spatial and communications difficulties that confront practicing managers can also be simulated.

At the most complex level of gaming are situations where the game is "enriched" by being integrated into two or more courses. In effect, the game is a "skeleton" used as a vehicle upon which to develop two or more courses or even an entire curriculum. One of the authors participated in the development of such a process where a "subfunction" game, PROSIM, was used as a base for a production course and a personnel course.[15] As sequential topics in the two courses were developed, corresponding changes in the game program were introduced to develop a dynamic aspect to an otherwise relatively static

---

[14]Sewall, Murphy A. "The Computer as a Teaching Assistant." *1975 Combined Proceedings of the American Marketing Association.* pp. 638-42.

[15]Hoagland, John S., and Pazer, Harold L., *loc. cit.*

game. Probably the most ambitious effort in this direction was the aim of the game developed at Carnegie-Mellon in which all, or most, of the courses in the business curriculum attempted to relate their subject matter to that university's game.

GAME ENVIRONMENT

The type of competitive environment is also a major variable in business gaming. Within this context, games might be structured as either deterministic or stochastic. Obviously, a deterministic game, to be challenging, must involve a high degree of complexity in the interrelationships used. On the other hand, the use of stochastic elements must be constrained if real effort is desired in the areas of process analysis and learning. Clearly, some features of the environment need to be depicted in terms of some degree of uncertainty, but if overdone, the participants are likely to perceive the game as little more than dice throwing.

There seem to be four separate types of competitive environments in which games can be structured. An appropriate analogy are terms usually applied to golf.

Medal play. In golf, medal play is used to allow each participant to play the course fully, with the best score winning. Business games can be structured in such a way that students each play against the structure of the game. Such a game may be highly complex, but the important feature is that every player competes in an identical environment that is not affected by the actions of any other participant. Students may be ranked in order of how well they accomplish the objectives of the game.

Match play. In golf, match play involves "head to head" competition. Standings are determined on the basis of the best score on each hole. The absolute score does not really matter, only the number of holes "won."

The match play is not precisely applicable to business gaming, but the spirit of the concept is preserved. The important feature of these games is that players compete against each other ("head to head," but usually there are more than two "teams" in the game at one time) within the game's environment. The results achieved by participants are affected by the actions of other participants as well as by the characteristics of the game. For example, agressive marketing action by some participants may lead to an expansion of their market shares, leaving a smaller sales potential available to other participants. As in match play on the golf course, standings are not determined by the absolute values achieved on the game's objectives. Rather, performance is judged by comparing results relative to other participants.

Par play. In some games, the participants are matched against one or more "synthetic" players whose decisions are prestructured in terms of some specific strategy, either on a normative basis or on the basis of some average level of past experience. One possible advantage of this approach is that different "par strategies" can be selected by the instructor on the basis of apparent player strategies.

In one of the most complex examples of a game involving synthetic competitors, students compete with three different artificial competitors.[16] Each competitor is actually a set of decision rules that respond to competition from the student player as well as the game environment. This game also contains its own set of rules for evaluating the results (establishing "par").

Walker cup play. The idea of intercollegiate gaming competition is comparable to the competition of teams from different countries in the Walker Cup. The most widely known such program is that of Emory University which was started in 1966.[17] That competition is essentially run by students in the Emory Graduate School of Business. These students administer the program, and the competing schools are selected from a wide geographical distribution. The host school does not enter a competitive team.

CAVEATS

Business gaming is only one of a large number of pedagogical tools available to instructors. Some consideration must be given to whether a proposed game is really the most appropriate method of accomplishing educational objectives.

Successful use of gaming requires a substantial investment in planning and preparation. Most current games use a computer program as a game environment and method of analyzing participants' decisions. It is important that a program being used at a specific computer installation for the first time be "debugged" and thoroughly tested by the instructor before introducing it to students. The fact that the program may function flawlessly at one institution is no guarantee that it will operate without a hitch at a new site.

Even for programs used by other instructors at the same school, a testing period is recommended for a new faculty user. Familiarity with the game and its behavior under a variety of circumstances is necessary in order to deal with the plethora of questions inevitably raised by students who must cope with both the analytic issues the game is designed to teach as well as the rules and procedures of the game itself.

It is difficult to anticipate all the combinations and sequences of decisions that students might attempt. Since participants are learning, they are apt to make errors that experienced practitioners would almost never make. Occasionally these errors fall into a realm of "irrational" behavior not contemplated by the game's designer. In such cases the computer program may fail to respond realistically (in rare instances the program may fail altogether). It is very useful if the instructor has the services of an experienced computer programmer who has some knowledge of business administration to deal with such problems.

Most games place a considerable administrative burden on the instructor. Decisions must be collected from participants, the game program must be run on the computer, and output must be distributed to students. As the number of participants increases, dealing with the quantity of output

---

[16]Sewall, Murphy A. "A Conversational Marketing Decision Game." *Decision Sciences* 7:358-65; April 1976.

[17]Jensen, Ronald. "Intercollegiate Business Gaming: The State of the Art." *1974 Proceedings of the Association for Business Simulation and Experiential Learning.* pp. 263-67.

alone can become a substantial task. The instructor must also develop policies for dealing with the mechanical problems of gaming. What should be done to penalize students who turn in decisions late? What should be done in the case of major errors in preparing decision forms or in punching decision cards (students frequently misplace decimal points or punch numbers into the wrong card columns)?

In "match play" gaming, it is inevitable that some participants will fall behind; as the game progresses, it becomes obvious that these students will not be able to catch up. Typical reactions of students in this position are to "give up" (fail to continue attempting to compete effectively) or to adopt desperation tactics. Either reaction tends to affect the competitive environment faced by other participants. Usually some elements of unreality will creep into the entire game (in the real world, a failed team would go bankrupt). Instructors need to consider measures for maintaining motivation among participants who are trailing in the competition. One approach is through scoring systems emphasizing comparisons with standards other than the results obtained by the best players.

EFFECTIVENESS

In virtually all studies that have compared business games with other methods of instruction (usually lectures or cases), no significant statistical differences have been found in the learning experienced by participants in the different approaches. More often, game participants exhibit greater enthusiasm for gaming instruction than students taught by other methods. In fact, one danger not mentioned previously is that some students may become overly involved in the game, to the detriment of other academic responsibilities.

Many of the instructors committed to the use of business games are frustrated by the failure to prove this method of instruction superior to other teaching methods. However, lectures, cases, and other standard teaching practices have a much longer history and have been accepted as effective for many years. The fact that these traditional techniques cannot be shown to be superior to gaming may also be taken as evidence that business gaming is a worthwhile alternative to other pedagogical methods.

The enthusiasm generated by gaming in comparison to other teaching methods is a factor favoring the adoption of games. On the negative side are the costs of using games. In addition to the administrative burden placed on the instructor, the per student costs of the computer processing tend to be fairly high.[18] At most four-year colleges and universities, computing facilities have sufficient excess capacity to support business gaming without difficulty. However, some consideration must be given to whether the benefits of gaming compared to more traditional teaching are worth the higher costs of implementation.

---

[18]Fisk, George. "Computer Aided Marketing Instruction." *Journal of Marketing* 35:28-33; January 1971.

CHAPTER 7

Modular instruction represents alternatives that can be developed at all educational levels, and this section of the Yearbook presents a challenge for such development. Teaching units, individualized instruction, and modular patterns in the classroom are not new to business teachers; most of them have experimented and developed many innovative alternatives. Modular arrangements that are adaptable to business programs at all levels from the secondary school through the senior college are discussed here. As the authors say in conclusion, "fear of the complexity" is perhaps the only barrier to more widespread adoption of such modules.

Modules in Business Education

HOBART H. CONOVER and WILLARD DAGGETT
New York State Department of Education, Albany
GORDON SIMPSON
State University of New York at Albany, Albany

The term *module* is used with varying meanings by educators. To serve as a basis for understanding the content of this chapter, the authors have adopted the following definition: *module*—an outline of content relating to a particular topic or course segment.

In this context a module is considered to be similar to a syllabus in that it prescribes subject matter to be treated. In the case of a module, the outline usually pertains to a fractional part of a course and is likely to be directed only to this limited skill or body of knowledge.

FORMATTING A MODULE

Philosophical statement. The basic purpose of any module is usually established in the form of a short philosophical statement. Whether the content is career oriented or of general educational value should be clearly indicated. In addition, the statement should provide suggestions that might be helpful to any teacher or guidance counselor in determining the suitability of the content and its treatment to any specified student objective.

Student performance goals. Another important feature of a module should be a clearly delineated series of expected student performance outcomes to be realized as a result of the study of the prescribed content. It is recommended that these statements be presented in behavioral terms and in language readily understandable to both teachers and students. It is desirable to provide students these performance goals early in their study of the module as a motivational tool and basis for eventual performance evaluation. Students gain considerable reassurance if they are able to understand clearly what will be expected of them as learning outcomes.

Outline of content. The central portion of the module usually consists of a topical outline, and in parallel columns, many suggestions for teaching procedures, recommended resources, and general reference materials. This portion of the module is teacher directed and should lead to a variety of supplementary materials suited to the topic under consideration.

A well developed module suggests learning activities that may serve as enrichment or to accommodate students who are especially adept in the content. This part of the module often serves as an "expansion joint" when modular scheduling is arranged in common time frames. It is not uncommon for some schools to move from one module to another each 5 or 10 weeks. Suggestions for extending or accelerating the content are especially valuable under these circumstances.

Like the performance goals, the student evaluation process should be clearly evident as part of any instructional module. Typically these two elements are closely linked so that students can be reasonably sure that by developing the prescribed proficiencies they will be successful in the performance evaluation. In fact, the student performance goals frequently specify the planned evaluation procedures. It is surprising how effective and student-motivating this linkage can be. Of course, this advantage need not be limited to modular curriculum design; it does, however, emphasize the desirability of giving students insights into the expected outcomes of any module or course.

ADVANTAGES OF MODULAR CURRICULUM DESIGN

Course content tailoring. Modular curriculum construction permits a teacher to select among a series of modules in the development of a local course of study. Modular construction also makes it possible to rearrange a sequence of topics to accommodate a particular teaching preference or differences in the background of students or classes. An illustration may help clarify these advantages.

A teacher of general business at the high school level may have at his or her disposal 12 modules suggested as likely content for a course of study. As a result of pretesting, the teacher discovers the content of three of the topics to be well understood by most students in a particular class. As a consequence, the teacher allocates time and develops plans for the school year based upon the remaining nine modules. Another teacher, faced with quite a different pretest experience, will build upon the background of that class by selecting other appropriate modules.

The question may be raised, How does this differ from practices followed in developing a course plan based upon a conventional syllabus? One principal difference seems to stand out: Student evaluation in modular curriculum is usually based upon the content of those modules selected by the teacher rather than the total array of topics, as would be the case in a conventional course of study.

In the development of instructional modules, curriculum specialists have followed a variety of time patterns. In certain instances modules have been developed to meet uniform time frames. Modules involving substantial bodies of knowledge are then planned so that one part of the content (Module I) must be studied before the second part (Module II) or third portion (Module III) of the total body of knowledge. Module I, for example, relating to "Principles of Insurance" would be a prerequisite to the study of "Life Insurance" or "Casualty Insurance," subsequent modules in the sequence. This design continues the modular advantage of fixed time frames, yet accommodates bodies of knowledge that require more extended blocks of time.

In other instances, the suggested time parameter for each module is governed entirely by the amount of complexity of the content to be covered. Under these circumstances teachers must select modules to accommodate the fixed time barriers established for the entire course. This often requires some slight time adjustment to accommodate the modules selected.

Matching depth of study to career needs. Conventional curriculum typically ties students to a particular course of instruction for at least a semester or full school year. The student is thus locked into a subject area without consideration of depth of understanding demanded by an envisioned career. A student contemplating a career as a programmer, requiring minimal typewriting skill, is often required to spend the same period of time developing this competency as a would-be stenographer who undoubtedly will spend a major portion of each subsequent working day at the typewriter. A high school student aspiring to a career as a warehouse or storeroom clerk, with little or no need to understand the process of closing a set of books, may be required to "endure" learning this competency along with the student who contemplates becoming a full-time bookkeeper. Obviously, with modular curriculum design, a school is able to prescribe instructional blocks much more closely allied to each student's particular career needs.

A slight variation of this advantage is related to the opportunity for interdisciplinary mixes. One or two modules of content relating to product display and advertising may constitute desirable preparation for the student who aspires to the operation of an automobile service station, beauty salon, or other small service-oriented business upon graduation from high school. Similarly, a module or two directed to business organization and management might be advantageous to the student who is planning a career in horticulture or small animal care. As modular curriculum design becomes more widespread, interdisciplinary ties of many varieties should become increasingly popular.

Motivating achievement by a success formula. Modular curriculum helps to motivate student success through a series of prescribed learning goals. As the student meets each learning goal, the evaluation scheme can have the effect of "patting the student on the back" and rewarding his or her accomplishment. Students are prodded by the desire to clear one learning hurdle after another and to complete the series of modules that comprise the program or course of study. This characteristic may also benefit prospective employers for it permits the school to report precise knowledge and skills each student is prepared to bring to a job. As a consequence, the employer is able to determine much more accurately whether the capabilities of the job applicant match the requirements of the position.

Opportunities for accelerated and independent study. Modular curriculum is particularly suited to independent study when learning materials can be provided that closely relate to the objectives of the module. Modular curriculum, supported by learning contracts, projects, and/or learning application packages, makes it possible for students to move ahead from one module to another with minimal teacher assistance. A course of study or entire career preparation may be accelerated depending upon the student's interests and unique learning capacity.

Opportunities for broadening the total learning experience. The limitations of a school day and choice of only semester or full-year courses keep students from sampling widely from the total learning experiences available in any educational institution. A business education major at the high school level may, for example, be prevented from profiting from more than five or six courses as the basis for career preparation. And outside the student's major area of study, there may be literally no opportunities to broaden the cultural experience. How many times have you heard a student say upon leaving high school, "I sure wish I might have had an opportunity to study art, or auto mechanics, or carpentry." This limitation is equally applicable to postsecondary institutions and is another of the penalties paid when students are confined to semester or full-year course offerings. Modular curriculum, obviously, is economical of student time and greatly expands opportunities for a broadly based educational experience.

May facilitate a learning continuum. A carefully sequenced series of modules relating to any subject field can establish a learning continuum that a student may follow with minimum difficulty. If topics and competencies have been arranged with due regard to difficulty and sophistication, the student should be motivated to move ahead to increasingly higher levels of learning.

It is important that curriculum specialists articulate program content at the high school and adult levels with that of the two- and four-year colleges so that students may progress easily from one level to the next. Students at the high school level, through effective modular design, should be encouraged to reach for competencies normally expected of two-year college students. And conversely, teachers seeking to assist students entering the two- and four-year colleges with content deficiencies, should develop modules designed to help overcome the specific student weakness.

Specially designed remedial instruction. Modular curriculum offers a special advantage to the student who may be experiencing a particular learning problem. A student having difficulty in business mathematics, for example, may benefit from an opportunity to brush up on the fundamental processes. With the aid of learning application packages or other self-study materials, such a student may even be scheduled for this remediation on an independent-study basis. Furthermore, a student experiencing difficulty with shorthand transcription may, because of poor English skills, gain considerable impetus from the study of one or more remedial modules directed to various aspects of English grammar and mechanics. A teacher fortified with modules of a remedial variety has an opportunity to help many students simultaneously with a variety of learning deficiencies.

Matching content to learning readiness. Some subject matter in a course of study is often more compatible with student interests as seniors than as freshmen, or the reverse. Modular design makes it possible to program content sequentially in instructional "blocks" over one or more years of a student's total school career. Content may thus be scheduled when there is greatest student readiness. This advantage is especially noteworthy in those business courses concerned with "living skills," where student receptivity to certain concepts and understandings is likely to come early in their teens, while other survivor competencies are more closely allied to their future adult years.

APPLICATION OF MODULAR CURRICULUM TO THE SENIOR HIGH SCHOOL PROGRAM

What might a high school program of study in business education look like if modular curriculum were available? The following illustration may serve as an example.

MODULES AVAILABLE TO ALL
Business and Nonbusiness Students

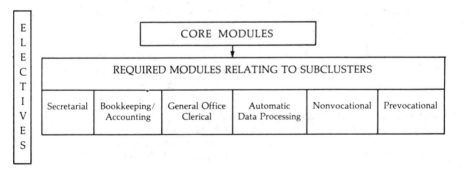

Core modules would be required of all business education majors regardless of their field of concentration. Greater depth of treatment of content is provided through specialized modules required of students majoring in a particular occupational subcluster such as stenography, bookkeeping and accounting, automatic data processing, and general office clerical. Nonvocational and prevocational sequences would also be provided, and all modules would be available as electives to nonbusiness students.

Illustrations of titles of modules that might be included in the various classifications are listed below.

CORE MODULES

Content Area	Illustrative Modules Titles
General Business and Economic Education	Political and Economic Systems The Role of Government Business Organization and the Healthy Economy Communication Systems Transportation Systems Credit and the Economy Introduction to Insurance Banking and Investment Consumer Awareness and Protection
Business Mathematics	Fundamentals Refresher The Business Cycle Banking and Finance Office Mathematics
Business Communication	Principles of Effective Oral and Written Communication Mechanics of Written Communication Personal-Business Communication Written Business Communication Basics of Oral Communication Public Speaking Application of Psychology in Oral and Written Communication
Recordkeeping	Introduction to Recordkeeping Maintaining a Checking Account
Typewriting	Keyboard Mastery Basic Typewriting Applications Introduction to Office Typewriting I
Business Law	The Individual and the Legal Environment Law and the Minor
Introduction to Automatic Data Processing	Introduction to Data Processing Components of Automated Systems Electronic Computer Systems Computer Data Banks and File Management

Illustrative Titles	Secretarial	Bkkg./Acctg.	Office Clerical	Automatic Data Processing	Nonvocational	Prevocational
Business Mathematics						
Personal Money Management					✓	
Recordkeeping						
Processing Receipts of Currency	✓		✓			
Processing Currency Payments	✓		✓			
Sales Records			✓			
Inventory Records			✓			
Purchases Records			✓			
Payroll Records	✓		✓			
Single-Entry Records for a Service Business			✓			
Wholesale Records			✓			
Personal Business Records					✓	
Bookkeeping/Accounting						
Double-Entry Records for a Service Business		✓		✓		
Double-Entry Records for a Merchandising Business		✓		✓		
Multi-Bookkeeper Systems		✓		✓		
Payroll Clerk						
Office Cashier						
Accounts Receivable Clerk						
Accounts Payable Clerk						
Notes and Special Merchandising Procedures		✓				
Completing the Bookkeeping Cycle		✓				
Bookkeeping/Accounting Peculiar to Various Forms of Business Organization		✓				
Interpretation of Financial Records and Reports		✓				
Internal Control Systems		✓				
Machine Accounting			✓			
Payroll						
Accounts Receivable						
Accounts Payable						
Billing and Age Analysis						
Office Practice and Procedures						
Adding/Calculating Machines	✓	✓	✓			
Machine Transcription (Level I)	✓		✓			
Reprographics	✓		✓			
Information Storage, Retrieval, and Management	✓		✓			

Illustrative Titles	Secretarial	Bkkg./Acctg.	Office Clerical	Automatic Data Processing	Nonvocational	Prevocational
Business Law						
The Law of Contracts	✓	✓	✓	✓	✓	✓
Personal Property	✓	✓	✓	✓	✓	✓
Real Property			✓		✓	✓
Transportation and Travel			✓		✓	✓
Family Protection			✓		✓	✓
Employer and Agency Relationships			✓			
Business Ownership			✓			✓
Typewriting and Word Processing						
Personal-Use Typewriting					✓	✓
Introduction to Office Typewriting II	✓	✓	✓	✓		
Intermediate Office Applications I	✓		✓			
Intermediate Office Applications II	✓		✓			
Advanced Office Applications	✓		✓			
Power Typewriting and Text Editing			✓			
Machine Transcription (Levels 2, 3, 4)			✓			
Word Processing Organizational Systems	✓		✓			
Automatic Data Processing						
Data-Entry Device Operation		✓	✓	✓		
Introduction to Computers				✓		✓
Computer Operations				✓		
Problem Solving/Programming Languages				✓		
Manual Bookkeeping/Accounting Applications				✓		
Accounts Receivable						
Accounts Payable						
Office Cashier						
Payroll						
Computerized Applications				✓		
Business Organization and Management						
Management of Human Resources						✓
Financial Management						✓
The Manufacturing Function						✓
Marketing and Distribution						✓
Management Decisions and Policy Making						✓
Shorthand						
Shorthand Theory	✓					
Speed Development and Pretranscription	✓					

Illustrative Titles	Secretarial	Bkkg./Acctg.	Office Clerical	Automatic Data Processing	Nonvocational	Prevocational
Speed Development and Transcription I	✓					
Speed Development and Transcription II	✓					
Secretarial Production I	✓					
Secretarial Production II	✓					
Human Relations and Job Success						
Verbal and Nonverbal Communication	✓	✓	✓	✓		
Human Behavior	✓	✓	✓	✓		
Job Seeking	✓	✓	✓	✓		
Behavior on the Job	✓	✓	✓	✓		

MODULARIZATION OF THE TWO-YEAR COLLEGE BUSINESS EDUCATION CURRICULUM

The content of the curriculum and makeup of the student body makes the two-year college business curriculum uniquely suited to modularization. Few two-year colleges have as yet implemented this step, however. This lack of receptivity has been more closely related to administrative problems than to educational limitations.

Financial accountability within institutions of higher education has tied them closely to the Faculty Teaching Equivalent (FTE). Using FTE as an index of productivity, the colleges have compartmentalized students into a time- and content-centered curriculum. This system, furthermore, assures the ability to measure whether each college department and faculty member is pulling his/her own weight.

Many educators feel that a modular curriculum cannot be effectively developed with the restraints caused by the need to maintain measurable FTE. This assumption is incorrect. Modularized curriculum can function effectively in a time-centered educational setting. The flexibility of such an organizational procedure allows it to function in nearly any educational setting. As pointed out in the introduction, the advantages provided from tailoring course content, providing for varying depth of concentration, motivating students by generally understood learning goals, and related periodic evaluation can be achieved in the most rigid educational environment.

Modularization of the two-year college curriculum offers several additional advantages. Two-year college programs tend to be more technical or specialized than those in secondary schools. With a modular curriculum, a student has the opportunity to profit from even more "custom tailoring" than in the traditional curriculum. Some students in a secretarial program,

137

for example, may wish to concentrate their advanced studies on power equipment, others may want to develop supervisory skills, and still others may want to sharpen their basic communication skills. Modular curriculum is much more adaptable to such varied concentrations than traditional structures.

Many college students are highly motivated and interested in proceeding at the fastest possible pace. The modular curriculum will enable them to do so. The module's philosophical statement, furthermore, will provide students with insights into its conformity with their particular learning goals. As a consequence, students will be less likely to take a course simply because it is "next in line" in the program requirements. This provides students the opportunity to make critical career decisions as they proceed through the educational program.

If the two-year college modular curriculum is well sequenced with that of feeder secondary schools and provides for pretesting as part of the design, needless waste of time and money can be avoided in the students' education. Unfortunately, overlap and waste of student time and money are still characteristic of many of our educational programs today.

APPLICATION OF MODULAR CURRICULUM TO THE TWO-YEAR COLLEGE PROGRAM

A wide variety of modular designs can be developed with the curriculums of our two-year colleges. The following is offered as one example:

MODULAR PATTERN FOR TWO-YEAR COLLEGE BUSINESS EDUCATION CURRICULUM

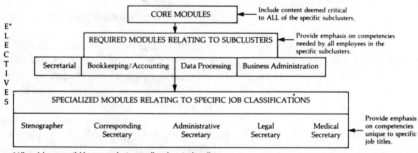

As with the high school design, the core modules at the two-year college level would be required of all business students regardless of their major field of concentration. Greater depth of treatment of content is also provided through specialized modules required of students majoring in a particular content area.

138

CORE MODULES

Content Area	Illustrative Modules
Business Organization and Management	Development and Characteristics of a Business Organization and Role of The Manager The Marketing, Financial, Production, Personnel, and Planning Functions of Business Relationships Between Business, Society, and Government Division of Labor and Flow of Authority Delegation of Responsibility and Communications
Macroeconomics	The Function of Price, Supply and Demand National Income and Production Savings, Consumption and Investments Multiplier Theory and Income Determination Money Systems and Fiscal Policy
Microeconomics	Alternative Economic Systems Profit Equilibrium; Analysis of Cost and Competitive Supply Imperfect Competition and Anti-Trust Policy Theory of Marginal Products and Other Economic Policies
Introduction to Data Processing	Development of Data Processing and Basic Computer Systems Advantages and Limitations of Computers Number Systems, Decision Tables, Flowcharting The Computer as an Aid to Decision Making
Principles of Management	Process of Management; Its Concepts, Behavior and Practices Management's Role in the Decision Making Process Human Factors in Organizing, Controlling, and Planning
Accounting I	Accounting Principles and Techniques Accounting Cycles Interpretation of Financial Statements Payroll Preparation and Taxation

CORE MODULES (Continued)

Content Area	*Illustrative Modules*
Business Law	Analysis of America's Legal System Law of Employment

Business Communications	Principles of Effective Written Business
	  Communication
	Writing Letters, Memoranda, and Reports
	Basics of Oral Communications
	Public Speaking
	Application of Business Psychology in
	  Writing

Human Relations	Application of Psychological Principles
	  to Personal Adjustment
	The Individual's Behavior Within a Group
	  or Institution
	Application of Behavioral Sciences to the
	  Work Situation
	Effect of Verbal and Nonverbal
	  Communications
	Techniques for Influencing Others
	Basic Principles of Human Relations
	Effective Techniques in Self-Motivation
	Development of Skills in Working with
	  Others
	Becoming an Effective Member of a Team

Public Relations	Overview of Public Relation Practices Employee Relations Development of a Company Image Effective Written and Oral Public Relation Techniques

Business Mathematics	Fundamentals of Applied Business
	  Mathematics
	Basic Mathematic Problems in Business
	  Operations
	Figuring Interest, Bank Discounts, Markup
	  and Markdown

140

REQUIRED MODULES RELATING TO SPECIFIC SUBCLUSTERS

Students will be expected to complete specific modules in this classification based on their program major or emphasis as noted below.

Illustrative Titles	Accounting	Business Administration	Data Processing	Secretarial
Typewriting				
Basic Skills for Operation and Care of the Typewriter	✔	✔	✔	✔
Development of Skills in Typing Personal and Business Letters, Forms, and Reports		✔		✔
Development of Typing Speed and Control; Application to Business Forms, Letters, and Reports				✔
Development of Typing Skills Consistent with Business Standards				✔
Mastery of High Speed Typing Techniques				✔
Stenography				
Shorthand Theory				✔
Reading and Writing Contextual Materials; Pretranscription				✔
Stenographic Skills Development; Emphasis on Speed				✔
Stenographic Skills Development; Emphasis on Basic Language Arts				✔
Intensification of Shorthand Skills Development (Speeds of 100-120 WPM)				✔
Transcription Techniques Commensurate with Office Standards				✔
Development of Office Production Standards (120-140 WPM)				✔
Records Management				
Technical Aspects of Records Management		✔		✔
Operation and Control of Storage Systems		✔		✔
Secretarial Practice				
Comprehensive Overview of the Modern Office		✔		✔
Simulation of On-the-Job Activities				✔
Transmittal Service, Records Management, Receptionist and Telephone Techniques				✔
Preparation of Business Reports		✔		✔
Attitudes and Traits Essential to the Successful Executive Secretary				✔
Personal Characteristics of a Successful Secretary				✔

Illustrative Titles	Accounting	Business Administration	Data Processing	Secretarial
Data Processing				
Basic Characteristics of Digital Computers	✔	✔	✔	
Computer Languages and Communication; Emphasis on Fortran II		✔	✔	
Concepts of Algorithms and Flowcharting			✔	
Basic Structure of APL and PL/1			✔	
Utilization of the Computer in Business Decision Making			✔	
Basic Structure of COBOL			✔	
Basic Structure of R.P.G.			✔	
Study, Design and Implementation of Business Systems			✔	
Advanced Study of Computer Hardware and Software Systems			✔	
Theory of Linear Differential Equations; Emphasis on Methods for Determining Solutions			✔	
Use and Functions of the Keypunch Machine			✔	
Setup and Operation of Various Keypunch Machines			✔	
Operational, Diagnostic, and Close-Down Procedures of Peripheral Equipment			✔	
Knowledge and Skills Used in Management Decision Making	✔	✔	✔	
Accounting I				
Accounting for Partnerships	✔	✔		
Accounting for Corporations	✔	✔		
Intermediate Accounting				
In-Depth Use of the Worksheet	✔			
Tangible, Intangible, Fixed, and Noncurrent Assets	✔			
Principles of Finance				
Raising and Using Funds in the Organization of a Business Enterprise	✔			
Financial Planning and Activities of Business	✔	✔		
Expansion, Merger, Consolidation, and Reorganization		✔		

Illustrative Titles	Accounting	Business Administration	Data Processing	Secretarial
Tax Accounting				
Current Federal Income Tax Laws and Regulations	✓	✓		
Concepts of Taxable Gross and Net Income, Deductions and Exemptions	✓	✓		
Business Law				
Law of Business Contracts	✓	✓		
Law of Sales	✓	✓		
Law of Agency, Partnerships, and Corporations	✓	✓		

SPECIALIZED MODULES

The following modules are designed for those students desiring in-depth concentration in a specific occupational specialization:

Content Area	Illustrative Modules
Cost Accounting	Techniques and Methods of Accounting Including Cost Concepts and Analysis of Costs Materials Control; Accounting for Labor Manufacturing Overhead; Job Order Cost; Direct Cost Analysis of Variance Profit-Volume Analysis, Capital Budgeting, and Break-Even Analysis
Principles of Marketing	Principles and Practices of the Distribution Process Channels of Distribution Product Pricing and Promotion Government Regulations Development of a Marketing Strategy Marketing Research and Development
Advertising	Role of Advertising in Business Characteristics of Advertising Media Advertising Layout and Production Planning an Advertising Campaign Strategy

143

Content Area	*Illustrative Modules*
Money and Banking	Nature of Money The Monetary System and Standards Commercial and Noncommercial Banking 　Institutions Relationship of Money and Banking to 　Prices and Economic Growth
Industrial and Labor Relations	Factors Affecting Labor/Management 　Relations Collective Bargaining Methods of Evaluating Jobs and Job 　Descriptions Wage Structures, Wage Surveys and Salary 　Determination Labor Law Designing, Organizing, and Installing 　Training Programs Employee Training Principles of Supervision Principles and Practices of Job Study
Retail Management	Principles of Retail Management Organization, Control, and Operation of 　Retail Establishments Principles of Merchandising Consumer Relations Stock Control Understanding and Influencing Buying 　Patterns Fashion Buying Forecasting Fashion Trends Domestic and Foreign Markets Textile Merchandising Non-Textile Merchandising Principles of Display
Insurance	Principles of Insurance Kinds of Insurance Insurance Law Principles of Life Insurance Principles of Automobile, Fire and Theft 　Insurance

144

Content Area	Illustrative Modules
Retailing	Overview of the Field of Retailing Types of Retailing Institutions Store Location and Layout Store Organization and Management Recordkeeping in Retail Establishments Customer Service Personnel Management Merchandising Techniques Merchandising Services Inventory Control and Valuation Markups and Markdowns Buying Practices Credit Sales and Management Pricing Policies
Principles of Real Estate	Introduction to Real Estate The Real Estate Broker's Office and Its Legal Environment Real Estate Management Valuation and Appraisal Subdivision and Development
Real Estate Law	Legal Aspects of Real Estate Deeds, Bonds, and Mortgage Analysis Taxes, Assessments and Title Closing Voluntary and Involuntary Alienations
Machine Shorthand	Mastery of the Keyboard and Theory of Machine Shorthand Advanced Development of Machine Shorthand Skills
Small Business Administration	Principles of Small Business Administration Starting and Operating a Small Business Recordkeeping and Finance in a Small Business Labor, Tax, and Other Regulations Profit and Cost Control
Data Processing for Retailers	Data Processing as an Aid to Retailers Point-of-Sale Data Recording; Backoffice Data Recording; Inventory Control; Perpetual Open-To-Buy
Display	Basic Principles of Display Design and Building of Interior, Window, and Point-of-Purchase Displays
Sales Management	Function of Sales Management Sales Forecasting, Organizing, and Planning Selection and Training of a Sales Force Management and Compensation of a Sales Force

145

Content Area	*Illustrative Modules*

Life Insurance	Principles of Life Insurance
	Basic Life Insurance Plans
	Types of Life Insurance Contracts
	Survey of Major Kinds of Personal
	  Insurance Coverages Available
	Computations of Rate-Making and
	  Reserves
	Policy Values
	Group Settlement Options
	Beneficiary Designators

Property and Casualty Insurance	Principles of Property Insurance Principles of Casualty Insurance Property Insurance Coverages Rating Involving Fire, Marine, Home- owners' and Commercial Policies

Medical Secretarial Practices	Introduction to Semitechnical Medical
	  Activities of a Medical Secretary
	Analysis of Medical Care Plans and
	  Related Forms
	Development of Skill in the Use of Office
	  Machines; Medical Filing Techniques
	Development of Medical Dictation and
	  Transcription Skills

Legal Secretarial Procedures	Comprehensive Legal Shorthand
	  Vocabulary
	Transcribing Bonds, Legal Forms and
	  Communications
	Development of Legal Forms (Wills,
	  Bonds, Leases, etc.)
	Rapid Dictation of Litigation Materials
	Structure of Courts

Personal Income Tax	Federal and State Personal Income Tax
	  Laws and Regulations
	Gross and Net Income, Deductions and
	  Exemptions
	Completion of Individual Federal Income
	  Tax Forms
	Completion of Individual State and Local
	  Income Tax Forms

Investments	Analysis of the Investment Market Investment Institutions and Security Exchange Methods of Investment Analysis

MODULARIZATION OF THE FOUR-YEAR COLLEGE
AND CONTINUING EDUCATION PROGRAMS

The arrival of competency-based education, alternative education formats, and the mastery learning concept on the teaching/learning scene brought to the four-year colleges and continuing education programs extensive use of curricular instructional units in the modular design. As in the high schools and two-year colleges, curriculum and instruction for many courses, from a specific subject matter area to a master's degree program, is being designed at the four-year college level in such a way as to provide greater opportunity for students to pursue collegiate study evolving around the student's individual learning style and rate.

The curriculum being devised generates specific objectives, behaviorally stated, for the students to master. Rationales are included to provide the college student with a concise statement as to why specific objectives are included in the module of study. Any prerequisites for the attainment of objectives are also explicitly depicted. In addition, a competency-based program may include a preassessment component that allows a student to skip instruction in those areas where he or she can demonstrate mastery prior to instruction. Finally, modular teaching-learning programs are usually more complete in their delineation of instructional activities than traditional programs.

ADVANTAGES OFFERED

Accountability. Competency-based programs by the organizational design tend to be more efficient than traditional programs, while their emphasis on behavioral evidence of competency grants them increased accountability.

Transferability. Since competency-based education is generally more explicitly described with detailed accounts of objectives, instructional activities, and evaluations, this type of teaching/learning is more transferable from one instructional setting to another.

Flexibility. The modular framework allows a great deal of flexibility both for the instructor and the learner. The instructor's role now becomes one of facilitator and/or orchestrator with the capacity to integrate comments and draw conclusions. He or she has the freedom to suggest, develop, and implement those instructional activities that will best aid the student mastery of the expected outcomes. The module included many activities, but selecting new activities and modifying existing ones is still a vital responsibility of the instructor if the program is to meet individual student needs and capitalize on both the instructor's and learner's special attributes.

The learner has the opportunity to apply those skills gained prior to instruction toward development of competency in the specific objectives that will be measured. The student may select, with the instructor's guidance, or elect to pursue the learning within a large group setting, a small group mode, or on an individual basis. He or she has the flexibility to select those instructional activities that will best satisfy his/her particular learning style and rate.

FORMATTING THE MODULAR PROGRAM

The organization of a modular program at the four-year college or continuing education levels is usually planned within a semester time frame. The format for a particular course would include the title, number, and course rationale. This rationale typically focuses upon society demands, the particular subject matter to be covered, and the client/learner to be served.

The next phase in the organizational framework is the presentation of those *units* or *clusters* of modules that encompass the course. Each unit/cluster outlines for the student the title, rationale, and general objectives to be met. As pointed out in earlier portions of the chapter, one may also view within the unit construction possible pre- and postassessment opportunities. Preassessment allows the learner to skip instruction in those areas where he or she can demonstrate competence prior to instruction. Preassessment may provide the learner with an estimate of his/her achievement status or the instructor with an estimate of the status of the entire class. Postassessment, on the other hand, provides for instructional accountability, learner accountability, instructor accountability and institution accountability. At this point in the module, provision for necessary remediation, whether open-ended or closed, must be evident.

Another feature of modular curriculum construction may be what are considered advance- and postcurriculum organizers. The advance organizer serves as an introduction to each module and, hopefully, serves to motivate the student to pursue the area of study. The postorganizer, however, seeks to link the learnings within the module to that of forthcoming modules.

The final phase of the organizational framework involves the syntheses of the unit/clusters into instructional modules. This involves the presentation of descriptive module titles and specific behavioral objectives as well as module prerequisites necessary to master the content. Distinct phases of instructional development in competency-based modules might be as follows:

PHASE   I   Identifying the level of objectives in the module

PHASE   II   Identifying the instructional aims relevant to the level of objectives

PHASE   III   Identifying kinds of instructional activities that will meet the instructional aims

PHASE   IV   Developing instructional materials for the various learning activities.

In capsule form, then, the organizational structure of a program of study on the four-year college or continuing education levels might be outlined as follows:

148

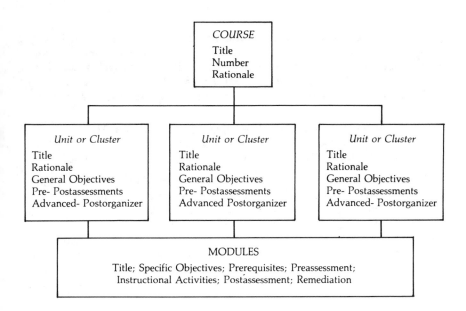

APPLICATION OF THE MODULAR PROGRAM

A wide variety of instructional activities is suggested for each module. The activities selected by the developer usually reflect four criteria: efficiency, effectiveness, interest level, and flexibility. While it is felt that student competence can be attained by participation in those activities listed in the module, instructors are expected to modify and/or delete activities to meet their own special skills and the specific needs of the students. While pursuing the module, the instructor as well as the learner should feel free to add appropriate activities that may aid in attaining the competencies.

The learning activities provided by the module developer should be organized according to their instructional purposes—revealing information, interpreting and clarifying, demonstrating, reviewing, and practicing. Many learning activities may be implemented under each purpose; *variety is the key*. This variety in instructional/learning activity allows for differences in learning and teaching styles among students and instructors. Secondly, it should prepare the student for competent performance in several demonstration modes.

The philosophy of evaluation in a modular program usually establishes preference for assessment at times appropriate to each student. Students should have the flexibility to take these final assessments when they perceive they have attained the module's objectives. This, then, paves the way for self-pacing on the part of the student. Selected students may elect to take the module preassessment, which in many cases is the same or similar to the postassessment. Preassessment, however, should not be used as a diagnostic instrument.

149

The use of modules in schools of business and business education on the four-year college level as well as in continuing education can be viewed today as a positive step toward alternative learning, individualization, and competency-based education. Modules may be designed in such a way as to serve the college student on the two-year, four-year, or graduate level with a minimum amount of subject matter duplication and loss of time and effort.

IMPLEMENTATION OF MODULARIZATION OF THE FOUR-YEAR AND CONTINUING EDUCATION COLLEGIATE CURRICULUM IN BUSINESS AND BUSINESS EDUCATION

A majority of the *core* modules, the *required* modules, and the *specialized* modules outlined for the two-year college are basic requirements for four-year college programs in business administration, which includes economics, finance, marketing, management; accounting; and business education. These modules, either taken individually or in combination/mastery level format, would become the subject matter clusters of the first few semesters of the four-year college program. The career path currently followed by many individuals pursuing postsecondary education involves the completion of "basic" modules that emphasize foundational content at the two-year level. This study is undertaken with the understanding of transferability into the four-year college program to complete the specialization, even extending to the fifth year, or setting of goals for continuing education.

The chart that follows depicts a sampling of modularization as projected for the four-year and continuing education levels. This pictorial illustration tends to interweave learnings mastered on the two-year collegiate level with those educational goals to be achieved by the student on the four-year and continuing education levels. Should the two-year collegiate program not be pursued, the first phase of the student's educational program on the four-year level would incorporate the modules derived previously for the two-year college. Students who desire technical/occupational education career instruction may enter the job market following the completion of those specific modules on the two-year college level or may select to follow a higher level program in business administration, accounting, or business education.

MODULES RELATING TO HIGHER LEVEL COMPETENCIES ON THE FOUR-YEAR COLLEGIATE LEVEL

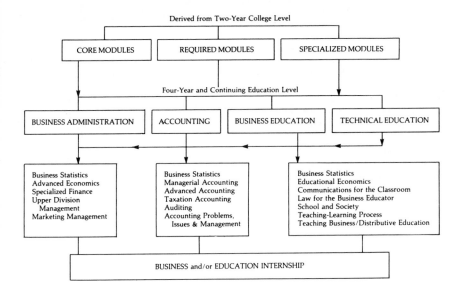

BUSINESS ADMINISTRATION covers preparation for entry into business or government and for admission to schools of law and graduate schools of business

ACCOUNTING course of study which meets the minimum requirements for taking the CPA examination and preparation for entry into accounting for industry or government

BUSINESS EDUCATION meets the B.S. degree requirements in teacher education with concentration in one of three areas: Accounting, Distribution, or Office Education

TECHNICAL EDUCATION includes preparation in a business-related career pattern of secretarial, retail, or clerical areas

151

MODULES DERIVED FROM THE TWO-YEAR COLLEGE LEVEL
(Core, Required, Specialized)

	Accounting	Bus. Admin.	Bus. Educ.	Technical Ed.
CORE				
Business Organization and Management		✓	✓	
Macroeconomics	✓	✓	✓	
Microeconomics	✓	✓	✓	
Introduction to Data Processing	✓	✓	✓	✓
Principles of Management	✓	✓		
Accounting I	✓	✓	✓	✓
Business Law I	✓	✓	✓	✓
Business Communications	✓	✓	✓	✓
Human Relations	✓	✓	✓	✓
Public Relations	✓	✓		
Business Mathematics	✓	✓	✓	✓
REQUIRED				
Typewriting	✓	✓	✓	✓
Stenography			✓	✓
Records Management	✓	✓	✓	✓
Secretarial Practice			✓	✓
Data Processing	✓	✓	✓	✓
Accounting II	✓	✓	✓	
Intermediate Accounting	✓	✓		
Principles of Finance	✓	✓	✓	
Tax Accounting (Personal)	✓	✓		
Business Law II	✓	✓	✓	✓
SPECIALIZED				
Cost Accounting	✓	✓		
Principles of Marketing	✓	✓	✓	✓
Advertising		✓	✓	✓
Money and Banking	✓	✓	✓	✓
Industrial and Labor Relations	✓	✓		
Retail Management		✓	✓	
Insurance	✓	✓	✓	✓
Retailing		✓	✓	✓
Principles of Real Estate	✓	✓	✓	
Real Estate Law	✓	✓		
Machine Shorthand				✓
Small Business Administration		✓		✓
Data Processing for Retailers		✓	✓	✓
Display			✓	✓
Sales Management		✓	✓	
Life Insurance	✓	✓	✓	✓
Property and Casualty Insurance	✓	✓	✓	✓
Medical Secretarial Practice				✓
Legal Secretarial Practice				✓
Personal Income Tax	✓	✓	✓	✓
Investments	✓	✓	✓	✓

BUSINESS ADMINISTRATION

Content Area	*Illustrative Module Titles*
Business Statistics	Descriptive Statistics Probability Theory Binomial and Normal Curves Point and Interval Estimation Hypothesis Testing Correlation and Regression Analysis

Advanced Economics	Wage Theories and Structures
	Labor Supply and Mobility
	Wage, Supply, and Employment
	   Relationships
	Impact of Unionism and Collective
	   Bargaining
	Influence of Geography on Industry,
	   Commerce, and Markets
	Regional and Urban Economics

Specialized Finance	Principles and Practices of Federal, State,
	   and Local Finance
	Governmental Expenditures, Borrowing,
	   and Indebtedness
	Taxation Principles and Policies
	Theory of International Trade: Barriers;
	   Balance of Payments; Commercial and
	   Financial Policy
	Corporate Financial Policy and Strategy

Upper Division Management	Personnel Administration and Human
	   Resource Management
	Labor Management Relations and Legal
	   Aspects
	Techniques of Collective Bargaining
	Introduction to Management Science:
	   Model for Establishing Policy and
	   Decision-Making
	Operations Management and Research
	   Applications
	Computer Applications for Business
	   Management

Marketing Management	Managerial Considerations in Marketing
	   Decisions; Evaluation of Alternatives,
	   Strategy, and Action in Profit Terms
	Marketing Research Design
	Channels of Distribution
	Marketing and Consumer Behavior
	International Marketing

ACCOUNTING

Content Area	*Illustrative Module Titles*
Managerial Accounting	Cost Concepts Used in Planning and Control Budgeting Financial Statement Analysis Use of Financial Accounting for Management and Investors
Advanced Accounting	Accounting for Price-Level Changes Financial Status of Estate Administration Trusts Receivership Accounting and Partnerships Accounting Problems from Consolidations Management Accounting
Taxation Accounting	Federal Tax Structure as It Applies to Individuals, Partnerships, and Corporations Elements of Tax Research Preparation of Tax Records State and Local Tax Structures as Applied to Business and Personal Income
Auditing	Fundamental Analysis of Auditing Contribution of Auditing to Financial Reporting Application of Audit Tools: Systems Flowcharting, Statistical Sampling, EDP and Others Professional Ethics and Legal Responsibility of Internal Control in Relation to the Auditor
Accounting Problems, Issues, and Management	Intensive Investigation of Accounting Theory Through Literature Financial Information Systems and Computer Programming Fiscal Control Systems Current Issues in Public Accounting Professional Examination Problems and Procedures

Content Area	*Illustrative Module Titles*
Educational Economics	Principles of Economics Development of the American Economy Economics of the Educational Structure
Communication for the Classroom	Business Communication Communication Arts Educational Communication Concepts Mass Communication and Education Instructional Media
Law for the Business Educator	Business Law Concepts Legal Requirements of Education Drug Use in American Society
Foundations of Teaching: School and Society	History and Philosophy of Education Social Foundations of Education School Organization for the Classroom Teacher Programs of the Secondary School Current Issues in Education
Foundations of Teaching: Teaching-Learning Process	Psychology of Learning Human Growth and Development Human Relations for Teacher Development Behavior Modification Alternative Teaching Techniques Measuring Intelligence and Evaluation Counseling and Personnel Services
Teaching Business/Distributive Education	History of Business/Distributive Education Development of Curriculum and Materials Learning Cycles of Skill Courses Learning Cycles of Basic Business Courses Learning Cycles of Distribution Courses Methods and Techniques for Teaching Business/Distributive Education Lesson Planning: Units, Daily Classroom, Performance Objectives, Evaluation . Audiovisual Equipment/Materials Field Participation

Content Area	*Illustrative Module Titles*
Practicum in the Area of Specialization	
Independent Study in Business and/or Education	
Field Studies in Business and/or Education	
Work Experience	
Supervised Student Teaching	
Professional Semester in Education	School Organization and Administration
	Educational Psychology
	Techniques of Teaching in Secondary Schools
	Techniques of Teaching Business/ Distributive Education
	School Internship
	Student Teaching

CONCLUSION

Curriculum modularization is still in its infancy. It appears that only fear of the complexity of the system keeps it from more immediate acceptance and implementation. Potential benefits from curriculum modularization are great, especially for students.

CHAPTER 8

"The future of society seems solidly based upon technology. Business education appears to be ideally positioned to continue in its now important role, making meaningful contributions to the task of preparing men and women—young, middle age, and senior citizens—for their everchanging future." Regardless of teaching specialty, every teacher must be aware of present-day technology. Those who have stayed on top of innovative technological change will want to read this to test the knowledge acquired; those who have avoided change with a "head in the sand" attitude must read on to become aware of what they have missed.

Technological Utilization in Business Education

MARY NEMESH

Anne Arundel County Board of Education, Annapolis, Maryland

ANNA NEMESH

University of Maryland, College Park

Innovation has become one of the watchwords in American education. Since Russia sent Sputnik into orbit, we as a nation have developed a powerful sense of urgency in regard to the improvement of our educational system. There has been great stress on technological improvement in the teaching process. Because of the rapid nature of change, attention has been focused upon the technology itself, rather than upon the people involved. As a result, it is much easier to make definitive statements about the quality and extent of educational technology than it is to make definitive statements about the humans involved in the system.

'Technology" is one of the most misunderstood words in our language— particularly when applied by educators to education. The misunderstanding is caused by a failure to view technology as a process at a sufficiently high level of abstraction. Business educators tend to define technology by its obvious manifestations: machines. It is an easy step from this to the simplistic view that if we have machines, we are using technology; and if we haven't machines, we are not engaged in a technological process.

The proper definition of technology, however, which educators must keep in mind when applying the term "educational practice," is given by John Kenneth Galbraith:

Technology means the systematic application of scientific or other organized knowledge to practical tasks. Its most important consequence, at least for purposes of economics, is in forcing the division and subdivision of any such task into its component parts. Thus, and only thus, can organized knowledge be brought to bear on performance.[1]

Using this definition, it is clear that educational technology may be applied at all levels of educational practice as an approach to solving practical problems—from the application of technology in planning the educational system as an emerging notion to preparing a module of programmed instruction in order to achieve a behavioral objective.

For the teacher, the new technology represents a multitude of changes. In the old system, the teacher's role was fairly well standardized and accepted. In the new system, the teacher's role must be redefined in order to utilize the changing technology.

EMERGING TECHNOLOGIES AS A DEVELOPING FORCE

Between 1900 and 1950, technology advanced to a more sophisticated level through progressive application of a series of innovations in method, machinery, and communications. "By 1950, aided by the acceleration of two world wars, industrial technology grew and developed, eventually transformed American society, philosophy, and art."[2]

However, during this same period, technology still had not been exploited to any great degree for educational purposes. Finn notes:

Technology only washed lightly upon the shores of instruction. In this time span when high speed printing techniques, radio, sound motion pictures, television, and other pieces of communication technology were invented, developed, and exploited, American education failed to apply these devices in quantity to the instructional process, and, of course, failed to develop the appropriate technological systems necessary for this application. There were always rumblings to be sure, as evidenced by the statement attributed to Edison in 1916 that the motion picture would replace the teacher. However, looked at from the vantage point of 1960, laboratories, project methods, libraries, and minute arrangements for audio-visual materials—the provisions to 1950—constituted what was still a pre-industrial technology for instruction.[3]

It is difficult to ascertain the precise reasons for the apparent reluctance to incorporate technology into education during this period. A number of reasons have been postulated. A common generalization states: "Education is conservative. It takes time to bring about widespread changes in content and methodology."[4] Still, another precise factor which may have contributed to the slow acceptance of technology and one which characterized general, overall thinking about the application of technology and the use of media in education was specialization in the production and administration of instructional technology and media.

During the 1950's the reluctance toward incorporating technology into education began to change. Improvements in hardware and refinements in

---

[1]Galbraith, John Kenneth. *The New Industrial State.* Boston: Houghton-Mifflin Co., 1967. pp. 12-13.

[2]Finn, James D. "Technology and Instruction." *Phi Delta Kappan* 41:371; June 1960.

[3]*Ibid.*

[4]Saettler, Paul. *A History of Instructional Technology.* New York: McGraw-Hill Book Co., 1968. p. 79.

accompanying software were being made. Finn noted that with the year 1955, American education was given "a sharp push into mass production technology. The time was ripe. There was a shortage of teachers; education and educationists were under fire from all sides; neotechnocracy was turning its attention to education; the race with Russia was underway; the natives were restless indeed."[5]

The Commission on Instructional Technology also recognized that developing technologies could do much to assist in the solution of a number of educational problems such as changes in job requirements, increased rate of school dropouts, movement toward integrating schools racially, attention to the long-neglected needs of the gifted, the retarded, and the educationally disadvantaged learners. In their report, they stated:

> Various innovations have been introduced as ways to break out of the rigid system which marches students, lockstep fashion, through a series of identical classrooms in which teachers do most of the talking and students have little opportunity to respond. . . . The aim of all these innovations—organizational, curricular, and technological—is to adopt instruction more precisely to the needs of each individual student. . . . Technological media can perform many of the functions involved in this process.[6]

The slow pace of applying instructional technology methods and developing new technologies for education was quickened. This has accelerated at a phenomenal rate in recent years, particularly since 1955.

With the advancement of instructional technology in education, much of the thinking regarding school administration and teaching has changed. In some instances, it has become an integral part of the instructional process. It has further caused new concepts to develop in the logistics of instruction. Such concepts have required new and different staff and a changing role for the teacher and administrator.[7] The goal is to create learning environments which are flexible, dynamic, and capable of responding to a wide variety of individual needs and learning styles through the use of media, personnel, and actual experience. Understanding technology also means understanding the erratic nature of change. There are no more forceful changes than the changes technology can make in our occupations. This generation wants to be educated for jobs. But educating learners for jobs is a difficult assignment because many jobs become obsolete in a short time, and others emerge. We can predict to some extent, however, the likely changes; and we can prepare learners with a few transferable skills which will be used to become more and more flexible as one supplements and modifies these skills which one took from high school for the ever-changing job requirements within clusters of jobs.

---

[5]Finn, *op. cit.*, p. 373.

[6]U.S. Congress. House Committee on Instructional Technology. *To Improve Learning*. Washington, D.C.: Government Printing Office, 1970. pp. 29-30.

[7]Finn, James D. "Instructional Technology." *NASSP Bulletin* 47:99-119; May 1963.

A NEEDS ASSESSMENT DERIVED FROM EDUCATIONAL TECHNOLOGY

Since there is no consensual definition of educational technology, it is important to identify its most common usages. Along with identifying the common usages, it is also important to identify the essential conceptual ingredients of educational technology.

Technology refers to the tools of our work and can be defined in the very narrow sense of hardware and machines or in the very broad sense of theory and knowledge.[8] Education refers to the general processes of learning that occur as a result of a wide variety of experiences from formal instruction to informal instruction to informal situations.[9] Thus, educational technology is a broad term for the tools and techniques used in general learning situations. It is often used synonymously with instructional technology; but instructional technology generally refers to the specific instructional techniques used mainly in formal, school-type learning situations, whereas educational technology refers to instruction and management and pertains to a wide range of learning situations.

In sum, the concept of educational technology deals with the implications and study of a variety of technologies as applied to the general process of learning. There are real problems in the use of hardware and complex instructional techniques, but it seems clear that the purpose of their use is to create a more humanized and responsive learning environment. Technology is considered a positive force because it helps to adapt instruction to a variety of learning needs.

EDUCATION AND TECHNOLOGY

If we are to prepare our students for the present and the future, we must look at the factors that are responsible for current conditions. The school environment of the twenty-first century will be a center of electronic marvels. Exciting methods of technological developments incorporated into the classroom can be so well implemented as to enable teachers and students in the educational system to do what has been impossible or very difficult: to assimilate the new machinery and its skill requirements and its rapid effect upon the technological "revolution" of our business and economic environment.

Technology presently enables the learner to participate in different environments and will increasingly do so. Television, through various distribution patterns, reaches most students in and out of school, but has yet to serve the learning process to its full potential. Telephone lines, now used primarily for conversations or specific audience communication, have the ability to carry information into virtually every school and home. No element of the educational process need be limited by the walls of buildings or organizational demarcations.

---

[8]Mesthene, E. G. "Technology and Humanistic Values." *Technology, Human Values and Leisure.* (Edited by M. Kaplan and P. Bosserman.) Nashville: Abingdon, 1971. pp. 42-57.

[9]*Ibid.*

Curriculum design and media utilization are inextricably interwoven. Purposeful integration of curriculum and media is ongoing and open-ended, with media professionals, curriculum consultants, teachers, and learners jointly designing instructional systems in which content and method evolve together. This process of scientific instructional design results in a more effective allocation of both the human and the material resources of the educational program.

Effective curriculum realization requires the interaction of media programs at every level. These levels include school, district, region, state, and even farther-reaching relationships, as technology makes these possible.

The vast array of educational innovations over the past two decades, which have been touted as panaceas by some overenthusiastic educators, have led many concerned researchers and developers to be more than skeptical about introducing "popular" new ideas. More often than not, the failure of an innovation in education to make a real impact on practice has resulted from its use by educators who have little understanding of its substance and who attempt to implement the innovation outside of its systematic context.

The purpose of this chapter is to attempt to dissuade business educators from mere bandwagoning activity by discussing the role of technological utilization in business education. The utilization of technology in business education should be thought of as one component of a total, systematic change model and not as something that, in itself, can significantly solve all educational problems. One of the major weaknesses in educational planning today is not the absence of reliable ideas, theory, and practice, but rather the reluctance or inability of too many educators to see the inextricable interconnections of innovations offered by researchers and developers to solve specific problems within the educational establishment.

Educational tomfoolery continues. The plea of this chapter is that technological utilization in business education be considered as any other educational innovations should be—within the concept of a total model for change.

To embrace technological tools in the name of modernity, efficiency, or effectiveness (in a limited, "performance" sense) is inadequate. Rather, we must realize that technology is enabling us to create totally new educational environments which both encourage and require new behaviors in the teacher and the learner.

As business educators, we can help learners trace technological change and analyze its influence on our lives. We can help learners to be conscious of change and of its erratic development. And, we can help learners develop attitudes which will enable them to "hang loose," thereby more easily coping with change as it occurs.

Teaching learners to understand technology and cope with it now and in the future is not easy. Yet, it is not impossible; and teachers can do it. All that is needed is to be alert to the world around us; to learn more about industry by reading and listening to those who know, and to enlist the help of the community. In addition, we must recognize the importance of technology in the lives of the young.

The outstanding evidence of technological development can be seen in new media such as television and the computer. Although audiovisual aids in the form of films and radio have been used for decades as supplementary teaching aids, it was only with the advent of the newer technologies that one could conceive in full the enormous impact these media could have on conventional classroom techniques. The use of audiovisual aids (such as filmstrips, tapes, projectors, charts) has influenced the traditional educational behavior of teachers. The introduction of multimedia systems, television, and computers calls for changes in the total teaching/learning process both in pedagogical methods and organizational and administrative procedures.

Strategic thinking is needed at all levels today: by the teacher in the classroom, where learning actually takes place and where new learning systems are to function; at the institutional level, which has to implement learning systems and provide for their functioning; at the levels where one is concerned with curriculum development, with the design and development of course material and with the large-scale dissemination of learning systems; and, last but not least, at the decision-making level, which is responsible for drawing up long-range policies.

To understand the policy implications of educational technology, one has to see its impact in the general context of reforms and innovations that are at present taking place in education. The preoccupation with the teaching/learning process constitutes one of the elements in the combined efforts to update education to the needs of modern society.

Educational technology is aimed at the interaction process between teacher, media, and learner. All our educational planning, educational management, or curriculum development will finally have to prove its validity by the effectiveness of the learning outcome, that is, the effectiveness of the teaching/learning process to meet the needs of both the individual and society.

The advent of a systematic approach to the teaching/learning process creates a need to assign to educational technology the design, organization, and evaluation of learning systems. This, in effect, materializes in the effort to produce prefabricated course materials, i.e., objectified learning units, which are utilized by the student, independent of the constraints of time, space, and personnel. Such packages contribute directly to:

1. Individualizing instruction; for example, self-contained learning packages for individual use in conjunction with audiovisual aids and/or other material assignments that are tailored to meet different learning styles. The design of the material allows the individual student to progress according to his/her own motivation and knowledge, which will, in effect, stimulate inquiry behavior and creativity.

2. Coping with mass student enrollments and contributing to the equality of educational opportunity; for example, learning systems that imply the use of mass media such as television or computer in conjunction with printed material can serve innumerable students at the same time over great distances and can be constantly repeated.

3. Democratizing the learning situation; for example, the procedures for developing course material necessitate defining precise educational objectives to be achieved by the learner. This enables students to more effectively understand what and why they are to learn and also gain a greater insight into the goals of education than they had in the past. Furthermore, self-contained learning packages are aimed at active student participation in the learning process, giving them a responsibility on the timing of their learning. Lastly, these learning systems assign new functions to teachers while freeing them from old ones, which will, in essence, reduce to a great extent, the old autocratic relationships in the classroom.

In summary, the utilization of educational technology in business education can contribute to the cost-effectiveness of learning, bridge the gap between teacher demand and supply, and improve the quality of the learning outcome. However, if the contribution of educational technology results "only" in an equal education for a greater number of students in possibly a shorter time and at a reasonable cost increase, we will have surmounted some of the problems we are facing in education today.

INSTRUCTIONAL TECHNOLOGY

The act of teaching is regarded as foremost in importance because it is under the direction and control of the teacher. The teacher is in authority and in a position to shape instruction to further the kinds of learning for which the instructional program has been designed. Furthermore, the teacher is also able to draw upon media to serve those ends.

Media convey ideas and information from self to others, selves, and things. The word is symbolically multimeaning. When used in media instruction, it may be defined as "devices" (hardware) plus use and user. For the more specific definition, "media" will refer to the mechanistic and electronic devices which are capable of producing and retrieving materials on a more or less permanent basis rather than those products which are transient in their endurance and retrievable potential.

Because media can be assigned one of several roles in teaching and can be made to contribute to a variety of teaching purposes and behavioral outcomes, the media requirements of each teacher tend to be personal and unique. One of the most productive ways of looking at teaching and uses of media is by analyzing the roles that business teachers assign to media as components of a larger context of instruction. Because the teacher is the major influence upon learning in the classroom, the teacher is in a position to determine what is to be learned at any time, how it is to be taught, what kind of activities are to be engaged in by the students, and how outcomes are to be evaluated.

Thus, media can be observed as environmental variables that affect the management of the classroom (such as grouping of students) and as instructional stimuli that influence behavior of students (such as levels of thinking). Directions and questions extend the influence of media by providing student choice in activities and responses, by raising levels of student thinking above the level of recall of knowledge, and by examining values and ideas of the affective domain. There is an acceptance of instructional technology, at the lowest level as tools to help perform instructional tasks and at the highest level as a systematic approach to instruction where media are vital and integral to the entire process.

MULTIMEDIA SYSTEMS

The advent of a systems approach can also be observed in that there has taken place a development from teaching aids to the use of media systems. With the introduction of television and, in the course of time, of other media systems, it has become more and more common to speak of media in general instead of audiovisual aids. The word is becoming increasingly used today as a generic term for the various conveyors of information. Media really embrace everything from the conventional media of chalk and blackboard to books, maps, and audiovisual aids, to the steno laboratory, TV sets, and computer. The term "new media" borders imprecisely on the classical teaching aids and refers to new products which have penetrated into educational institutions in the last 15 years. For decades, the medium, under the label "audiovisual aid," was seen as a supplementary tool of the trade—whether it was a map, a slide projector, tape, or film—for use by teachers in their efforts to convey information. This instructional process might be described as a medium-supported teaching system.

The introduction of the "new media" decisively alters this constellation. The medium itself has become an autonomously functioning conveyor of information. Steno and typewriting laboratories, TV educational programs, and "classical" as well as new learning machines can be programmed so that they can take over the task of conveying the information themselves. If certain accessories are used, e.g., accompanying texts, then these media can assume an interactive relationship with the pupil that is independent of the teacher, though of course the degree of freedom in the relationship is controlled and limited. Under these circumstances, the teacher no longer remains the main purveyor of information. This type of instruction could be called a medium-integrated system. The advance from a medium-supported to a medium-integrated instruction system offers a major point for consideration when one is evaluating general trends in the use of media for teaching purposes. There can naturally be no talk of "replacement" of the teacher by the machine—a common ·and ill-considered conclusion often drawn in this connection.

The change from teaching aids to media systems points to developments which will only be fully operationalized in the years to come. With regard to hardware, these crystallize at present in the move towards multimedia systems, i.e., the development of learning packages. Where people previously tended to view educational media in isolation, seeing every new medium as a cure for all ills, there is a growing awareness of the limited scope of individual media. Their disadvantages, but also their particular advantages when combined in a package, are being realized. Thus, it is no longer a question of global commitment to any single medium, but one of deciding which ones can best be combined for achieving specific learning goals.

A fully equipped multimedia system has a very complex assortment of sophisticated equipment and facilities and often requires special technical and architectural provisions not present in most conventional educational institutions. Such a system might make use of films, closed-circuit TV, slides, audiotapes, overhead projectors, projection walls, and/or TV monitors. It might easily include dial access information, retrieval systems, and CAI facilities. Yet, multimedia systems can be installed in a far more simple form. Any combination of public television and/or radio teaching with local working groups, written work, and text material is a multimedia system, just as is any structuring of teaching around special texts, loose-leaf files and working instructions, special tape cassettes, slides, or single-concept films. In fact, it is precisely this less costly form of media combination, more flexible in terms of time and space, which is currently receiving much attention in some European countries. The design of these learning packages follows the methodological procedures of classical programmed instruction. Programmed instruction, although it is no longer propagated in its classical form of teaching machines, nevertheless has had a very strong influence on curriculum development in that it has provided a set of procedures which introduce the empirical approach to curriculum design.

Furthermore, it is to be expected that the multimedia approach itself will expand to include new fields and activities. If current educational problems are to be overcome, we shall have to foster this movement and see that these new points of departure move beyond their experimental and planning stage and are put increasingly into practice. Many innovations in education can today be developed only by means of empirical trial and revision. The challenge is to recognize the potential inherent in, and peculiar to, media, and to exploit them and integrate them rationally into the teaching/learning process.

Audio-video retrieval systems. Audio-video retrieval systems utilize a delivery source of media transmission by means of audio and video playback equipment that supplies many reception areas on a closed circuit. This is usually but not necessarily confined to a central listening-viewing area. Several systems are currently in use such as (a) a dial-access or touchtone signal utilized by the student to obtain delivery of service in carrel or study area, (b) a direct telephone request to a delivery center for transmission to a specified area, (c) an automated delivery on a scheduled basis, either manually or time-clock controlled, or (d) combinations of these. The retrieval system is a complicated, somewhat inflexible, extremely expensive system to buy and maintain. It is capable of delivering many audio-video units simultaneously, and its delivery capability is limited only by the number of playback units available. It also has the capacity to serve many students at the same time by varying the number of viewing sets available.

Since this system is designed for large group use rather than individual control of the playback equipment, it delivers the "whole" of something. Much like commercial radio or television, each unit is presented in its entirety. The student's dial-up may either activate the remote mechanism to playback or, if the unit is already in progress, it tunes in at whatever point the unit is then playing. The audio-video retrieval systems have a tremendous impact on the teaching/learning environment in business éducation. The successful and progressive business educator will implement the system to complement the program of work as determined by the behavioral objectives set forth in a program area.

Individual audio applications. Without a doubt, the audio machine and materials have contributed markedly to the individualization of instruction by making lesson elements available to students outside of regular group instruction patterns. Individualized instructional materials have been developed across the board in business education.

The reduction of cost and size, coupled with an increase in operating convenience, have made cassette audio-recorders checkout items for individual student use in open classrooms, business education laboratories, or out-of-school assignments. The point to be made is that it is common for students to have individual access to the tools of recorded sound anyplace, in or out of school, which heretofore were not available to our students.

In addition, listening stations and/or carrels in the business education environment provide the individual student access to audio information sources without direct pupil manipulation of the materials or machines. The student has an accessing device, either a dial or a touch-tone panel, and a headset. The information sources are contained in a bank of audio-tape recorders which are activated by signals from the student's station and send programs out in response. These kinds of audio-tape recordings are, of course, used in the laboratory environment: the audio-passive in which the student hears the lesson presentation and follows instructions by himself if oral response is indicated, and the audio-active in which the student records on his own track. This type of setup works very well with the disadvantaged student since the student can work at his own pace, setting his own goals and objectives within his learning capability.

Videotape recorder (VTR). The videotape recorder, commonly referred to as VTR, is making a significant impact and contribution to business education activities in the classroom environment as well as to programs related to professional growth and development through in-service learning. This magnetic recording device makes it possible to record activities or programs for immediate use and/or to store the tapes for future presentations.

The VTR system employs a camera similar to those used by commercial and/or educational television, except that it is portable, much less complicated, and less expensive. The tapes may be reused many times with numerous playbacks of each program, with little or no deterioration of picture or sound quality.

In a large school system, it is impossible for a total staff of teachers and supervisors to visit and observe a particular teaching situation or innovative study. To overcome this particular obstacle, portable VTR equipment helps to make viewing of these activities not only possible, but practical. The situation can be videotaped for subsequent viewing and discussion by small or large groups.

166

In conclusion, the use of the video recorder (VTR) has greatly enhanced a school's flexibility in gaining access to televised lessons and educational programming. Business educators can benefit from the utilization of the VTR within the classroom environment as well as in-service learning. The potential utilization of the VTR is unlimited based upon the business educator's resourcefulness, creativity, and ingenuity.

Sound-on-paper systems. In the sound slide system, the audio presentation is accompanied by pictures projected either on a wall screen or in an individual viewing unit. This accelerated movement towards individualized instruction has led to the introduction of new and refined ways of creating a sound dimension to paper pictorial and verbal materials. The most common of these is the audiocard machine. The audiocard is quite similar in appearance to a data processing card. It contains a magnetic strip along the lower edge. Essentially, the audiocard is a flashback with sound and is operative by being inserted in a slot on the machine in which a transport mechanism then moves it through the slot. Through the use of a headset and/or speaker, up to 15 seconds of sound can be played back. Its uses are myriad. The audiocards can be shuffled to separate mastered from unmastered examples for drill purposes such as business math applications. Business teachers have found the audiocard systems to be one of the handiest and most utilized of the audiovisual media in the subject for which they are appropriate, such as business math or accounting, and in schools where they are available.

Dial access systems. The prime objective of the dial access system is to provide direct and individual access to the entire collection of audiovisual materials at whatever time is most appropriate to the learning process. All current trends in instructional organization indicate the need for such availability. If team teaching, flexible scheduling, self-directed learning, and conceptual or inquiry curriculum in business education are to have their potential impact, students must have independent—and individual—use of appropriate instructional materials in all formats. Through the use of a dial access system, a teacher or a student has the capability to request any available program, either audio or video. The material is, in effect, directed through an electronic switching system to any of the remote terminals throughout a particular school district.

There are several factors that a school must consider when contemplating a video dial access system. First, commercially prepared video materials that every television distribution system can use are scarce. Secondly, most materials used individually by students must be locally produced within a school district.

However, dial access has led directly or indirectly to some exciting changes in the instructional programs of many school districts. An increased awareness of the entire range of media available has developed. Students as well as business educators are experimenting with media production as never before. Individual students, in ever-increasing numbers, are utilizing instructional materials that formerly were available only on a group basis in the classrooms.

In conclusion, whether it is through a complex automatic dial access system or through the use of cassettes and individual projectors or viewers, schools everywhere should provide such availability. The demands of today's curriculum and today's instructional organization are such that the schools can no longer ignore the need of individual access to media; it is a need that can be fulfilled with proper planning and implementation.

Closed-circuit TV via microwave, cable, satellite TV. Closed-circuit TV by way of microwave, cable, pickup of standard band TV, or a central dissemination system normally services (but is not restricted to) classroom monitors or similar reception areas elsewhere. Many school systems across the nation, both local and statewide, use this method to mass-deliver instructional units for class viewing. The transmission is generally made from the central delivery system via wave-lengths unobtainable on home sets. The usual procedure on such systems is to schedule on a time-basis the transmissions available during that time frame. Such systems have many advantages in the capability of setting up a two-way transmission between distant points, thereby permitting interaction from students gathered in one location with a teacher broadcasting from distant points. Although this type of capability is presently limited, it is easy to believe that there will be a day when satellites will be used to a greater extent to service geographical areas via microwave.

Closed-circuit television is unique because of its design, in which coaxial cable or microwave is utilized to transmit signal or images and/or sound to predetermined receiver or monitor locations. The system is contrasted with the public broadcast of images or sound to basically undetermined and nonselective receiver locations. The salient feature of closed-circuit television is the element of control exercised over its reception and hence, it is to be hoped, over its utilization. Like the retrieval systems, closed-circuit television has the tremendous advantage of being able to transmit to many students simultaneously.

In its basic form, cable television, commonly referred to as CATV, consists essentially of an assortment of high-powered TV antennas usually located on a large tower in which signals from these antennas are amplified and distributed over coaxial cables to homes, schools, hospitals and libraries. Schools with developed educational media programs will find cable television very useful to facilitate the distribution of many multimedia materials between buildings. Other schools that draw upon the multimedia resources of area or regional media centers may well find cable television to be an outstanding high-speed retrieval vehicle. Schools sharing a computer housed some distance away may find that the local CATV operator will provide them with free interconnection to it, thus saving the schools the usual and considerable expense of leasing access lines from the telephone company. All of these are possible, and many school districts are establishing pilot projects with their local cable operator to find out the applications that are most feasible in their localities. The closed-circuit television as well as educational television has led to a systems approach to teaching and learning with computer-assisted programmed instruction as well as the Educational Communications Systems multiservice national network capability.

168

In conclusion, with the rapid technological advances in television recording and transmission, the educational programmer is able to receive programs from permanent satellites via ground-based relays from state, regional, and national program banks. However, programs must be scheduled at appropriate times from the teachers' point of view; this would involve having a videotape recorder in every school that can pick up programs beamed by satellite and replay them when wanted. Each school and/or community would need receiving equipment—TV and radio sets, plus audiotape and videotape recorders for local use. The benefits accrued to business educators in the utilization of closed-circuit TV via microwave, cable, or satellite are unlimited. A variety of business education topics have been televised; they range from general introductory series to courses in accounting, credit, insurance, typing, and shorthand. Also, we find that for the most part the majority of work has been done with lessons originating in a studio and being viewed by students located in many classrooms within different buildings or individually at home.

Television is a multiple medium device. The business educator can use television to view effective and dynamic teachers at work. Weak spots in the curriculum can be bolstered and lesson loads can be eased by the introduction of well-prepared television plans. If it is wisely and imaginatively used, closed-circuit television can play a major role in broadening and enriching the education of our students. It holds great promise for education, especially business education in the modern age.

Votrax voice synthesizer. The votrax voice synthesizer, a talking computer, is being utilized to tutor the blind and visually handicapped in vocational classwork. A project called VOCAB, developed jointly by the Office of Research and Extension Services of the School of Education at North Carolina State University, Raleigh, and the North Carolina Department of Human Resources, Division of Services for the Blind, is aimed to help the blind attain skills in accounting and data processing. Both blind and visually handicapped students communicate with the specially designed instructional programs via typewriter-like keyboard, receiving messages from the computer by means of a synthesized voice response. The electronic voice system interfaces with data communications equipment which converts the output of the computer or other digital device into electronically synthesized human speech.

At the outset, students are taught the keyboard by means of four cassette tapes, developing the typing skills essential to communicate with the programs. Students call the computer over the telephone, identifying themselves and the lessons they need. In the interim, the computer reads a section of the lesson by means of the votrax voice synthesizer. The student is then asked a multiple-choice question about what he/she has just learned; the student types in the number of his/her choice. The computer, in turn, transmits new information based upon the student's response, thus providing immediate feedback to the student.

With the advent of the votrax voice synthesizer, vast new possibilities for instruction of the blind and visually handicapped student can be developed.

Computers. The ever-increasing dependency of education upon the computer seems inevitable because it helps meet the needs of students for greater individualization of instruction and greater relevance of subject matter. Computers fall into two major categories: the object of instruction and the vehicle for instruction. As an object of instruction, we are concerned with learning about computers and data processing. In general, we find these courses at the secondary level. They, in turn, fall into two categories: the first category includes the how to course, which teaches how to use computers for problem solving in courses such as math and science and how to operate the equipment in courses such as business education and data processing. There is, of course, an overlap because most courses teach at least some problem solving and some equipment skills. The second category includes the appreciation units, which teach about the potential and power of computers.

Using the computer as the vehicle for instruction, either as the total or partial instructional delivery system, is relatively new. Delivery systems refer to two broad categories, namely, CAI (computer-assisted instruction) and CMI (computer-managed instruction, commonly referred to as data-managed instruction or DMI).

Computer-assisted instruction consists of programmed instructional sequences presented to students by means of a computer. The student interacts with the computer directly, usually at a terminal (typewriter and/or video). Computer-assisted instruction can be extremely responsive to student learning needs by branching each student through a lesson sequence contingent on responses to questions in the lesson. The computer keeps complete records of all responses and gives performance summaries to teachers and/ or other school personnel. It is important to realize that, given sufficient educational software (material and strategies), CAI could account for the major substantive learning of a student. The teacher, of course, should be involved in planning the system and supervising its operation. A well-planned system frees the teacher from routine teaching tasks so that more time can be spent working closely with individual students. The implications of such a system for the structure, process, and form of education are indeed enormous.

In the computer-managed instruction approach, records of a learner's learning experiences and needs are maintained by the computer. The business educator can utilize the data to prescribe various learning activities for the individual student and for group activities as well. In the CMI approach, a natural extension of student data files can be kept by schools, and this fits in well with the training and experience of today's teacher.

Programming the materials for the computer is a highly specialized skill, but it has tremendous flexibility for interplay between student and computer teacher, allowing for assimilations of other media and immediate response. It is of itself the nearest one may get to the one-to-one teacher-student relationship via media apart from a human teacher. The values it loses in personality-to-personality are counterbalanced by the quality the programmer can design into the instructions.

The level of service a computer can provide is determined by the design and quality of the software. Creating programs envelops students who enroll in vocational data processing; therefore, the students must have a working knowledge of the programming language COBOL for vocational business data processing to be used to model the process. Support software, commonly referred to as canned programs, is designed so that students must supply the required information at the beginning, at some intermediate point in the program, or supply answers that the program responds to. The computer simulates physical processes not so easily obtainable in a laboratory and prints extensive results.

The computer has been utilized by teachers and administrators with in-school administrative processes. Teachers use the computer in the preparation of tests and in marking students' responses. Administrators can update and access student records via computer as well as develop a scheduling package within a school district using the network utility for attendance, student report cards, school accounting, and school payroll. The potential of the utilization of the computer not only in instruction but also administrative application is limited only by the knowledge and imagination of the teachers and administrators using the system resources.

Using time-sharing methods, a single computer can provide simultaneous instruction for a large group of students, each working independently and in his own sequence at a teletypewriter or other terminal connected to the computer. The computer processes the students in rotation, but with such great speed that each student feels he/she has the machine's undivided attention. Many school districts are moving in this direction.

Computer use does not mean dehumanizing. In fact, data from studies thus far indicates that one of the strengths of the computer in the instructional environment is that it greatly humanizes the students' educational experience. As business educators, we need to incorporate the teaching of business data processing into our curriculum, concentrating on developing computer operation skills and utilizing programming as an educational tool.

Terminals. A relatively new term in the data communications vocabulary is the intelligent terminal or, more precisely, intelligent terminal system since it includes a number of modular components such as CRT's, printers, and tape or disc drives. A terminal is a machine that enables you to "talk" and/or "communicate" with the computer. It has a keyboard for input, something on which it can display output, and a connection to the computer. Thus, a data terminal can be defined as a device used to input and output data. The intelligent terminal is one that can be programmed to perform certain functions that would otherwise require the services of the central processor to which it is attached.

There are two basic types of terminals—one that types output onto paper, and one that displays output on a TV screen. Terminals that type output onto paper are referred to as hard-copy terminals. This type of terminal provides the user documentation of source programs, making it possible to check the status of such programs. In addition, a hard-copy of one's work is useful to the user/learner who desires to save a printed copy or type out a particular file.

Terminals with screens are known either as video terminals or CRT (Cathode Ray Tube) terminals. The CRT consists of the display unit and a connected keyboard, which may be integral to the unit or connected by a few feet of cable. The CRT and keyboard are usually the same whether the unit is a stand-alone or cluster type. Keyboards come in a variety of layouts in terms of key designation and position. A number of general-purpose function keys (as many as 24) may be on the keyboard. Their function is determined by the program set up in the associated processor. The video/CRT terminals produce output more quickly than the hard-copy terminals. These (CRT) terminals are useful when you are doing a lot of work for which the end result is important; immediate feedback is possible, which is displayed on the screen. Working with this type of terminal allows the students to receive and see responses immediately. Whatever is displayed on the screen, however, must be kept in some sort of digital storage so that it can be displayed continuously, even for hours.

Some terminals are connected directly to the computer by wires which run between them. Other terminals are connected to the computer over the telephone. This is accomplished through the use of an acoustic coupler. An acoustic coupler is an instrument which converts the terminal and computer signals into sounds which pass through the telephone lines. A telephone and a phone number connecting directly to the computer are needed for this system layout. However, there may be several numbers needed, depending on how far away the computer is. If these three elements are present, you are ready to dial in, interacting with the computer.

What can be done with an intelligent terminal system depends a great deal on the processing unit. With a small processing unit on a CRT-type terminal, the device is primarily a CRT display. As the processor and the memory expand, the capabilities also expand.

Processors may include simple controllers, microprocessors, minicomputers, and small- to medium-scale computers. Most CRT-oriented terminals have microprocessors, which are communications oriented. Software systems support these terminals as well as function in a real-time, on-line mode. This support makes it easier for the average user to take advantage of the opportunities available through teleprocessing. The data processing student can program into the terminal error-checking routines and data validation routines. Typical inquiry/response applications may include credit checking, reservations, inventory status, and account status. Inquiry/response tends to be a simple application if not combined with other tasks.

In summary, intelligent terminal systems can do any terminal job previously done by older hardwired terminals—visual display, keyboard entry, inquiry/response, time sharing, remote batch, remote printing, and a host of other functions. Since many intelligent terminal systems use minicomputers as their stored program "controller," they can be used as stand-alone general-purpose computers as well as terminals. Data processing students can, therefore, preprocess data, create new programs, do calculations, and perform other such tasks without interrupting the central processor.

Because of the proliferation of computer terminals and/or input/output devices, it is important that data processing students be exposed to a reasonable sample of the basic types presented. A data processing program should be broadly based, preparing students for immediate entrance into employment.

Many school districts are moving toward updating the data processing program. A modern, up-to-date central processing unit capable of serving multiple units, terminals in sufficient numbers to serve its users without inordinate delay, and a modern communications network to service them (students) is feasible if concerted effort is made toward the betterment of data processing education. The Anne Arundel County Public Schools' vocational data processing program has installed a computer systems network in each comprehensive high school; the equipment configuration includes four CRT's, a data recorder, a line printer, and four acoustic couplers in each of the 12 schools, with the central processing unit housed at the vocational center. Students are receiving training in computer operations as well as data-entry operations and programming skills.

Calculators. Technological innovation is the key word in the calculator market. Sophistication of technology is combined with operational simplicity and continued equipment improvement.

THE DUAL READ OUT. The dual read out, commonly referred to as a display and print calculator, is designed for business and commercial applications which require additions, calculations, costing, and conversion involving units of measurement. This calculator features the standard ten-key keyboard which includes digits 1 through 9, a 0, and a decimal point. Calculations and results may appear on the display screen when the display key is engaged. As the term "dual read out" implies, one has the option to switch the calculator on print. When engaged in print, the calculations and results are printed on a paper tape. This enables the learner to check accuracy and also provides a record of the results. Its wide range of capabilities and ease of operation makes the dual read out calculator highly desirable not only in modern offices but also in the business mathematics laboratory, office training laboratory, and/or accounting laboratory where speed and accuracy in a variety of calculations are necessary. In many instances, the capability of maintaining a tape record of all computations and results may be considered desirable but not required; the student has the capability with the dual read out calculator to provide a tape record when instructed.

THE PROGRAMMABLE CALCULATOR. The programmable printing calculator, referred to as a data processor, can accumulate data, make decisions, solve problems, and execute programs automatically. Programs are recorded onto magnetic cards after instructions have been initiated via keyboard. Once recorded, the program can be read many times and the calculations are performed automatically. The keyboard is simplistic. The processing of data is rapid and efficient. Utilization of this type of equipment in advanced business education classes such as accounting has tremendous application.

The creativity and ingenuity of the teacher will determine the successful and/or effective usage of the programmable calculator in the business education environment.

WEIGHTS, MEASURES, AND METRIC CONVERSION CALCULATOR. The metric conversion calculator is the most recent development. This type of calculator not only handles weight, measure, and metric applications but also handles business calculations. Several companies have developed the metric conversion calculator. This is a very timely calculator to incorporate into the business education curriculum as the nation moves towards metrication.

Reprographic/reproduction equipment. The business environment has been inundated with new types of reproduction equipment over the past several years. This has had a tremendous effect not only in the business world but also in the educational realm. Today's business managers are beset with decisions regarding the type of reprographic system best suited to their organization and the type of equipment to purchase. This same decision faces the office worker who must decide which type of available equipment is best suited for each reprographic job for which he/she is responsible.

The term "reprographics" refers to all the processes, techniques, and equipment employed in the multiple copying and/or reproduction of documents. Conventional reprographic devices such as stencils and photocopiers are still being used by many businesses and educational institutions. Among the recent developments is the electronic stencil maker, which duplicates the subject matter from an original onto a stencil. When this has been accomplished, the stencil can be utilized for reproduction not only in black and white but also in color on any stencil printer. The originals consist of line composition, tone composition, or a combination of both.

As the electronic stencil maker functions in two modes, a line and tone mode, shades of gray ranging from black to white can be reproduced. In addition, areas darker than a certain shade of gray can be reproduced as black or areas lighter than that shade as white.

Line originals can be done by a typewriter, line printer, or drawing lines with a pen or pencil. Tone originals are photographs and/or pictures; the shading is similar to a photograph. By keying the control settings to dots and symbols, the set-up procedure for line and tone work has been accomplished. A stencil is made with a stylus through which an electric current flows. When a stencil is made, carbon should be removed from it. The machine makes a line stencil and stops automatically when the stencil is complete. In addition, transparencies for use with projectors can be produced at the same time a stencil is made. Having this dual capability is a time saver for the teacher.

Some schools include in their office training classes (1) ways to paste up copy for duplication to avoid retyping, (2) cost factors to consider in arriving at a decision on methods of copy preparation and duplication to use for special jobs, and (3) specific ways in which office workers can help to keep duplication costs under control. Through discussion and practice, students are able to envision the problems encountered in the business world in regard to types of reprographics equipment to purchase, whether equipment selected should be centralized or decentralized within the organization, and the best means of resolving the problem of paste-up, cost factors, and control factors. Increasingly, business educators are placing more emphasis on the study of flow-of-work and cost control procedure within various reprographic systems, as well as in all aspects of office work. Many school districts cannot afford an electronic stencil maker so they utilize available equipment to create a flow-of-work. However, school districts possessing monies for such equipment have utilized the electronic stencil maker within the office training classroom as an integral part of the program; some school districts have implemented a program in reprographics for a semester, utilizing reproduction equipment. As business educators, we must keep abreast and inform our students of the technological developments and the effects of these developments in the business world.

Media typewriters. Automated and/or media typewriters are single-element typewriters coupled with recording tools, such as magnetic tape or magnetic card, that enable the typist to type the material, then edit, correct, and store it so that it can be played back for later use. If you operate an automatic typewriter, such as a mag card, memory, or electronic composer, you will be able to produce individually typed letters or copy letters automatically from a master original. The recorded copy can be played back on the same typewriter, error free, at speeds ranging from 150 to 185 words per minute.

Automated and/or media typewriters can enhance the business education program; however, because of the expense involved in purchasing them, automated typewriters should not be used as regular typewriters. Effective and realistic activities should be planned in which the students receive a real perspective of the use of automated typewriters. In today's business world, the basic procedures for the operation of automatic typewriters are very similar for the different brands and models. Most manufacturers offer training, in-house or at the site, in the use of the equipment.

Word processing. Word processing, a coined phrase from Germany, refers to the operation of electronic typewriters utilizing magnetic memory. Word processing is the latest step in the search for more efficient use of business machines and secretarial time.

Basically, word processing is a term used to describe equipment (the use of such machines as word processing typewriters, combined with audio-dictation equipment) and organized systems (office routine) to facilitate the handling of words or texts, generally resulting in greater productivity in office procedures. The magnetic media power typing equipment is often housed in "word processing centers," in a further effort to rationalize office procedures through differentiation and specialization of secretarial functions. One of the primary functions of these products is to increase productivity of both the typists and the professional staff so that the many documents required by industry or educational institutions can be generated. In this way, productivity is enhanced through decreased time required to complete the various editing cycles involved in the creation of a document and decreased time expended in proofreading by author, writer, or typist.

One should not assume that word processing is just the current terminology for a typing pool. Nor should it be assumed that large numbers of staff or reorganization changes are needed to introduce word processing.

Word processing can best be defined as a clerical operation that combines people, procedures, and equipment to transform ideas into printed communications. Typing activities are centralized through dictation equipment and power of automatic typewriters. Under this system, the secretary's function can be divided into two specialized branches:

1. Keyboard unit to yield written communications
2. Administrative secretarial duties (telephone communication, public contact, filing, research reports, statistics).

Thus, freed from dictation and typing, administrative secretaries can provide increased administrative service to managers, who in turn can enlarge the scope of their activities.

A component of word processing is the equipment system. Dartnell's Glossary of Word Processing Terms defines a "word processing system" as a combination of equipment and personnel working in an environment of job specialization and supervisory controls for the purpose of producing typed documents in a routinized, cost-effective manner. [10]

Utilizing word processing equipment in the business education environment, we business educators should be aware that the system consists of input and output equipment designed to function together. An input system comprises dictating equipment that can be classified as discrete media or an endless loop system. The discrete media system utilizes magnetically coated belts, discs, or tapes in cassettes and cartridges. A desk-top model for dictation and transcription may be employed, or a centralized PBX with dictation phoned into recording units can be utilized in the correspondence center; the belts, discs, or tapes containing material that has been dictated can be transmitted by messenger to the correspondence secretary for transcription.

The endless loop or tank-type systems are characterized as continuous-flowing tapes that do not have to be reloaded or ever touched by the transcriber. In fact, the tape is sealed in a tank. The machine itself consists of several loading tanks and desk-top transcribers. The monitoring panel contains dials that indicate which tank is in use, which one is idle, and the amount of backlog materials that remains for each tank to be transcribed. Like the discrete media systems, the endless loop system can be utilized individually by a person who generates a tremendous amount of dictation; or it can be centralized where many individuals in an organization can be word originators.

The output equipment for word processing can be classified as follows:

1. Automatic typewriters that capture keystrokes on magnetic media, used for straight, repetitive output that involves little or no text editing for automatic playback

---

[10]*Dartnell's Glossary of Word Processing Terms.* Chicago: Dartnell Corporation, 1977. p. 54.

2. Stand-alone text editors that operate independently, permit changes and corrections to be made on documents, and are not connected to other machines

3. Stand-alone display editors that have a cathode ray tube display screen, enabling the operator to see what is being typed so that corrections can be made before entering it into the system

4. Communicating text editors that are capable of communicating with other text editors, computers, and other special terminals via a telephone line

5. Shared-logic systems that consist of multiple terminals and are computer-based with a central processing unit, in which operators can use the CPU simultaneously

6. Time-sharing services that permit usage of computers located elsewhere (you pay for the service as you use it).

Business educators must remain aware of the changing scene in word processing with the ever-increasing technological developments and advancements. Although the equipment may not be within budget constraints, it is necessary to keep abreast of the changes in this field so that students can be well informed about what they will find in the business world and what they may be asked to use.

Priorities and emphases. In making decisions on priorities, a set of questions such as the following deserve consideration.

1. Should motion pictures, filmstrips, radio, and other such media already adopted be taken for granted, or should they be reexamined for currency and logistical adequacy?

2. Should emphasis be placed on the newer technologies such as CAI and ITV, individually prescribed instruction be intensified, or should these undergo more extensive feasibility, operational suitability, and effective testing?

3. Should efforts to diffuse instructional technology and increase its effectiveness be time-phased from the elementary school, which is more open to innovation, to the high school and college which are more conservative and less open to changes in teacher role and ritual?

4. Within the formally structured and certified educational systems, should emphasis on the employment of instructional technology be directed among those schools serving the culturally deprived student population, or should it be directed among those schools serving the family-reinforced docile, compliant, and thus more teachable student population?

5. What changes are required in teaching rituals and functions in order to increase allocations of time to learning activities of students directly related to "new media" and in teachers' expectancy images of students so they are perceived as human beings with primordial capacities to learn, "turn on" and develop on higher levels?

6. What balances and directions are required in the development of the newer and more complex technologies of instruction and/or their employment for both the essential individualizing and the essential socializing processes of education?

Beginning with the implementation of technology, the business educator must be provided the means to recognize the needs of students who will learn under his/her guidance and the means to understand and have at his/her disposal the sources of a wide range of information to support learning. Considerable planning and thought must be given to the multimedia systems which assist in using vast sources of information. Analytical devices must be utilized for matching each student's needs with the particular learning process that most effectively encourages the progress of the individual student.

Educational technology makes possible the reformation of our schools— but only if we business educators view technology in a sufficiently broad context. The wide array of approaches, techniques and methods demonstrate evidence of a pragmatic response to the challenge. The challenge is to meet the needs of the individual student.

CONCLUSION

The future of society seems solidly based upon technology. Business education appears to be ideally positioned to continue in its now important role, making meaningful contributions to the task of preparing men and women—young, middle age and senior citizens—for their everchanging future.

Technological progress and change will affect society—including education in general and business education in specific—to a greater extent in the future than will any other variable foreseen. One way in which technological progress and change will affect the needs of the individual is related to the ways it shifts the characteristics of the work force. As a result of technological innovations, the world of work has become a complex and massive matrix of vocations. Because of this complexity, the individual will require continuing orientation to the world of work.

Educators have begun to recognize the necessity to initiate programs that provide students with an active and realistic view of the world of work that includes social and technological problems. These programs would simulate problem-solving activities conducted in the world of work and society, with the business educator providing the means (the learning environment) and the students finding the ends (solutions).

The disparity among academic, business education, and vocational education is dated. If the educational system is to be designed to focus on problems related to technology and society, crossing social and economic boundaries, programs must be established which merge the field of knowledge presently organized into separate subject areas.

Any successful application of these developments is likely to require a more active coordinative role at the state level. There is a need for much more cooperation within and among school districts than has commonly existed.

Implications for business education. As part of the total educational system, business education will be responsible for helping to meet the needs brought about by technological change and progress and the changing meaning of work in our future society. Therefore, these factors will shape business education internally by affecting the curriculum and course content of business education in the future.

Technological developments in business education can be expected to have an impact on every aspect of school operations and to affect pupils, teachers, administrators, and government officials alike. To meet this challenge, state and county departments of education will have to acquire considerably more expertise in the newer technologies than exists today in most states. This expertise must be more than knowledge of how to thread film in projectors or to operate teaching machines or even the ability to run a computer center. It must include a familiarity with, and an ability to apply, systems analysis and design procedures in matching the technology to the total needs of individual districts or a cooperating group of districts.

There is little question that technology and its utilization will eventually change the entire pattern of business education; however, the ability of districts to cooperate and the quality of governmental leadership and coordination will determine whether the change comes swiftly and efficiently, or whether it stumbles through a protracted, costly, and disorganized period of trial-and-error learning before the true benefits of technology are recognized.

Future of business education. Business education must bridge business and technological literacy so that all students are successfully functional in the society of the future. It will be the responsibility of the business educator to update continually the technological concepts taught in order to parallel the change and progress in the world of work.

Change cannot take place unless people bring it about, and people make up the most unchangeable elements in education. If the exciting educational experiments of today are to become realities of tomorrow, there must be a revolutionary change in educating teachers.

Many things are possible through technology. A major responsibility of educators is to develop the instructional use of new technology. At the same time, business educators must remain flexible in planning by keeping before them the values of a broad curriculum reaching individual learners. The greatest problems we will face are not in introducing and implementing technology, but rather, in fostering appropriate curriculum changes which will require multimedia utilization. Curriculum change means "people change," and "people change" is the first order of business.

CHAPTER 9

Community-Based Projects in Business Education

The business education teacher is a community resource and therefore can be instrumental in the development of alternative business education projects within the community. Our Yearbook authors view this contribution from two directions. First, they look at the vast opportunity in what can be called independent study on the part of the postsecondary school learner. The business teacher becomes the focal point around which many types of independent study projects can develop. Then next is a look at the business teacher as a resource contributor to the development of community programs or projects of varying types which require a degree of business expertise. There are numerous roles the business teacher can assume beyond that of the teacher/lecturer or study mentor. The philosophical viewpoint of business education has always projected this type of teacher involvement, and it is important that the alternative opportunities be highlighted.

Section A: Independent Study Projects

Arkansas State University, State University

One of the chief virtues of independent study is its flexibility. Through independent study projects, individual differences in interest, ability, and experience can be met, difficult schedules can be circumvented, and a variety of special educational needs can be attained. Independent study courses may be fitted to any time schedule. Such courses and/or study permits expansion of the program of studies at minimal costs.

Independent study may be administered by a learning center, by individual instructors, by administrative officers, by guidance counselors, or by evening or adult school personnel. Several independent study formats are possible at both the high school and college levels. Some of the common ones are programmed instruction, supervised correspondence study, individual study projects, individually prescribed instruction, and work-related studies.

PROGRAMMED INSTRUCTION

Hundreds of programmed instruction courses have been developed in the last two decades; however, the flood of courses does not ensure good materials or courses. Good developmental methods require that the materials be tested with a great deal of precision with clientele groups for which they are intended. Aside from ensuring reliability and validity, a major problem is the selection of suitable courses for a particular individual or group. Prerequisite background and level of content are primary considerations.

Programmed courses are taken several ways; however, programmed instruction as an independent study format can best be handled by a learning center manned by one or more persons trained in learning center work. If a sufficient number and variety of courses are stocked in such centers, the most appropriate for each individual can be selected by trial.

If properly developed, programmed instruction courses should be entirely self-teaching after the student understands procedures. Literacy, of course, is required except for a few low-level courses based on other symbols.

SUPERVISED CORRESPONDENCE STUDY

Supervised correspondence study was "invented" in 1923 in the Benton Harbor School (Michigan). It is now used in well over 1,000 high schools and in many community and four-year colleges.

This instructional format was created to serve students' educational needs which could not be accommodated in conventional classroom courses. The format can extend the program of studies by hundreds of courses. It is especially useful where too few students want a course to justify a class, where no qualified teacher is available, where the instructor is already fully scheduled, or where the student cannot fit an existing course into his or her schedule. Small schools especially find it a useful way to enrich programs. For example, dozens of small high schools in Nebraska and other Great Plains states supplement their programs of study by supervised correspondence study.

Sources. Two general sources of correspondence courses are available—the private correspondence school and the correspondence departments of colleges and universities. Most schools which utilize supervised correspondence study depend upon the private schools for these courses. They offer the greatest array of subject matter in business and other fields. Several thousand courses are available at the secondary and adult levels.

Schools such as the American School (Chicago, Illinois) and the International Correspondence Schools (Scranton, Pennsylvania) have an extensive list of courses and may also tailor-make courses by selecting and combining off-the-shelf units. The National Home Study Council (1601 Sixteenth Street, N.W., Washington, DC 20009) accredits these and about 100 other correspondence schools. Names and addresses of these accredited schools can be obtained from the Home Study Council. Correspondence offerings may be sold as separate courses or whole curriculums. Tuition in private correspondence schools includes all textbooks and other necessary instructional materials such as kits of learning exercises if applicable. Many high school courses published by the American School are already organized as one-half or one Carnegie unit. The local school may have to determine how much credit to allow in other courses.

A limited list of courses may be found in correspondence departments of certain university extension divisions. About half of these departments offer high school-level courses; most of them offer college-level courses. Credit is already designated. Textbooks usually have to be ordered separately for university extension courses. As volume of enrollment in private correspondence schools is usually much greater than in university correspondence courses, the private schools have greater opportunity to field-test and improve their instructional materials.

How supervised correspondence study (SCS) works. A local faculty member is appointed as "SCS coordinator." In small programs this is a marginal assignment, although there may be released time. The coordinator usually holds a teaching credential, but need not be qualified to teach the subject taken by the correspondent—the qualified course instructor is at the correspondence school.

The coordinator is an "administrator" who arranges space and time for study and serves a liaison role between each local student and the one or more correspondence schools in which local students are enrolled. The tuition and instruction fee set by the correspondence school may be paid by either the student or the local school. The coordinator takes care of enrollment details. The course packages should be sent to the coordinator for distribution to appropriate students.

Either the SCS coordinator, another teacher, or a guidance counselor may counsel students in selecting appropriate courses. The SCS coordinator explains procedures and helps each student get started. As correspondence courses are designed for independent study, literate and motivated students should be able to work independently. Usually, the courses selected are electives, and students select only courses in which they are interested. By arrangement of scheduled time and place for study, the coordinator helps each student "keep on track."

Finished assignments are returned to the coordinator who records the completion and forwards the assignments to the correspondence school for evaluation (grading), correction, and further instructional assistance. The corrected assignments are returned within a few days, and the coordinator passes them on to the appropriate student(s). This provides a good time for the coordinator and student to review and benefit from the comments made by the distant instructor.

While one assignment is at the correspondence school, the student continues working on the next one. When the course is finished, the coordinator administers the final examination if one is required. After it is graded by the correspondence instructor, marks are entered on appropriate forms and credit is given toward graduation if that is an objective.

The coordinator is not expected to give subject matter assistance to the student; that service is the role of the correspondence instructor. In small programs, the coordinator may, if time permits, give a small amount of such assistance in areas of competence. Other qualified instructors on the faculty may also be a local subject matter resource. However, this situation should not be allowed to become a tutoring arrangement that utilizes too much time of already busy instructors. Such assistance should be reserved for crucial and specific help to move a student past a difficult point.

Under this system some students may take as little as a half unit; others may take several units or courses. This system is especially good for students wishing to pursue specialized vocational careers for which the local school is not equipped or staffed. The system is also good for occupational exploration. It can bring introductory subject matter to the student, and it provides a good basis for determining additional interest.

A number of adult and continuing education programs at the secondary and college levels use supervised correspondence study. This method allows a student to progress at his or her own rate if meeting a semester or graduation schedule is not important. It is a flexible method, especially convenient for people with heavy or irregular schedules.

A primary consideration, as in all courses, is the selection of courses suitable to the interest and ability of the student. As all correspondence assignments are to be completed satisfactorily, there is no "floating through" a course. However, lazy students may (and usually do) drop these courses. While dropout rates in independently pursued correspondence courses are relatively high, the supervised arrangement usually results in a 90 to 95 percent completion when the coordinator is a proper stimulator.

INDIVIDUAL STUDY PROJECTS

These projects are usually developed locally, although some are available from publishers. They can be tailored to individual needs, interests, and ability levels. Those who develop their own can gradually accumulate a list of projects or units from which students can select. Able and advanced students can be invited to propose their own independent study projects subject to instructor approval. This is especially good for projects not yet developed and for extending the breadth or depth of those already developed.

Some business teachers develop and accumulate dozens of short-unit projects that may be used with classes or in independent study. Some projects may require an extended period of time to complete; others may require only a few hours of time although the clerical and administrative load increases as projects are shortened. Students may select enough short units to constitute a semester or year's work. Interested students may select specific units to strengthen grades, to make up for absent periods, or for other purposes.

Academic and life-related projects. *Academic* projects are designed as learning exercises with or without relation to work the student may be doing. *Life-related* projects have a bearing on or are derived from an occupational (or other) activity or interest of the student. Either type may use largely library and in-school resources, or they may depend upon experience on the job, in the community, or other outside activity. They may combine the two. Academic projects are more likely to be *theoretical* although they can be very *practical.* They may fill an "academic requirement" which may not be of interest to the student, or they may fill a real, immediate need or a clearly perceived future need. All of these elements, of course, have great bearing on motivation.

Illustrative titles of six projects suitable for business studies include:

1. Learning Proofreader's Marks (probably academic unless student has an actual or anticipated need for the skill)
2. Report Writing (may be either academic or life-related)
3. Selecting a Bank (probably academic even though work would be largely in the community; certainly a "practical" learning activity)
4. Causes of Stock-Market Cycle (academic and/or life-related)
5. Developing a Personal Insurance Plan (could be either academic or life-related)
6. Organizing a Mailing List (could be life-related or academic exercise).

Characteristics of good project outlines. Outlines of short, well-planned independent study projects need not occupy more than a single typed page. Semester-length projects may require longer outlines. Essential elements of the contract are:

1. Goals and/or Objectives: An overall statement of what the student will learn
2. Behavioral Objectives: A breakdown of objectives written so that the student will know when they have been mastered
3. Reference or Study Materials: These may all be assembled in a package (brown envelope) or may be in libraries or other diverse places
4. End product to be expected
5. Schedule: Final due date and checkpoints. Checkpoints may be at regular intervals or at stages of progress through the unit.

A sample project outline for "Writing Minutes" is given in condensed form. This should serve as a guide for those who wish to develop their own.

WRITING MINUTES

Behavioral Objectives:

1. To learn what information is essential for the preparation of minutes of a meeting.
2. To organize the necessary information in an acceptable minute form.

References:

1. R. Row: *Legal Forms*, pp. 97-126.
2. Eckersley-Johnson, Ed.: *Webster's Secretary Handbook*, p. 36.
3. Other appropriate texts and information.

Procedures:

1. Study references.
2. Examine and study formats and content of several different types of minutes in appropriate minute books or records.
3. Attend several business meetings of clubs, committees, city councils, school boards, and similar organizations. Try to see the format and content of these minutes.
4. Take notes of these meetings including essential information required for preparation of the minutes in their usual form.
5. Draft the minutes of each meeting attended.

6. Compare your draft with actual minutes as prepared by the official secretary. Seek comments of secretary on draft.

7. Submit final minutes of three different business meetings with backup notes to instructor for evaluation.

INDIVIDUALLY PRESCRIBED INSTRUCTION (IPI)

IPI is a form of independent study using programmed instruction, supervised correspondence study, or other modes of instruction. Achievement tests are used to identify weak subject areas if the general educational level is to be determined. Within each subject, diagnostic tests assess areas needing remediation.

The effectiveness of the system depends upon (1) the availability of reliable diagnostic instruments and (2) the availability of appropriate instructional materials. For adults, this format works quite well in a learning center that has an ample supply of off-the-shelf instructional units and diagnostic tests. IPI is especially useful with adults preparing for the GED tests. In business education, IPI is useful for getting acquainted with students transferring into a program. It is a useful format for mid-term entries and for preparing any student for placement or for meeting any terminal general examination. Students aspiring to take civil service tests can identify weak areas in advance and can strengthen them through IPI. It is usable, of course, with any class of students working on an independent study basis.

WORK-RELATED STUDIES

A beneficial format of community-based independent study can be attached directly to the work or occupation of the learner. Most jobs above the very routine and repetitive serve as excellent bases for such projects. Employees can bring their job-connected challenges and problems to the educator. Together they can work out plans and procedures for doing the work faster, easier, and/or better. This type of study normally helps solve a problem or improve efficiency. However, it may deal with a potential problem not yet recognized by management. It may be a feasibility study and can even be focused on problems or higher levels of management or more advanced job descriptions.

Such studies can combine theory and practice in an applied situation. The learner brings the problem. The educator opens up learning resources, study and research methods, problem-solving procedures, and evaluation strategies. Data is generated from the work environment. Work and study are integrated in a most meaningful way.

One university using this format has a master's program catering to a specialized group of executives scattered across the nation. These executives go on campus for two 2-week periods per year. While there, they review the work done in their studies and map out work for the next six months. The professors and students (executives) keep in touch by mail, telephone, and cassettes between on-campus visits.

This format, based on reality combined with theory, provides strong motivation, useful learning, and a totally meaningful experience for the learner. For the instructor, it provides a useful interface of theory with reality. It is, undoubtedly, one of the most effective learning formats in independent study.

Section B: The Business Teacher as a Community Resource

NELDA C. GARCIA
University of Texas at Austin, Austin

A widely held belief in business education is that the gap between the classroom and the world of work should be bridged. Advocates of this position usually see two alternatives for doing so: (1) bring a community resource into the classroom as a guest speaker, or (2) send the student out of the classroom to work in a business environment. A third alternative, however, for bringing the business student and the business world together is to send the teacher out into the community as a representative of the classroom and as a resource in the community.

The business teacher serving as a community resource can derive valuable benefits which also contribute to the profession of business education. Like the sociologist who uses the community to conduct field research, the business teacher can use the community to conduct primary research, that is, to acquire first hand knowledge based on observations and practical experience. Although teachers from different academic areas commingle in an educational environment, community involvement requires it. The expertise found on an advisory board, for example, is a cross representation of fields and disciplines. This could enable the business teacher who served on such a board to develop interdisciplinary perspectives and cross-cultural understandings that reflect the makeup of the community. In short, community-based projects need the business teacher's expertise and professional service.

Another benefit of community involvement is that insights or expertise gained can be applied to classroom instruction. Teaching is not confined to the classroom; neither is learning. Leaving the classroom to go to the people, as one business educator indicates, "helps me help my·students." Involvement in the community provides meaningful experiences that enrich subject matter and improve teaching effectiveness.

CHOOSING AN ALTERNATIVE

The decision to leave the classroom as a means to bring the school and the community together poses many variables, some administrative and others philosophical-psychological. Choosing not to leave the classroom, for example, can be attributed to the school administration's policy requirements, the teacher's busy schedule, or the teacher's philosophical-psychological preferences. As to the last factor, many business teachers place overriding

186

concern on the students and their classroom instruction. To be absent from the classroom without due cause, of course, is to abuse the privilege of administratively sanctioned classroom absences and to neglect the students. While it is recognized that some teachers abuse the privilege of approved absences, other teachers simply prefer to remain in the classroom. For these teachers bringing a community resource into the classroom, not vice versa, may be the best alternative.

Given administrative sanction, however, most teachers will choose to leave the classroom for various professional purposes. Choosing to leave the classroom, but not to be an active contributor, is one alternative. Preferring to be "an outsider looking in," a passive participant in an audience rather than an active participant in a conference program, for example, is nonetheless a professional alternative. A common approach is to leave the classroom for active involvement in a professional endeavor. Choosing to become an active community participant, a doer, a community resource, is an alternative. Posed with these alternatives, which one should a business teacher choose? And why?

Before attempting to answer the above questions, it is first necessary to identify some of the major factors influencing the teacher's decision to become a resource and the available alternatives for doing so. The teacher's job requirements and the administration's philosophy are two such influences. To fulfill certain job requirements, for example, on-the-job supervisors have to be active participants in the business community where products from their training program are placed in part-time employment. Supportive administrative philosophy may view a teacher's community-professional service as useful to the educational institution that the teacher represents and useful to the community that benefits from these services.

The most influential factor in the decision-making process, however, is the benefits that the business teacher can expect from such involvement. If school administrators recognize the value of community service and the contributions it can make to the school, the community, and the teacher; and if business educators recognize the need to direct students toward realistic concepts, such as those experienced in internships and cooperative work-study arrangements; and if the business teacher can recognize that students do benefit from these business-school arrangements, does it not follow that the business teacher also benefits from community involvement?

IDENTIFYING COMMUNITY PROGRAMS IN NEED OF THE BUSINESS TEACHER'S ASSISTANCE

The choice to become a community resource poses procedural questions: How can the business teacher identify the community-based projects in need of professional assistance? Where in the community can the business teacher be of service? What type of professional service can the business teacher provide? To become a community resource, therefore, the business teacher can follow certain identification-selection procedures that will help determine how, when, and where to become involved in the community.

The first step in the identification process is to become familiar with the needs of the community. The use of such sources as a community services directory or a telephone directory can help identify community programs, service organizations, and activities. A community services directory for Austin, Texas (population: 321,900), lists as many as 284 resources for services in the areas of health, welfare, recreation, and education. The agencies/organizations are listed alphabetically and cross-indexed using 50 categories. Under the "Employment" category, for example, there are 19 service organizations listed, one of which has nationwide familiarity and may interest business teachers concerned with the vocational rehabilitation of the handicapped, i.e., Goodwill Industries.

Service organizations are also listed in the yellow pages of the telephone directory under such categories as "Voluntary Services," "Associations," or "Social Service Organizations." The telephone directory can also be used to identify government departments which can provide a list of programs that have national affiliations and depend on voluntary services.

A community is composed of spheres of activity concerned with the educational, occupational, political, religious, or social needs and interests of its citizenry. Businessmen and women serving as guest speakers in a business classroom, for example, enable the business teacher to gain familiarity with business-related activities in a community. The political sphere in a community, however, may be less known to business teachers unless, of course, steps are taken to bring government-related activities into the class-room; e.g., government resources can be brought into the classroom, students can be assigned to an independent study project on the legislature, or the business teacher can choose to become a resource for a government-related project.

A clearer understanding of community program services can be gained by interacting with people who are involved in different community spheres of activity. A woman executive, when asked how she became involved in community service, indicated that her work included counseling women on career interests and led her to offer a course in career choices, which is now in popular demand at the Austin Women's Center.

Community programs that need the business teacher's professional background, skills, and knowledge can also be identified by consulting city government personnel. A service organization operating a government-funded project forms a contract with the city. Since the city oversees the program's operation to ensure its successful outcome, city personnel are informed about its objectives and needs. The human resources department—which most cities of considerable size now have—can help the business teacher identify programs in need of the business teacher's assistance. Of 23 social programs listed by the human resources department in Austin, Texas, more than half needed the professional services of business teachers. Some of the programs needing business teachers to volunteer professional service were The Association for Retarded Children, The Women's Center, and Big Brothers/Big Sisters. Many of the programs in need of business teachers are concerned with rehabilitation, the elderly, and youth employment.

Before the teacher makes the decision, however, prospective programs should be evaluated in terms of their relevance to business education, to the professional needs of the teacher, and to the social needs of the community. Together, the three criteria can help the business teacher determine where assistance is most needed. Community programs in need of the business teacher's services may be concerned with new developments in legislation and new directions in education: the vocational rehabilitation of the handicapped, training programs for unemployed youth, small business management, and so on. Community involvement with programs in these areas can increase the business teacher's working knowledge of new laws. These laws not only give rise to community-based projects but also affect teaching.

Vocational rehabilitation of the handicapped. Legislative developments, such as The Education for All Handicapped Children Act of 1975 (EHC Act), require that business and vocational education be provided to all handicapped students. By 1980 public instruction will need to be revised so as to accommodate handicapped students in regular classroom settings, i.e., mainstreaming.

Participation in civic organizations geared toward rehabilitating the handicapped for employment purposes may enable teachers to gain experience in providing occupational training to the handicapped. Goodwill Industries, for example, provides a comprehensive program that includes work orientation; vocational evaluation; work, personal, and social adjustment; and job readiness, placement, and follow-up. Community service to organizations such as Goodwill, therefore, can provide the business teacher with practical experiences that can be related to teaching handicapped students in business and vocational education classes.

Unemployed youth. Working with manpower development programs that upgrade vocational skills can acquaint the business teacher with the economic plight of unemployed youth—the dropouts of society. Most teachers have had students who dropped out, but few teachers will ever encounter them again. What has become of them? And how many business teachers have the opportunity to assist out-of-school youth who wish to stay off the economic slag heap?

Currently, school dropouts are being helped by certified business teachers who are teaching full-time in a business-related vocational skills program in Corpus Christi, Texas. Under the Comprehensive Employment Training Act (CETA), youth programs are being offered to combat the problems of unemployed youth. The CETA community-based project in Corpus Christi is conducted by Operation SER (Service, Employment and Redevelopment).

Community-based projects that assist the economically disadvantaged, primarily the Spanish-speaking population, are conducted by Operation SER. Seeking to improve the socioeconomic status of its Spanish-speaking students, SER places major emphasis on the attainment of gainful employment. Over half of the people served by SER—148,000 have been assisted since 1966—are high school dropouts. SER, with 101 offices in the nation,

189

operates employment training centers to open career opportunities and upgrade the vocational skills of its participants.

Small business management. The economic survival needs of minority entrepreneurs and small business owners in the American economic system have received much attention in recent years. Traditionally, the college business administration curriculum has been geared toward the corporate structure rather than the small business owner. Lack of business training or managerial know-how is a factor behind the high rate of small business failure. The educational needs of the small business owner, therefore, represent an area where the business teacher can be of service.

Management training for the small business owner is of primary importance to the Office of Minority Business Enterprise (OMBE), the National Economic Development Association (NEDA), and the Service Corps of Retired Executives (SCORE). These nationwide programs, through a network of local organizations, stimulate small business enterprise in the private sector. They provide management/technical assistance to the entrepreneur or small business owner. SCORE's executives volunteer their business-professional expertise and services to businesses that cannot pay for professional management counseling. Regarding the demand for women executives especially, a SCORE chapter president has stated that "about 5 percent of our membership includes women, and they are needed now more than ever."

Equally important is the role of the business teacher in providing entrepreneurial education. Selected schools in Houston and Dallas, for example, are fostering awareness by developing curriculums and courses in entrepreneurial education. The Dallas Entrepreneurial Training Program, an HEW funded project in joint cooperation with the Texas Office of Minority Business Enterprise, is a pilot program for an 11-state area. OMBE officers are observing the Dallas project's progress to consider duplicating the program in their states.

The business teacher, therefore, can increase awareness of business ownership as a career. A small business can contribute to the economy when it creates jobs and provides employment. Business ownership can provide occupational incentive for those who are not in the economic mainstream, primarily disadvantaged ethnic groups and women. The practical experience gained by assisting the small business owners with their problems can help the business teacher develop units of instruction in these areas.

Women in employment education. Since young women represent the majority of students enrolled in business education classes, trends in the employment/education of women provide major implications for business teachers. Women are heavily clustered in office clerical occupations. Occupational forecasts for the 1980's show an increased need for employees in these occupations. Unfortunately, few women come out of school prepared for a business career at the executive or managerial level. If business education is to respond to the needs of women, special focus needs to be placed on developing women's potential for executive positions in government, business and industry.

It can be seen from what has already been stated that the business teacher can be of assistance to the community, and that involvement in community programs relates to business education and provides professional benefits for the business teacher. In the final analysis, the business teacher's professional background, interests, and attributes play a major role in the selection of a community-based project.

Determining how and where a business teacher can serve as a community resource is best summarized by a woman executive. When asked what procedures a business teacher could follow to become a community resource, she gave the following suggestions:

1. Take an active approach if you have something to offer. If you wait until someone asks you (although, of course, this can be regarded as an honor), you won't do it!

2. Look at a situation and take the initiative to propose your ideas or a plan to correct the situation.

3. If something challenges and interests you, *you can find the time*—for that one night a week.

4. Choose an activity that is going to be rewarding. Otherwise, there is no future or meaningful reason for developing the expertise.

BECOMING A COMMUNITY RESOURCE

The business teacher may be given responsibilities that require serving in different capacities. As a community resource, the business teacher can render professional service in the following capacities:

1. As an executive advisor—to set policy for decision making and long-range planning

2. As a resource person and consultant—to solve problems and develop effective approaches for problem solving

3. As an educator, teacher, advisor, and counselor—to develop human resources through manpower development training programs

4. As an intern—to gain practical experience through the application of academic principles in community situations

5. As a public relations person—to learn about the community and to teach the community about business education.

Any capacity in which a business teacher serves for a community-based project will provide learning experiences and will utilize the business teacher's professional background. As a community resource, the business teacher can draw upon five professional disciplines: (1) business administration—for example, accounting, (2) office administration, (3) business communications, (4) management, and (5) business education. Putting business training into practice helps the business teacher develop expertise in these academic areas. Subsequently, the developed expertise can be applied to classroom instruction. For example, serving in an advisory capacity to set up personnel policies for recruiting, screening, and selecting employees draws upon a management background. The expertise developed in the academic area, personnel management, can then be applied in an office management class. Also, the personnel experiences can be incorporated in modules of instruction on "Standards for Employment" and used in office-related classes.

Becoming a community resource: an illustration. The role of the business teacher as a community resource can be analyzed in terms of the service capacities required by a community-based project, the utilization of a professional background to perform the different services, the development of expertise in academic areas, and the application of the newly acquired experience to other situations.

To become a resource, however, it is first necessary to identify the types of services that a community resource may be asked to perform. Accordingly, the ways in which a business teacher can serve as a community resource for a community-based project (such as the National Urban League) are indicated by the executive director of the Austin Urban League. They are as follows:

1. Planning and developing training programs to provide secretarial, data processing, or other types of training for individuals who are unable to pursue a college degree program

2. Serving as a volunteer teacher in the training program; or, as a classroom visitor to expose individuals to the world of work

3. Serving on an advisory committee for the training program

4. Using expertise to upgrade the training course offerings or curriculum

5. Assisting in the development of fiscal accounts in terms of acceptable accounting principles

6. Developing and maintaining an accounting system for membership payments

7. Lending research support (e.g., analyzing, drafting, and typing grant proposals)

8. Training staff (e.g., secretarial or bookkeeping staff)

9. Developing internship arrangements to serve as tutors in remedial skill development.

The business teacher's professional background can be utilized in many of the above ways. A pattern of examples: by serving as a consultant, the management area is put into practice; by writing a grant proposal, business law and business communications training are put into practice; by developing an accounting system, the business administration or accounting area is applied.

Developing fiscal accounts or maintaining an accounting system are further examples of activities that can be applied in basic business courses, especially bookkeeping. But the expertise ·gained in developing an accounting system for a community project can also be utilized by the teacher when rendering service in other professional capacities, for example, when serving as a consultant for a small business or accounting firm. As a final example, by providing instructional services such as counseling and assisting unemployed youth with job entry skills, the business teacher is learning about the community (the National Urban League, its history of institutional strength, and the black community it serves) and teaching the community about business education.

Learning, relating, applying. The business teacher, by providing professional service as a community resource, can bring the learning experiences back to the classroom. Listed below are some examples of how a community resource person experiences learning situations and how experiences can be related to business education courses and applied to modules of instruction in the classroom:

1. The office procedures teacher serving on an advisory board as a recording secretary is learning, by performing communication tasks/activities; is relating, by drawing upon report-writing training; and is applying, by using the experiences in a business communications or business English class.

   The experiences can also be adapted for other classes, in shorthand, for example, for units on "Taking Minutes in Shorthand."

2. The business law teacher working with a community-based project that operates under a government contract can gain practical experience in drafting a proposal to obtain funds and form a contract (learning phase); utilize business law training to develop expertise in "Writing a Contract" or in "Evaluating the Outcome of a Contract" (relating phase); and use the experiences to enrich instruction in a business law class—"How Not To Write A Contract" (applying phase).

   The practical experiences that can be gained by the business law teacher are extensive, e.g., analyzing equal employment opportunity laws, writing affirmative action plans, constitutional bylaws, ad infinitum.

The role of the business teacher as a resource for different community-based projects is summarized in the chart on page 194. Reference to the column captioned "Task Performance" shows how becoming a community resource for small business owners can involve the business teacher in providing technical management assistance. The managerial assistance is relevant to courses in career education, entrepreneurial education, and the free enterprise system. The teacher's expertise developed by assisting small business owners can be used to develop modules of instruction on such topics as "Small Business Ownership" or "Managing a Small Office."

Serving as an intern for a service organization concerned with the handicapped can result in observational tasks or in lending teaching assistance to handicapped persons who seek occupational training. Doing apprenticeship training in a service organization for the handicapped has relevance for all courses. Instructional strategies can be developed, from the experiences learned as an intern, to provide instruction for a handicapped student in a business class. Modules developed on "Providing Occupational Training and Opportunities for the Handicapped" can benefit the teacher and the handicapped student. The community-acquired experience can place the business teacher several steps ahead in awareness and teaching methodology/preparation. Becoming aware of different types of handicaps, for example, can lead the business teacher to develop methods on how to teach a handicapped student and prepare instructional materials that are individualized for the handicapped student.

The practical experience gained from a teaching internship with a service organization for the handicapped (learning), and its relevance to business education or teaching strategies (relating), can be used by the teacher to

193

THE BUSINESS TEACHER AS A COMMUNITY RESOURCE

Community-Based Projects	Professional Service Capacity	Professional Background	Task Performance	Courses	Learning-Teaching Applications Modules
An Advisory Board Council Committee	Executive Advisor Committee Member, Chairman Resource Person	Management	Policy making Personnel recruitment, selection, job descriptions Decision making for program operation	Office Management Office Procedures	"Employment Standards for the Office Employee"
A Service Organization: The Handicapped: Retarded Children Goodwill Industries	Officer, e.g., Recording Secretary Intern Teacher Advisor	Office Administration Business, Office, Vocational Education	Taking/transcribing minutes Observing, assisting, teaching handicapped persons Developing instructional strategies	Office Procedures All Courses	"Taking Minutes" "Providing Occupational Training/Opportunities for the Handicapped"
Small Business Owners, Entrepreneurs: OMBE NEDA SCORE	Resource Person Consultant Educator Teacher Advisor	Management Business, Office, Vocational Education Accounting	Providing technical management assistance Setting up management systems: Office, Records, Equipment/Supplies Accounting Systems Analyzing statements Budgets Filing tax returns	Career Education Entrepreneurial Education Free Enterprise Office Management Office Procedures Bookkeeping Accounting Finance	"Small Business Ownership" "The Private Sector in the American Economic System" "Managing a Small Office" "Financial Statements" "Money Management for the Small Business Owner, Consumer"
Unemployed Youth: CETA Projects Operation SER	Resource Person Consultant Educator Teacher Advisor	Business, Office, Vocational Education	Developing, conducting, upgrading vocational skills training programs, courses	Career Education Office, Business, Vocational	"Gainful Employment" "School Leads to Jobs, Careers"
A Service Organization: Women's Center The National Urban League	Resource Person Consultant	Management Business Communications Business Law	Analyzing, writing research grant proposals	Business Communications Business Law	"Report Writing" "Writing a Contract"

enrich instruction for the handicapped in business courses (applying). Analytical-judgmental learning and the transfer of that learning contributes to the professional growth and development of a community resource, the business teacher.

DERIVING VALUES/BENEFITS

In the past, more has been said about utilizing community resources by bringing them into the classroom than about sending the business teacher out to the community as a resource person. The involvement of the business teacher in community programs benefits not only the community as a whole but also the individual teacher. For instance, increased awareness results on the part of the business teacher who becomes conscious of the ways in which the business-civic community is alive and everchanging. The student benefits as a recipient of the teacher's newly gained practical experiences, perspectives, and insights. The school administration benefits when the ongoing community activities are related to the school environment, and the community benefits when its businessmen and women and civic leaders become aware of business education as a profession and contributor to the community.

Contributions to the business-civic community result in recognition both for business education as a profession and for the individual business teacher. As an illustration of the latter, the National Economic Development Association (NEDA) in Phoenix, Arizona, gives an "Outstanding Educator of the Year" award for contributions to the business community. Since the image of business education is of concern to business educators, the business teacher who is contributing professional service to the community needs to be rewarded.

In conclusion, the role of the business teacher as a community resource is perceived positively and receptively by business-civic leaders in the community. Serving as a community resource enables business teachers to utilize the business-civic community as a training ground to gain practical knowledge and experience, to relate that community-acquired knowledge and expertise to business education, and to apply community-developed expertise to improve teaching effectiveness. The role of the business teacher as a community resource is an effective approach to professional growth and development.

CHAPTER 10

Teaching and Learning by Means of Achievement Levels or Competencies

Competency and achievement are always the goals of those who teach skills. As society looks toward accountability and competency-based education, the business teacher, who has always been concerned with vocational proficiency, takes another look at what has already been accomplished. What has developed and is developing concerning competency evaluation at secondary and higher education levels are examined in this chapter. The efforts made within the public school systems of our country are reviewed from the standpoint of properly training vocational business students for employment and/or for entry to fields of higher learning. Efforts in higher education to recognize those who qualify for advanced learning—not only through competency obtained at previous levels but also for life experiences that have brought about individualized achievement—are emphasized. The business teacher at each level should be aware of current activities in the profession that are affected by competency-based education.

Section A: At the Secondary School Level

CARL E. JORGENSEN
Virginia State Department of Education, Richmond

It is unusual for any educational practice to gain wide acceptance within a short period of time. Nevertheless, the use of performance objectives and criterion-referenced measures have become accepted for defining the products of professional education programs, teacher education programs, military training, and vocational education programs in just a little more than 10 years. There have been many outside pressures on all levels of instruction to provide accountability statements that provide evidence of the effectiveness of programs and document the contributions made to each individual served in the program.

The demands for accountability have also brought pressures for better articulation so that students may pursue and complete educational goals in a more orderly fashion. Duplication of effort and wasting students' time by not allowing them to reach their goals as quickly as possible has been caused by a lack of articulation. Educational organizations, citizens groups, and even legislatures have spoken out regarding the lack of articulation, the failure to meet student needs, and the poor use of tax dollars. The development of competency-based education (CBE) programs provides real promise for better articulation.

A GROWING INTEREST IN COMPETENCIES

Among the individuals who have created an interest in competencies, performance objectives, and the development of sound vocational education have been Robert F. Mager and Kenneth M. Beach, Jr. Sparked by their books on *Developing Vocational Instruction* and *Preparing Instructional Objectives*, vocational educators began to refine their programs and take the lead in providing assistance to other teachers from other disciplines as their principals and administrators began to request lesson plans and course outcomes in terms of measurable objectives. To some degree, business educators have always used measurable interim and terminal objectives for evaluating skills for business and office occupations.

An additional dimension to the use of performance objectives is the development of a competency-based educational (CBE) program. This approach considers the complete program; it provides a systematic approach to instruction that will meet accountability demands. In business and office education the system includes job standards as described by the employer and employee as well as other objectives related to employability, work ethics, skills, and knowledge. It is a system that provides feedback for purposes of updating the program to meet current needs of the employment community. The use of this approach in occupational preparation provides a standard for measuring the proficiency of each individual student completing a program.

To date, large expenditures have been made to develop the resources for competency-based programs. The result can be seen from the following:

a. Catalogs of performance objectives, criterion-referenced measures, and performance guides

b. Teaching guides and courses of study which now state outcomes in measurable terms

c. The use of CBE programs for instructing military personnel

d. Most programs for preparing personnel in the health field now using CBE

e. Some teacher education programs now using CBE to measure student outcomes

f. Numerous vocational education programs at the secondary and postsecondary levels that are now CBE programs.

A review of the professional literature shows a continuing interest in competencies and measurable objectives. William John Schill pointed out that measurable objectives are one of the long-standing components of occupational programs.[1] It is not difficult to identify the preparation needed for a particular occupation and measure the extent to which an individual

---

[1]Schill, William John. "Teaching to Measurable Objectives." *American Vocational Journal*, November 1974. p. 98.

meets the entrance requirements of an employer. However, Schill emphasized that in addition to terminal measures "we would still need measurable sub-objectives in order to develop a teaching strategy." This is one of the essentials of CBE materials. It is interesting to note that in 1974 there were other articles and publications giving attention to competencies. The *Industrial Education* issue of April 1974 described a system for implementing a per-formance-based approach to drafting. The system was described and formats for preparing objectives and developing modules were illustrated. The 1974 *National Business Education Yearbook* gave attention to a performance-based system of education as it applied to typewriting.

That all areas of instruction were beginning to focus on CBE can be seen by other publications such as the *Educational Technology* magazine, which contained an article describing CBE and identifying ways in which this educational system could assist teachers to meet many demands being made on education.

In vocational education the interest in CBE is reflected by extensive projects. One of these, a statewide project in Massachusetts, was described by William Kyros.[2] The project developed under the Management Infor-mation System for Occupational Education is designed to make terminal objectives, TERMOB's, available for teachers in all vocational programs in Massachusetts. The TERMOB's "represent flexible statements of job-entry skills that are required by business and industry." In addition to the terminal objectives, a number of enabling objectives are included. This is an advan-tage for secondary teachers for they can select objectives and then involve themselves with instructional strategies and teaching procedures that will enable their students to achieve these objectives. The teacher can thus spend more time on teaching activities rather than development of objectives.

By using TERMOB's, data can be provided that justifies the cost of occupational-preparation programs through a cost-benefit analysis. Such an analysis points out immediate economic benefits as well as long-range positive noneconomic effects on the community. Kyros also points out that this system has many positive effects for it provides the basis for a dialogue with employers, advisory committees, and lay citizens to examine the relevance of programs. Thus, there is a means for program revision to reflect technological changes.

COMPONENTS OF A COMPETENCY-BASED PROGRAM FOR SECONDARY SCHOOLS

In order to understand the contributions made to students, an examina-tion of the components of CBE in the secondary program is necessary. Nine components that contribute to a successful program are described.

Occupational demand. For any program of occupational preparation to be offered, there must be opportunities for employment upon its com-pletion. The Education Amendments of 1976, Title II, Vocational Education, prescribe a national and state system for collecting information related to

---

[2]Kyros, William. "TERMOB: Performance Objective with a Bigger Bite." *American Vocational Journal,* May 1975. p. 41.

supply and demand in the labor market. State Occupational Information Coordinating Committees, which are given this responsibility, are made up of individuals from various agencies including department of education, employment commission, department of labor, industrial development commission, and similar agencies. Once a demand is identified, it is possible to explore the need for occupational-preparation programs.

Assessment of students. The development of programs in business and office education as well as other areas should be based on student demand for certain programs. It is necessary to determine the extent to which the needs of students for occupational preparation have been met and determine interest in occupational areas where there are opportunities for employment. Student interest should not be the determining factor for offering a program; although individuals speak about a mobile population, research studies continue to show that most individuals who complete secondary occupational-preparation programs are not willing to leave their community in order to secure employment. A study of 1976 completions of occupational-preparation programs in Virginia who were unemployed showed 88 percent were not willing to move from home in order to secure employment although they were willing to commute if necessary.

Job analysis. The purpose of occupational-preparation programs in the secondary school is to prepare students to meet the needs of potential employers. Although analysis of business and office occupations has shown a wide variation in specific skills required by employers, it is possible through job analysis to identify the major duties and tasks to be performed by a worker. It is also possible, through job analysis and working with field reviewers from industry and education, to validate the duties and tasks as well as develop guides for acceptable performance.

Developing performance objectives and enabling objectives. From a job analysis that includes tasks that are important and difficult to learn, it is possible to begin writing objectives. It should be recognized that few secondary teachers have the time for this kind of research, and thus it is recommended that teachers use information from studies that have been made on a national, regional, and statewide basis. The objectives for a particular cluster of office occupations, such as secretarial occupations, may be reviewed by an advisory committee made up of employers and workers from a particular community.

Employability skills, work ethics, and job-seeking skills. After selecting the appropriate objectives identified by research and advisory committees, teachers must next identify the employability skills, work ethics, and job-seeking skills needed by students who are to secure employment and advance on the job. These items are not usually found in the research on job skills and duties completed in the community. Performance objectives and enabling objectives must be developed for these areas of the instructional program.

Curriculum development. Given the performance objectives and enabling objectives for a particular occupational cluster, along with performance objectives related to employability skills, work ethics, and job seeking skills, it is now necessary to organize these objectives into a logical sequence. This procedure will allow for an integrated instructional program in which related tasks are taught simultaneously as well as in a logical progression. This will result in instruction focused on job preparation rather than isolated skills.

Development of learning units (modules) and performance guides. It is possible to develop individual learning units once the curriculum has been identified and organized. These learning units will list performance objectives, criterion-referenced measures along with activities that will enable the student to achieve the objectives. These units can be used as a basis for group instruction or for individualized instruction. With objectives and evaluation measures identified at the beginning of the unit, students will usually be able to complete learning activities more quickly and experience success with the instructional unit.

Identification of instructional materials. This is completed along with the development of the unit of instruction. However, because of its importance, it is separated in this chapter. There are a variety of texts, reference manuals, practice sets, and simulations available to business teachers. An examination of these materials is necessary to determine which materials may be more effective in assisting the student to reach the objectives of each unit. While teachers may wish to develop their own materials, there is rarely enough time in any day or week to develop all the materials needed for CBE.

Evaluation, review of objectives, and revision. Any program of CBE requires the teacher to assess the student achievement as a result of the instructional system. Modifications may be needed so that students will progress more rapidly or achieve a higher degree of success. The business community should be involved through advisory committees to determine that the objectives are still appropriate. New technology or changes in business practice will create a need to rewrite objectives.

VOCATIONAL-TECHNICAL EDUCATION CONSORTIUM OF STATES

One of the delivery systems to assist with implementing CBE is the Vocational-Technical Education Consortium of States (V-TECS). This is a cooperative effort to develop catalogs of performance objectives, criterion-referenced measures, and performance guides for purposes of curriculum development in specific occupations. The consortium, administered by the Southern Association of Colleges and Schools, consists of 16 states and two associate member agencies. The member states are Alabama, Delaware, Florida, Georgia, Indiana, Kentucky, Louisiana, Maryland, Michigan, Mississippi, Pennsylvania, South Carolina, Tennessee, Virginia, West Virginia, and Wisconsin. The Air Training Command, U.S. Air Force, and the U.S. Naval Education and Training Command are associate members.

As outlined in the *Fourth Progress and Information Report* of July 1977, the catalog development includes the following:

> For each (occupational) domain, a state-of-the-art study is conducted and preliminary lists of tasks and tools and equipment are developed based upon

the review of existing literature. These preliminary lists are refined by extensive interviewing of incumbent workers and supervisors. The occupational inventory is then compiled and administered to a random sample of incumbent workers. Responses are obtained relative to task performance, task time-spent, task difficulty, and tool and equipment utilization. . . . writing teams . . . determine those tasks to be converted to performance objectives. A field review version of the catalog . . . is prepared, field tested, and refined.[3]

Once these catalogs are developed, they are made available to each state in the consortium. The member states assume the responsibility of printing and distributing the catalogs within their own state. To date, a number of catalogs have been prepared which have implications for business and office education. Catalogs under development or completed include the jobs titled: Bookkeeper, Hospital Ward Clerk, Data Processing, Programmer, Bank Teller, Legal Secretary and Court Reporter, Executive Secretary, Word Processing, Secretarial, and Clerk Typist.

States participating in the consortium agree that catalogs will not be distributed to any teacher except through in-service programs designed to assist the teacher with the use of the catalog and with the implementation of CBE. Catalogs can be used for program design as they contain major classifications called "duty" areas, and these are broken down into "task" areas. These can be used by the teacher in the development of outlines for programs, courses, and units of instruction. Each catalog contains a table related to task difficulty and time spent performing each task. This is helpful in selecting tasks to be included in an instructional program. For each task in the catalog, performance objectives are stated in behavioral terms. These assist the instructor to determine the manner in which the task must be performed satisfactorily. For each task there is a criterion-referenced measure followed by a performance guide to assist in designing instruction and evaluating the student. When a task is involved, the catalog includes an instructor's checklist. An equipment checklist in each catalog also assists in planning classroom laboratories and in determining the need to upgrade existing facilities.

BUSINESS EDUCATION VIEWS THE COMPETENCIES
NEEDED BY SECONDARY STUDENTS

On almost every regional and national program for business educators appears a topic related to new technology in the office, the changing nature of office work, word processing, office landscaping, or records management technology. Topics such as these reflect the effort of business educators to prepare students for office careers as they exist in business and industry. However, teaching assignments of secondary teachers allow little time to visit new facilities, study new technology, change objectives, and design classroom instruction around office systems as found in one's community.

The need to look to the future and prepare for technological change was pointed out by Jeffrey Stewart, Jr., in an article, "Business Education in

[3]Lee, Connie W.; Hinson, Tony M.; and Rohrbach, J. Jerome, Jr. *Fourth Progress and Information Report of the Vocational-Technical Education Consortium of States.* Commission on Occupational Education Institutions, Southern Association of Colleges and Schools. July 1977. p. 1.

the 1980's and Beyond."[4] A number of challenges were presented. Reviewing current practices, he observed, "A careful look at our own curriculums reveals a curious lack of relevance when compared with actual business practice and employment patterns." He continued, "Electronics technology has accelerated during the past five years to the point that office machines as it was taught until 1973 is now obsolete. Data processing as it was taught until 1973 or 1974 is obsolete." CBE and an organized manner of continually updating competencies can assist the business teacher to meet the challenge of aligning curriculums with current practice. Stewart further challenges business educators to "bring classroom practice up to the state of the art." He recommends that we use classroom practices that have been identified to be successful by current research.

Still another challenge given by Stewart is, "State the minimum outcomes of each vocational business program." This presents another reason for secondary teachers to use an approach of CBE. Research-based catalogs of objectives can assist in meeting this challenge.

Students in many business teacher education programs are being introduced to competency-based education through one widely used methods book, *A Teaching Learning System for Business Education*. The coauthor of this book, Adele F. Schrag, said the book was "the synthesis of the research done by about 50 other people."[5] The book identifies a system with eight steps that help the new business teacher function in a CBE setting to improve students' learning outcomes.

In 1976 a statement was released by the Policies Commission for Business and Economic Education, "This We Believe About Competency-Based Education." This commission includes representatives from the National Business Education Association, Delta Pi Epsilon, and the American Vocational Association. The CBE statement called attention to the individual assistance given to each student, and it specifically stated beliefs related to CBE implementation in an occupational-preparation program.

Thus, we are able to see a change taking place in instructional programs at all levels as more attention is focused on the students in our education programs. Individuals outside the education community who ask for an accounting of services offered to each student have also influenced a move to CBE.

ONE STATE'S APPROACH TO IMPLEMENTING CBE

It is not possible to make a major change in the approach to teaching and bring about immediate change by teachers in the classroom. Response to any radical change is almost always resisted, causing frustration to those who wish to implement the change. Therefore, the change in programs in business education in Virginia has been gradual. In-service activities conducted over a period of years have been directed toward assisting teachers to better meet the needs of students in occupational-preparation programs.

---

[4]Stewart, Jeffrey R., Jr. "Business Education in the 1980's and Beyond." *American Vocational Journal*, October 1977. pp. 48-50.

[5]Beale, Wendy. "Conversations with . . . Adele F. Schrag." *Business Education World*, September-October 1977. p. 22.

Development of occupational-preparation programs. In 1965-66, pilot programs were started in Virginia to explore the use of a block of time for occupational preparation. The teachers who were in these programs developed many materials that could be used in an integrated occupational approach to business and office occupations. The teachers in 13 programs met periodically, during each school year as well as in the summer, to identify appropriate teaching approaches and curriculums.

In February, 1968, *Suggested New Curriculum Patterns for Office Occupations Education* was released by the Virginia Business Education Service as a reference guide in developing occupational programs in business education using a block-time approach. The guide contained outlines for instructional units, teaching suggestions, and prerequisites for each unit, along with standards of achievement; these were competencies needed for successful completion of the unit. Prerequisite to implementing this approach in any school was a provision for in-service education for teachers in the program. Summer workshops were offered beginning in 1968 (and continuing to the present) related to this instructional approach with upwards of 250 business teachers attending workshops one summer. In addition to this, workshops and classes were offered for individual school divisions by business teacher educators. The Annual Summer Conference sponsored by the Virginia Department of Education also continued an in-service program with more than 400-500 teachers participating in the summer to discuss teaching approaches, integrated projects, development of skills, and other items of interest to teachers in occupational-preparation programs.

Projects developed by teachers in the late 1960's and early 1970's (when published materials were not very plentiful) were printed by the Virginia Department of Education and made available to all programs. Materials that were teacher-developed contained standards of achievement and performance measures by which the student and the teacher would know that the work had been completed satisfactorily. Teachers visited businesses and studied office systems as projects were developed. However, it was realized that most business teachers would not have the time to carry out this type of activity. Although there were 200-300 teachers visiting in the community to validate jobs and competencies, this did not provide an organized way to develop competencies.

Using V-TECS to implement CBE. In 1972, Virginia was invited to explore the possibility of entering a consortium to develop catalogs of objectives to be used in curriculum development for occupational programs. Business education, with the largest vocational program area in Virginia, was influential in identifying the potential for such a system and the assistance that could be provided through this system. Virginia became one of the charter members of V-TECS.

During the interim period of entering the V-TECS consortium and the receipt of the first catalogs, curriculum materials prepared for business teachers were developed using standards of achievement to measure student progress in each unit. Five teaching guides in broad areas such as typewriting, shorthand/transcription, and data processing were also prepared. An objective appeared in the five-year improvement plan for the Division of Vocational Education related to the preparation of course outlines for all approved courses. The approach in these outlines included the identification of terminal objectives for each course with certain enabling objectives. With extensive work to be done on these outlines before their completion in 1980, the research-based V-TECS objectives are helpful to committees.

Upon receiving the first catalogs and having them printed in 1976, it was necessary to provide in-service education. Before this could be accomplished, teacher educators needed to be trained. The Business Education Service designed an in-service program to instruct teacher educators and local supervisors; 45 business educators received the in-service training in 1976. With this group of individuals prepared, it was then possible to begin planning workshops and conferences for the next year.

During the summer of 1977 over 700 business teachers participated in initial in-service education. The workshops included an introduction to CBE, an opportunity to use a V-TECS catalog to prepare individualized training plans for students with specific objectives, work on analyzing simulated materials to determine which V-TECS objectives could be achieved through this medium, study of other ways in which the objectives could be used to improve traditional occupational-preparation programs, and evaluation of instructional materials using the V-TECS catalog. The sessions were all presented using a CBE approach. This included a general purpose, objectives, pretest where appropriate, and evaluation of every session to determine if its purpose had been accomplished.

This massive in-service was followed up by eight regional meetings to introduce the concept of CBE to business teachers who had not attended summer workshops and to present sessions on testing and grading in a CBE setting and additional and subordinate objectives needed by CBE for teachers who had attended a summer workshop. Well over 1,000 teachers attended these sessions in the fall of 1977. Additional workshops were offered for school divisions during the 1977-78 school year. The program continued with numerous workshops in the summer of 1978, at which time the emphasis in advanced CBE workshops was the analysis of current published instructional materials to determine which materials could be used to achieve the CBE objectives and the preparation of performance objectives related to job-seeking and employability skills.

An approach to assist teachers. To secure teacher support in the move to CBE, the approach in Virginia has been to show teachers how their present program can be strengthened and improved through the use of a CBE approach. The development of all in-service programs has focused on the ease of adapting the present program to meet individual student needs through CBE. The approach to occupational-preparation programs originally developed in Virginia was to emphasize the opportunity to provide for individual differences within the block-time class and the flexibility to change job objectives when it appeared necessary in order to assist the student to succeed in the program.

To assist all vocational services in implementing CBE, a suggested course outline was prepared to be used as a model in conducting workshops. Business education also funded a project through one institution of higher education to develop the modules to be used in the preservice program for business teachers.

The approach outlined for Virginia may not work in every state, but it emphasizes the need to use many avenues to reach teachers. It also points out the importance of having an ongoing program that will prepare new teachers for the CBE learning environment.

CHALLENGES FOR THE FUTURE IN CBE IMPLEMENTATION

With the implementation of CBE as a delivery system for people in vocational education, there are many challenges. The secondary program as taught within a fixed structure of time is not consistent with the philosophy of CBE. In almost all cases it will be necessary to use competencies within the structure of the school day as presently organized. This may mean that additional competencies will be achieved by certain students and that the use of competencies may, in fact, prove to be a help to the teacher who has talented and gifted students in a given class.

There are many educators who feel that performance objectives must be written only for cognitive and psychomotor level learning activities— that it is not possible to write performance objectives for the affective domain. However, this is not true; it is possible to write objectives which demonstrate that students appreciate, understand, and have a good attitude. Robert Mager, in his book *Goal Analysis*, describes the process that might be used to develop objectives in the affective domain. While this does require additional effort, it is necessary to teach and measure effectiveness in the areas of work ethics, employability skills, and job-seeking skills in a total occupational-preparation program.

Teachers usually have a very full teaching load and there is little time for program modification. It will be necessary to provide assistance and instructional packages that will enable teachers to easily use a CBE approach. Certain business education instructional materials being prepared for printing by 1980 have identified competencies within the text material to be used by students. This will provide for an easier transition to CBE.

Traditional grading and report cards do not lend themselves to an easy application of CBE. It will be necessary for teachers to devise ways of interpreting the achievement of competencies into the traditional grading systems. There are some localities trying the use of report cards on which competencies appear. This is a step in the right direction.

The identification of specific minimum and mastery levels of performance is difficult for many tasks. It will be necessary for teachers to use judgment and knowledge about their own community in setting levels of achievement for a given program. The use of advisory committees will thus become more important in this type of delivery system.

CONCLUSION

Although there are challenges in a CBE program, the satisfaction of achieving goals based on job standards as well as evaluation based upon these standards will prove to be a real motivating device for students. Teachers will also experience more satisfaction from being able to measure the quality of their product using research-based objectives.

When an instructional approach can assist business teachers to work "smarter" rather than to work harder, when teachers can see the benefits to students, when teachers perceive a change to be a help in performing their job, and when teachers see that an approach will help them demonstrate they are doing an outstanding job, then you will have teachers who are eager to learn and use CBE.

Section B: At the Postsecondary Level

PAUL H. STEAGALL, JR.
James Madison University, Harrisonburg, Virginia

In reviewing recent literature in education for the seventies, two major topics are in evidence. First, American education is in "deep" trouble. The cover story of *Time* magazine (November 14, 1977) is "High Schools in Trouble." Taxpayers spent $144 billion in 1977 on public education, and they are worried about whether they are getting their money's worth. Signs do indicate that student achievements in math and verbal skills are on the decline based on nationwide test scores. Some educators say that the reason for this is that more low achievers are taking the College Entrance Examination Board's Scholastic Aptitude tests than in the past. But how do we explain the fact that the number of high achievers on SAT tests (those scoring over 600) has been dropping, and the scores of top students—valedictorians and salutatorians—show a similar decline? It could be that American education is called on to try and solve too many of the problems of society—racial injustices, drug usage, improving America's underclass, and on and on. The solution proposed most often is "back-to-basics" with requirements of minimal competencies in essential skills before graduation.

The second topic that has attracted great attention is competency-based education (CBE). Programs in CBE give major emphasis to the identification of performance objectives based on occupational competencies that have been validated by task analyses of workers in the field. This is nothing new in vocational education, but it seems to be getting greater attention in the literature. What is new is that CBE is becoming more popular in higher education.

In 1975, Westbrook and Sandefur surveyed member institutions in AACTE to determine the extent to which they were involved in competency-based teacher education (CBTE).[1] Of the 570 AACTE members who returned the survey, 296 institutions (52 percent) indicated they were operating CBTE programs.

According to Houston and Warner (1977), during the past five years 26 states have revised their teacher education and certification standards to include the "approved program approach."[2] Of the states utilizing the approved program approach, 17 either have developed CBTE standards or were encouraging the development of CBE through their approved program approach.

The two topics just mentioned and at least a dozen national reports have verified that our schools are in a state of crisis and reforms are called for. These national reports endorse the need for alternatives in public education.[3] CBTE is just one of the alternatives in higher education. An increasing number of educators are now concluding that some learning can and should take place out of the classroom and away from the schools. This section will explore some of the alternatives used by students to earn college credit, diploma credit, and advanced placement in subjects at the postsecondary level.

ADVANCED PLACEMENT PROGRAM, COLLEGE-LEVEL EXAMINATION PROGRAM

The Advanced Placement Program of the College Entrance Examination Board began in the early 1950's and is one of the largest and better known examination services used by colleges. Students who have achieved advanced preparation through special advanced high school courses, independent study, or other means may take the examinations. Many colleges grant credit and placement for satisfactory work on the examinations; some grant placement only; others do not have a policy on granting credit for these examinations. The AAP examinations are normally three hours long and consist generally of two parts: objective and free response. Examinations are available in such areas as art, biology, chemistry, English, French language, mathematics, music, physics, and German and Spanish literature.

Another service provided by the College Entrance Examination Board is the College-Level Examination Program (CLEP). The CLEP examinations are 60 minutes long (general examination) or 90 minutes long (subject examination). The general examinations are in English composition, humanities, mathematics, natural sciences, and social sciences. A long list of subject examinations are available, including the following business subjects: computers and data processing, business management, accounting, business law, economics, marketing, and money and banking.

[1]Westbrook, D. C., and Sandefur, W. "Involvement of American Association of Colleges for Teacher Education Institutions in CBTE Programs." Phi Delta Kappan 57:276-77; December 1975.

[2]Houston, W. Robert, and Warner, Allen R. "The Competency-Based Movement: Origins and Future." Educational Technology 17:15-16; June 1977.

[3]Smith, Vernon; Barr, Robert; and Burke, Daniel. Alternatives in Education: Freedom to Choose. Bloomington, Ind.: Phi Delta Kappa Educational Foundation, 1976. 172 pp.

Many colleges and universities give credit and/or advanced placement for CLEP examinations, but policies vary widely across the country. Some colleges give sophomore standing for satisfactory scores on four of five or all five CLEP general examinations. Some colleges limit the number of credits given for general or subject examination to 15 units; some 30 units; and others, almost no limits. The names of colleges and universities that honor CLEP test scores are available from the Program Director, College-Level Examination Program, Box 1821, Princeton, NJ 08540.

CAEL—COOPERATIVE ASSESSMENT OF EXPERIENTIAL LEARNING

One of the more important new trends in American higher education is the idea of awarding credit for experiential learning. This learning usually results from such activities as work experience, volunteer work, travel, community service, military experience, and homemaking. These activities may occur either in programs sponsored by an educational institution or in learning that occurred prior to enrollment with an institution. Adults who have been out of school for several years are likely to bring such learning to an institution when they elect to enter or return to a college or university.

Experiential learning has emerged as a major area of concern for faculty and other professionals, as they are confronted with new roles and responsibilities. It was because of this concern that in 1974 a research and development project known as Cooperative Assessment of Experiential Learning (CAEL) began. The purpose of the project was to discover techniques, processes, and procedures for valid and reliable assessment of experiential learning. It was also concerned with the training of people to perform such assessment and to design and conduct programs in a way compatible with good assessment.

In September 1976, CAEL was chartered by the Regents of the State of New York for the purpose of fostering experiential learning and the valid and reliable assessment of its outcomes. CAEL is now an educational association of 250 institutions of higher education and other educational organizations.

How do students identify prior learning that might be acceptable for college credit? How do the college administrators and faculty evaluate the prior learning for possible academic credit? A series of publications that provide guidelines for faculty and student assessment of learning are now available from CAEL. A review of some of the highlights of a publication by Aubrey Forrest may offer answers.[4]

Most adults have learned many things through noncollege experiences that are equivalent to what is taught in a college or university. The important thing to remember is that colleges generally do not give credit for the experience itself, but rather for the knowledge and skills attained as a result of the experience. Some examples of the knowledge and skills that might be appropriate for adults seeking credit and the probable evaluations by the college are as follows:

---

[4]Forrest, Aubrey. *Assessing Prior Learning—A CAEL Student Guide.* Columbia, Md.: CAEL, 1977. 110 pp.

Salesperson. A person has read for and passed the appropriate state examinations and worked for several years in real estate. This person has also worked through a self-instructional textbook in salesmanship and participated in on-the-job training workshops. A member of Toastmasters International, the individual has given a number of speeches to service clubs; has been president of the local chapter of the Junior Chamber of Commerce and the Lions Club; is presently an elected member of the City Council; has been involved in the field of photography for over nine years, winning several awards at amateur photography showings and investing several thousand dollars in photographic equipment.

This individual wants to move up into a management position, but the company requires a college degree. All past learning should count towards a degree, which may result in receiving college credit in the areas of real estate appraisal, sales, photography, and public speaking.

Personnel manager. Another person rose to the personnel manager's position of a local branch of a nationally recognized company after nine years in personnel administration. This individual has written several articles for a professional journal in the field of personnel management. For several of the nine years this person lived and worked in Brazil. Preparation for that work utilized a self-study course in Spanish and Portuguese. This person should be able to find a college that will give appropriate recognition or credit in the areas of personnel management and foreign language.

Secretary. This person worked as a secretary for six years and then accepted a full-time position as an office supervisor for three years. She married, moved to a new location, and was not employed for several years, recently resuming working as a secretary. For the past four years this individual has been a volunteer aide in the psychiatric ward of a general hospital and has taken in-service courses while working closely with a psychiatric social worker in addition to reading several standard textbooks and numerous articles on the subject of abnormal psychology. This person now wishes to pursue a degree in psychology. Creditable recognition for the subject areas of abnormal psychology, secretarial science, and office supervision could be given for her prior experiences.

These are just a few illustrations about the kinds of prior experiential learning for which some individuals may seek credit and for which some colleges may be willing to give credit or recognition. Although the procedures vary among institutions, there are certain general characteristics commonly found in most institutions that give credit for this type of learning. Some of these are:

1. The student is required to identify the prior experiential learning that may be creditable or recognizable.
2. The student is usually asked to relate the learning to degree objectives.
3. The student is usually asked to document or verify the learning experiences.
4. The student may be asked to assemble a portfolio that serves as a petition to the institution for credit or recognition.
5. Most institutions require some evaluation of the prior experiential learning.

6. The evaluation of the student's portfolio is made by an official or committee representing the institution.

Colleges use various techniques to measure prior experiential learning. Many colleges require that the measurement of learning that relates to the traditional subject areas be conducted by means of a CLEP examination in cases where they are available. Other appropriate techniques used by some colleges are as follows:

Observation. An expert observes the behavior of the student as he/she performs. The expert may use a rating scale to record the activity as it occurs. If it is inappropriate to have an observer present, then the behavior might be audiotaped or videotaped for later evaluation. This would permit several experts or a committee to evaluate the competence claimed.

Product assessment. This assessment usually involves the use of rating scales or forms. The rating is a measurement of a product that a person has produced rather than an observation of a person's performance. The assessment of a product might include such items as reports, musical compositions, paintings, and other projects and work samples.

Oral interview. This is a face-to-face situation in which the interviewer asks questions of the student that are designed to obtain an evaluation of the knowledge, skills, or values relating directly to the learning to be measured. The oral interview can be especially useful in the measurement of such skills as creative problem-solving ability, oral translation of a foreign language, ability to compare and contrast ideas, and ability to express complex concepts.

Objective written examination. The most common form of objective written tests consists of a series of questions, with several options as answers for each question. The student is asked to choose one of the options as the correct answer to each question. An example of this type of test is the licensing examinations used by various state boards and professional associations such as nursing, real estate sales, certified public accounting, law, etc. Besides the CLEP examinations, many colleges use the final examinations in existing courses to measure learning in some subject areas.

Essay examination. The student is expected to organize and write answers to a series of questions or assignments. The answers on an essay examination may be used to measure either the amount of knowledge a student has in a subject area or the ability to use that knowledge. This technique would be appropriate for measuring many of the skills as listed for the oral interview.

Performance test. In a performance test the student is required to perform specific tasks in a situation designed and set up by an examiner. Some examples include typing and shorthand tests, office machines tests, electronic equipment operation, sports and physical fitness skill tests, and listening tests in music.

Simulations. A simulated situational test is frequently used to measure very complex competencies or several competencies at a single time. Some examples include simulated business exercises, role-playing situations, management games, and the use of simulated trainers. It is particularly

210

appropriate in the measurement of such abilities as analytical thinking, goal-setting, risk-taking, interpersonal competence, and planning.

Those adults who have been out of school for several years and who are considering entering or returning to a college or university should be aware of this important new trend in higher education. More and more colleges are receptive to the idea of awarding credit, advanced standing, or some other kind of recognition for the learning acquired through noncollege experiences. Students, faculty, and other persons desiring resource materials to assist in the identification, documentation, and measurement of college-sponsored experiential learning may write to CAEL, American City Building, Suite 403, Columbia, MD 21044.

INDIVIDUALIZED EDUCATION

Individualized education is the term most frequently applied to the nontraditional programs described in the growing literature on this topic. Many workshops, seminars, and meetings have been conducted on individualized or student-centered learning. The Center for Individualized Education at Empire State College (State University of New York) was established in the fall of 1974 to coordinate study in this area. Empire State College and seven other institutions are participating with the Center in a "network" designed to implement academic programs which recognize and provide for individual differences of students. The Community College of Vermont; Bunker Hill Community College, Massachusetts; Metropolitan State University, Minnesota; New College at the University of Alabama; the State University of New York College at Brockport; Rockland Community College, New York; and the University of Minnesota have members on a Task Force which works in coordination with the Center. The Center facilitates the ongoing activities of the Task Force which, thus far, has resulted in a number of workshops for faculty as well as a Faculty Internship Program.

The individualized education programs at the eight institutions differ in many ways; yet, there are many similarities. Generally, in all the programs, the student can pursue a degree without being a full-time student, resident on a campus, or enrolled in a series of specified classes which are prescribed for the completion of a predetermined major. The programs at Empire State College and one of the other institutions are briefly described to illustrate their developmental activities. A description of all eight programs is published in a catalog edited by Morris and Pellows.[5]

Empire State College (S.U.N.Y.). Empire State College of the State University of New York was created in 1971 and mandated to develop alternative approaches to higher education. The college has no campus, no one central location. Instead, it has a variety of structural units—learning centers, learning units, mentors-on-location, and cooperative relationships with other institutions and organizations.

---

[5]Morris, Michael M., and Pellows, Merrill J. *Individualized Education Resource Catalog.* Saratoga Springs, N.Y.: Empire State College Distribution Center, March 1977. 218 pp.

Empire State College offers four degrees: A.A., A.S., B.A., and B.S. The associate's degree requires 16 contract months, and the bachelor's degree requires 32 months. Progress toward degrees is measured in contract months —one contract month equals four weeks of full-time study, four semester hours of credit, or one course in a four-course system.

The student has great flexibility in designing, with faculty advice and consent, a degree program that suits his or her background, interests, and goals. Assessment of prior learning is a major part of the college's approach to alternative forms of higher education. Advanced standing toward the degree can be achieved not only through traditional means of courses and standard tests but also through describing and documenting what has been learned through work, travel, reading, community service, and other educational experiences. As many as 26 contract months toward the bachelor's degree or 10 months toward the associate's degree can be awarded through an assessment of prior learning.

Approaches to individual instruction have been developed through contract learning, modular programs, and independent study. The learning contract is negotiated by the student and a mentor. It describes the goals of the student, how they are to be achieved, what resources will be used, how long it will take, amount of credit to be earned, and how the goals will be evaluated. The student moves through a series of contracts in fulfillment of a degree program. Modules prepared by the college faculty or other scholars direct the students to a wide range of educational resources and guide them through readings, tapes, films, and field experiences. The student may also use independent study courses by enrolling in participatory colleges of the program for credit or receive tutorial instruction while using independent study materials. A variety of alternative routes to learning are available at Empire State College.

Metropolitan State University. Metropolitan State University, formerly Minnesota Metropolitan State University, was authorized by the Minnesota state legislature in May 1971. By design, the university focuses on alternative approaches to educating adults rather than duplicating already existing higher education opportunities. The programs are student centered, highly individualized, and competency-based.

The assessment of competencies gained through life experiences is an important component of Metro U. Applicants for this upper-division institution must have at least two years of college or its equivalent in demonstrated competencies. Once enrolled, many students use their jobs and home activities as a part of their education.

The student begins a program at Metro U. by enrolling in an Individualized Educational Planning Course (IEPC). The course is designed to assist students (a) to identify their current competencies and learning needs, (b) to understand university policies and assessment procedures, (c) to learn the principles of self-directed study, and (d) to design their upper-division degree plans.

The degree plan specifies those competencies gained by the student prior to admission and those the student plans to attain while enrolled at

Metro U. The plan also specifies the learning strategies to be used to attain competencies, the techniques that will be employed to assess the competencies, and the names and qualifications of the experts who will evaluate each of the competencies. Once this is successfully completed, the student is accepted as a candidate for the bachelor of arts degree, the only degree awarded by Metro U.

The student must now generate documentation in support of each of the competencies in the degree program. Working with a faculty advisor, the student begins to implement the degree plan using a contract learning model.

Metro U. does not have a traditional campus but uses existing facilities in such places as the First National Bank of Minneapolis, the St. Paul YWCA, Brookside Community Center, and the Control Data Corporation. Students are encouraged to include independent study and internships in their learning plans. Over 80 percent of the students are employed on a full-time basis and are generally employed in professional or management positions.

Instead of a credit-based letter grade transcript, the university records educational progress in terms of the competencies the student achieves. The student is ready for graduation when he or she has successfully demonstrated attainment of each of the competencies listed in the degree plan.

SUMMARY

In summary, what is important today is that an increasing number of educators are now concluding that some learning can and should take place out of the classroom and away from the school. A wide variety of action learning programs have emerged, including schools without walls, social internships, and career education programs. In another 10 years, if the present trend continues, optional alternative programs in higher education will be commonplace and their support substantial. Educators are setting new goals and attempting to meet the needs of a rapidly changing society. While the standard college or university will continue to be the major higher education institution in America, it will not be the exclusive one. Other types of schools with widespread educational options and many types of alternative programs will develop. The coexistence of both types of schools and programs should strengthen American education as a whole.

NBEA EXECUTIVE BOARD

OFFICERS

President: ROBERT POLAND, Michigan State University, East Lansing, Michigan

President-Elect: DORIS Y. GERBER, Office of Superintendent of Public Instruction, Olympia, Washington

Secretary-Treasurer: CARL E. JORGENSEN, State Department of Education, Richmond, Virginia

Past-President: GORDON F. CULVER, University of Nebraska, Lincoln, Nebraska

Executive Director: O. J. BYRNSIDE, JR., NBEA, Reston, Virginia

EXECUTIVE BOARD MEMBERS

Eastern Region: ROBERT L. GRUBBS (EBEA President), Coraopolis, Pennsylvania; MARION W. HOLMES, Philadelphia, Pennsylvania; JOHN S. NIGRO, North Haven, Connecticut; MARY B. WINE, Washington, D.C.

Southern Region: ANNELLE BONNER (SBEA President), Hattiesburg, Mississippi; LOIS E. FRAZIER, Raleigh, North Carolina; CHERYL M. LUKE, Columbia, South Carolina; MARGARETT A. HUGGINS, Clinton, Mississippi

North-Central Region: GARY D. RUGE (N-CBEA President), Green Bay, Wisconsin; JOHN KUSHNER, Detroit, Michigan; DAVID J. HYSLOP, Bowling Green, Ohio; THOMAS B. DUFF, Duluth, Minnesota

Mountain-Plains Region: JOSEPH A. NEBEL (M-PBEA President), Omaha, Nebraska; MARGARET H. JOHNSON, Lincoln, Nebraska; OSCAR H. SCHUETTE, Denver, Colorado

Western Region: ED GOODIN (WBEA President), Las Vegas, Nevada; DANIEL G. HERTZ, Bozeman, Montana; ROBERT J. THOMPSON, Los Altos Hills, California; MONA NOBLE, Mountain Home, Idaho

NABTE Representatives: HARRY H. JASINSKI (NABTE President), Aberdeen, South Dakota; JAMES ZANCANELLA, Laramie, Wyoming

Ex Officio: ARTHUR H. RUBIN, New York, New York

PUBLICATIONS COMMITTEE

OSCAR H. SCHUETTE (Chairman), Denver, Colorado; NONA BERGHAUS (Secretary), Emporia, Kansas; THELMA C. HOYLE, Weston, Massachusetts; REBA K. NEEL, Ruston, Louisiana; GORDON A. TIMPANY, Cedar Falls, Iowa; ROBERT POLAND, East Lansing, Michigan; and O. J. BYRNSIDE, JR., Reston, Virginia